HOUSE
PLANT

HOUSE PLANT

PRACTICAL ADVICE FOR ALL HOUSE PLANTS, CACTI AND SUCCULENTS

CONTENTS

INTRODUCTION

Science has proved it: house plants make us happier and healthier. When studies tell us that plants can purify the air, lift our mood, and reduce our stress levels, we have every reason to fill our homes with wonderful, happiness-inducing plants of every shape, size, and colour.

With so many different varieties on offer, there is a plant – or twenty – to suit everyone: elegant, blossoming orchids; dinky little cacti and succulents; delicate trailing plants; floor-standing palms and foliage plants… the list goes on and on. It's hard to resist the urge to simply fill any and every available surface with a random assortment of greenery, but the best house plant displays are those that go that one step further: thoughtful, curated arrangements that can create a mood within a home, be it a cosy little oasis or a dramatic, architectural plant display.

As much as we may want to, we can't all turn our homes into a full-scale botanical garden. Instead, we need to be a little more inventive. Poor light? Look for unfussy foliage plants, such as cast iron plants or snake plants, that can survive in a shadier spot. No free surface space? Plant up a miniature garden inside a glass terrarium, or go all-out and create a hanging garden with macramé planters and kokedama.

And, once you've designed your plant-filled home, how exactly do you keep the plants in peak condition? With this book, you'll be able to care for whichever plants you choose, keep them healthy and strong, and take cuttings to share with friends and family (or to grow your own collection). Treat your plants well and, no matter how large or small your collection, you'll be rewarded with an indoor garden you can enjoy for years to come.

DESIGNING WITH HOUSE PLANTS

THE RULES OF
HOUSE PLANT DESIGN

How you choose to design your house plant collection depends on your personal style, imagination, and the space you have available. With so many variables, the possibilities are almost endless, but for your displays to be successful, follow these key principles.

1 CARE COMES BEFORE STYLE

A healthy plant is a beautiful plant. When designing for a particular space, always choose plants that you know will thrive in the light, temperature, and humidity conditions provided by that space. There is no point taking the time to arrange the perfect display only to watch the plants within it begin to wilt and die because they are unhappy in their location.

2 THINK NATURAL

Be inspired by nature. Consider where and how a plant would grow in the wild, and try to emulate that in your display. So, if a plant thrives on a damp, semi-shaded forest floor, provide it with a position that offers a similar environment. If it trails from high branches, place it in a hanging container. If it grows aerial roots without compost, build that into your display. Whatever its natural circumstances, use them as inspiration.

3 HARMONY AND CONTRAST

Strike a balance between harmonious and contrasting design features. Familiarise yourself with the three key elements of design (see pp12–17), and harmonize or contrast them as needed to achieve the effect you want. Harmony can create a balanced, unified appearance, while contrast will add interest and dynamism to a display.

DESIGNING WITH
SCALE

To put it simply, scale refers to the relative size of objects in a design. A plant may be large or small, but its relationship with neighbouring plants or objects is what defines its scale. Correct use of scale is key to any successful design: a tiny cactus and a weeping fig, for example, would be totally out of proportion with each other. Get the scale right, and you can create interesting relationships between the plants in your display.

WHAT IS SCALE?

Scale describes your plants' sizes in comparison with one another. It is closely related to proportion, which describes the size of your plants within an overall display. Plants of a similar size are harmonious in scale, while those of different heights contrast in scale. Scale is relative: any two plants can share the same contrast of scale, provided that they maintain the same proportions.

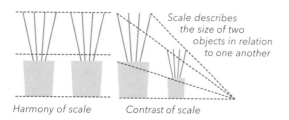

Scale describes the size of two objects in relation to one another

Harmony of scale   Contrast of scale

DESIGNING WITH
HARMONY OF SCALE

Harmony can reinforce pattern, so use plants of the same scale to echo and exaggerate existing patterns within your living space: the symmetry of a windowsill, the staggered surface of a flight of stairs. Maintaining the same scale across a display while varying other design elements creates a harmonious pattern that unites your plants.

1 The uniform scale of these three kentia palms allows the display to echo the outline of the steps.

2 This cluster of three very different trailing plants is given cohesion by its harmony of scale (left to right: donkey's tail, string of pearls, and mistletoe cactus).

DESIGNING WITH
CONTRAST OF SCALE

Grouping plants of different sizes offers a chance to manipulate the eye and generate a sense of movement. Perhaps you want to sweep along a windowsill or table, or conjure an impression of height, or lead the eye into a particular space. Use contrast of scale to create a sight-line between your plants and draw attention to a focal point within your grouping.

1 A sequence of ever-larger bromeliads creates a line of visual interest along a windowsill, with a smaller one at the end just to playfully challenge the order.

2 The extreme contrast of scale between the little missionary plant and the imposing Swiss cheese plant is given cohesion by the mid-sized fiddle-leaved fig, which unifies and balances the display.

DESIGNING WITH
COLOUR

Within Nature there are many different colours, shades, and tones for you to work with. Colours have emotional properties too: greens, the predominant colour of plant design, are restful and reassuring; reds and oranges suggest warmth and energy; white evokes purity and calm. Use them to set the mood for your space.

1

WHAT IS COLOUR?

Colours in isolation behave differently from colours in combination, and the colour wheel shows how those relationships work. In between the primary colours of red, blue, and yellow lie all the shades they make in combination (so, for example, green sits between blue and yellow, which combine to make green). Towards the centre are progressively lighter tints, while as the circle progresses outwards, the shades get darker.

The colour wheel shows all colours, along with their hues, tints, tones, and shades.

Adjacent colours work in harmony, as they share the same range of hues and tones.

Opposing colours on the wheel can create contrast and vibrancy.

DESIGNING WITH
HARMONY OF COLOUR

For a calm, ordered arrangement, plants need to blend gently with one another colour-wise. A strict colour palette of greens is refined, but you may need to vary other elements to avoid a dull display. Broadening your palette to adjacent colours allows a wider range of moods to be conjured, while retaining serenity and order. Cool hues generally suggest a sense of space.

1 A palette of purple flowers and foliage harmonizes this group of different plants, setting a gentle yet welcoming mood.

2 The rattlesnake plant's variegated green leaves offer some interest when paired with the fiddle-leaved fig behind it.

2

1

2

3

DESIGNING WITH CONTRAST OF COLOUR

Warm colours can make spaces appear more intimate. As they contrast directly with green, they also add drama to a plant display. Use them to draw the eye in to your display, or to create bold, vibrant relationships between your plants.

1 The vivid orange moth orchid picks up on the terracotta pots, and stands out as the focal point in the display.

2 Make an air plant display pop with a few red-coloured varieties.

3 Pinks and greens contrast in this delicate yet colourful design.

DESIGNING WITH TEXTURE

While it can be a subtle design feature, texture offers a vital sensory element in a display. A plant's surface type determines how it interacts with light and shadow, which gives it a unique presence: for example, velvety leaves have a soft, matte appearance, while smooth, glossy foliage presents a crisp, bright, clean-cut image.

WHAT IS TEXTURE?

Texture describes a plant's foliage, and the effect it creates when interacting with light and shadow. While it adds a seemingly tactile dimension, texture should primarily remain a visual design element: some plants, like the bunny ears cactus, may look soft, but you would not want to touch those fine spikes.

Feathery

Velvety, matte

Plump, fleshy

Smooth, glossy

Spiky, rough

DESIGNING WITH HARMONY OF TEXTURE

When a group of plants interact with light in the same way – absorbing or reflecting it, offering similar textural patterns of light and dark – there is a unity achieved that brings the composition together as a whole. A thoughtful combination of similar textures offset by other contrasting elements creates interest, although too much repetition creates monotony.

1 Pairing the structurally different, but equally glossy, fern arum (left) and radiator plant (right) builds a strong relationship that is reinforced by similarly glossy containers.

2 The *Myrtillocactus* (left) and rattail cactus (right) contrast in almost every regard, but their matching spiky textures offers a point of harmony.

3 A seemingly random sprawling group of air plants is given unity by the similarity of their textures.

4 Texture can harmonize a contrasting colour palette, linking the two purple velvet plants with the *Echeveria* (left) and *Kalanchoe* (right).

DESIGNING WITH CONTRAST OF TEXTURE

Bringing diverse textures together builds excitement and tension, as each texture brings a different mood to the display. The relationship between the different textures needs to be carefully balanced, however, in order not to simply suggest chaos. The light and shadow should work across the design in such a way that the eye is drawn to the contrasts but can also see the rhythm in them.

1 Fleshy, plump succulents contrast interestingly with the pretty fronds of moss; the voluptuousness of the succulents is accentuated by the delicacy of the carpet and reindeer mosses.

2 The dominant, rougher texture of the golden polypody's velvety leaves is sandwiched between the softer, more elegant Boston fern (left) and the fine foliage of the delta maidenhair fern (right).

1

2

3

4

1

2

CHOOSING
CONTAINERS

A great plant arrangement is as much about your choice of pots as it is about your choice of plants. By keeping your plants potted up in plastic containers with good drainage holes (see p320), you can easily swap one decorative outer pot (known as a "sleeve") for another until you find which one suits it best. That might mean a container that harmonizes (or contrasts) with the plant's colour or texture, one that gives the plant a unique outline, or another quality entirely. Keep swapping between pots until you find your perfect match.

1

2

The Agave's dramatic foliage is emphasized by the bold, geometric pot

The Sedum's diminutive size is offset by a vividly patterned, eye-catching pot

THE PERFECT MATCH

Successfully pairing plants with pots takes practice, as you learn what works and what doesn't. While neutral containers can offer a unifying backdrop for your plants, a bold container choice that emphasises one or more of the three design elements, scale, colour, and texture, can become a focal point in itself, highlighting your plants' best features and tying them in with the surrounding environment.

3

ONE PLANT, THREE POTS

As the paddle *Kalanchoe* on the left shows, the choice of container completely changes the plant's visual impact:

1 The tall, smooth pot gives the plant an architectural outline, while the pale colour sets off the vivid variegated (two-tone) leaves.

2 A textured pot contrasts with the smooth foliage, while the terracotta picks up on the plant's warm red tones.

3 A metallic pot enhances the kalanchoe's strange, almost alien appearance.

The Opuntia's round outline and spiny texture contrasts with the smooth, straight-sidedpot, while its bright green colour harmonizes with the light green pot

The spiny Euphorbia finds an almost comical textural contrast in a soft fabric pot sleeve

The flowering Echeveria makes a statement in a stripy monochrome pot

The Kalanchoe's colourful foliage clashes perfectly with the bright, solid blue pot

The tips of this Echeveria harmonize with this bright orange pot

DESIGNING WITH
CONTAINERS

Be adventurous with your container choice. Almost anything can be used as a container or outer sleeve: as well as regular pots and terrariums, try repurposing old household items for conversation-starting display.

1 This rustic white tray harmonizes with the dusty appearance of the air plants it displays.

2 A glass terrarium can display an entire miniature garden, allowing it to be admired from every angle.

3 These glass baubles act as tiny hanging terrariums for the ferns and trailing plants within.

4 Try planting spring bulbs in glass jars to show off their root systems as they grow.

5 Add drainage holes to the base of a clean food tin to create a statement cacti container.

6 A vintage jug makes a curious decorative sleeve for an orchid.

7 Wall-mounted containers turn these two staghorn ferns into living pieces of art.

8 Repetition of three is a tried and tested design device. This row of three neat geometrical pots results in a smart, symmetrical display.

1

2

3

4

5

6

7

8

DESIGNING FOR
BRIGHT
LIGHT

If you're lucky enough to have lots of bright light in your home (see pp308–309), take advantage of the possibilities by designing stunning displays of sun-loving plants. Fill up an empty window from top to bottom with lush greenery, or create a hanging garden beneath a skylight. Just remember to make sure your chosen plants can cope with the level of sunlight they are exposed to (see Plant Profiles, pp132–301).

1 Combine a mixture of sun-loving plants of different sizes and shapes to create a windowsill display that makes the most of the bright light levels.

2 Propagated cuttings (see pp124–25) make a pretty and practical display in a bright area out of direct sun.

3 Hang vanda orchids (see p147) in front of a window to show off their roots, which can be displayed without compost.

4 In the wild, many orchids trail from high tree brances. Echo that by hanging them beneath a skylight, out of direct sun.

5 This colourful, multi-level orchid display fills a small window with blooms.

6 A hanging herb planter makes practical use of a kitchen window.

1

4

2

3

5

6

DESIGNING FOR
LOW LIGHT

Don't despair if your home does not receive a lot of bright daylight. Many plants prefer filtered sun, and some can even thrive away in areas of light shade (see pp308–309), since many of them would naturally grow in the low light beneath a forest canopy. Use this as inspiration when designing for low light, adding touches of lush greenery to evoke a woodland landscape in your living space.

1 Large, glossy-leaved foliage and climbing plants trained up walls brings a touch of the jungle to an urban home.

2 Orchids that would naturally grow under dense forest canopies, such as this moth orchid, are well-suited to low light.

3 This small display of woodland plants will thrive in filtered sun/light shade (L–R: golden polypody, mind-your-own-business, Cretan brake fern).

4 Keep a bowl of damp pebbles near a collection of lush feathery forest ferns to keep them looking hydrated and fresh (L–R: crocodile fern, Boston fern).

5 Add flashes of colour to a low-light display by using flowering plants and variegated leaves (such as those of a polka-dot begonia, centre).

1

DESIGNING FOR
HUMIDITY

Most moisture-loving plants need regular misting and care, but what if you could display them in a ready-made humid space in which they could thrive? Use humidity to your advantage and be adventurous in your designs: dare to turn a kitchen into a jungle, or take over the bathroom with ambitious living walls and displays, where the steam will naturally mist humidity-lovers like ferns, bromeliads, and air plants.

1 Contrast the bright foliage of a bathroom bromeliad display with the addition of a humidity-loving Amazonian elephant's ear.

2 Assemble a kokedama string garden (see pp80–83) in humid areas of your home (L–R: Boston fern, spider plant, Cretan brake fern).

3 A trailing string of hearts plant adds a touch of atmosphere to a bathroom counter.

4 Use a humid spot to keep feathery foliage lush and fresh (L–R: mind-your-own-business, delta maidenhair fern, and string of pearls).

5 Since air plants draw moisture from the air, display them in a humid room in a wire frame or on a stand (see pp44–47).

6 Carnivorous plants love moist, boggy environments, so will thrive in a humid space.

1

4

2

3

5

6

DESIGNING FOR
SPACE

Any living space, large or small, offers plenty of opportunities to get creative with house plant design. If you have no free surfaces, create a colony of hanging plants above your head. If you have bare walls, swap artwork for architectural displays of plant-filled shelves. With a little imagination, you will find more and more ways to turn any space into an indoor oasis.

1

1 If you want to hang non-trailing plants from the ceiling, use decorative containers that will look attractive from below. Hang climbing plants from rafters, if your home has them, to allow the foliage to grow up and along the beams.

2 Climbing plants aren't just for the garden; you can also train them to indoor walls to fill an empty space.

3 Fill a tall set of shelves with a curated selection of plants to create your own "green library".

4 Assemble a lush collection of hanging plants to create a "living curtain" of foliage.

5 Create a miniature garden in a tiny space using a terrarium (see pp60–63 and pp96–99). Display it at eye level, where the detail can be closely admired.

6 Almost any space is up for grabs when designing plant displays. A staircase, for example, shows off your plants at eye level and from above as you walk down.

4

2

3

5

6

DESIGNING FOR
WELLBEING

There is far more to house plant design than visual beauty. Plants aren't just decorative objects: they are capable of lowering our stress levels, filling our homes with fragrance, and even ridding the air we breathe of harmful pollutants. Follow the advice on these pages to make the most of these benefits.

HOW HOUSE PLANTS HELP

Multiple studies have shown that there are tangible psychological benefits to keeping plants in indoor spaces such as homes and offices. After spending time living and working alongside plants, those taking part in the studies found that, on average:

- their mood levels improved
- they felt less stressed
- they felt more productive
- their attention span improved (in some studies)

DESIGNING FOR
MINDFULNESS

Modern life doesn't always offer enough opportunities to enjoy the Great Outdoors, especially for those of us living in built-up urban environments with little daily access to parks or woodland. Studies have shown that living and working in a plant-filled environment can noticeably boost mental wellbeing (see below left). By adding touches of greenery throughout your home, especially in the places where you spend the most time, you will create a more calming atmosphere in which you can go about your daily life. In particular, keep plants near any windows that look out onto built-up areas to bring nature into your view.

1 A plant-filled home can provide a psychological boost when access to nature is otherwise limited. For the full effect, create an indoor jungle packed to the rafters with foliage to stimulate your mind and improve your mood.

DESIGNING FOR
THE SENSES

Fragrant house plants add an extra sensory dimension to any plant design. We often bring bulbs and other scented plants into our homes during the darkest months of the year to remind ourselves of the sights and smells of spring. Position them in a front hallway for a bright, fragrant welcome, or near a door so that you will catch a hint of fragrance every time you pass.

1 Nelly Isler (left) and brassia orchid blooms both provide a burst of scent.

2 Stephanotis is a classic plant choice when designing for scent.

3 Thyme bushes release a wonderful fragrance when brushed against in passing.

4 Combine scented and non-scented plants to create a larger display without an overwhelming amount of fragrance (L–R: peace lily, scented hoya, scented cyclamen).

5 "Force" grape hyacinth bulbs for scent and colour during winter (see pp328–29).

1

1

2

3

4

5

Bringing it all together
The more you design houseplant displays, the more bold and creative your arrangements will become. Keep in mind how to work with scale, colour, and texture, and select containers that will complement your plants and your living space. For example this indoor oasis creates harmony with its all-green colour scheme, and contrast between the shaggy texture of the plants and the clean lines of the apartment.

HOUSE PLANT
PROJECTS

DESERTSCAPE

Grouping your cacti and succulent collection together in a single container is a great way to show off their different characteristics. The container does not have to be deep, as cacti have shallow root systems, but make sure it has adequate drainage; adding a layer of gravel beneath the compost will help prevent waterlogging if your container has no drainage holes.

WHAT YOU WILL NEED

PLANTS
- Selection of cacti, succulents, and plants with similar care needs, such as bunny ears cacti, golden barrel cacti, and African spears

OTHER MATERIALS
- Shallow decorative container, preferably with drainage holes
- Fine-grade gravel
- Activated charcoal
- Peat-free cactus compost
- Pebbles and small stones, to decorate

TOOLS
- Small tray, for watering
- Spoon or small trowel
- Dibber
- Protective cactus gloves
- Small paintbrush, for dusting

1 Water the cacti and other plants thoroughly by placing them on a small tray filled with water. This will encourage the roots to make good contact with the new compost.

2 Pour a layer of gravel, approximately 2.5cm (1in) deep, into the base of the container. Mix in a few spoonfuls of activated charcoal to prevent the growth of fungi. Top with an even layer of cactus compost, 5–7.5cm (2–4in) deep.

3 While still in their pots, arrange the plants on top of the compost until you are happy with their placement. Allow plenty of room for growth. Once you like the arrangement, remove the plants, remembering where you intend to plant them.

4 Select your first plant. Using the dibber, make a hole in the compost large enough to fit the plant's root ball. Wearing gloves, remove the plant from its pot and gently tease the roots to release excess soil. Repeat for the remaining plants.

5 Using a spoon, carefully fill in any gaps between the plants with compost. Firm the compost down using the back of the spoon or the dibber.

6 Decorate the surface of the compost with pebbles and small stones.

HOW TO MAINTAIN

TEMPERATURE 10–25°C (50–77°F)
LIGHT Sun/Filtered sun in summer
HUMIDITY Low
CARE Easy

WATERING Water your cacti when the compost is completely dry. Depending on the conditions of your living space, this will usually take 3–4 weeks. Soak the compost completely, but take care not to overwater, especially if your container does not have drainage holes, as this could cause root rot. Do not water at all between October and March.

MAINTENANCE AND CARE Gently brush off any compost caught in the spines of the plants with a soft paintbrush. Place on a sunny windowsill from autumn to spring; move the display further away from the window in summer, when the heat can become too intense. Watch out for draughts in winter, and relocate if necessary.

SUCCULENT GLOBE

Made with two compost-filled hanging-basket frames, this living globe seems to defy gravity. Low-growing, rosette-shaped plants work best for this project, as they help maintain the display's spherical outline, but you could also try adding a few trailing plants near the bottom of the globe to create a living waterfall effect.

WHAT YOU WILL NEED

PLANTS
- A selection of small succulents, such as echeverias and sempervivums
- 2-3 trailing plants, such as *Curio rowleyanus* (optional)
- Sustainable decorative moss

OTHER MATERIALS
- 2 coir fibre liners
- 2 x 25cm (10in) hemispherical wire hanging baskets
- Peat-free cactus compost
- Florist's wire
- Strong cord, twine, or chain
- Florist's pins

EQUIPMENT
- Baking sheet or wooden board
- Wire cutters
- Sharp scissors
- Dibber (optional)
- Deep tray
- Plastic funnel, for watering
- Jug

1 Place a coir fibre liner inside each basket. Fill with compost up to the top of the baskets. Pack it in as tightly as possible, because any air pockets that remain could cause the coir fibre to sag later.

2 Hold the baking sheet against the top of one of the baskets. Quickly and carefully flip the basket and sheet over, and place them directly on top of the other basket. Ease out the sheet, taking care not to let any compost leak.

3 Use florist's wire to attach the outer edges of the baskets to each other at regular intervals. They should now form a secure "globe". Loop a piece of strong cord around one of the baskets' bars, ready to hang up the globe later.

4 At the opposite side of the globe to the cord, cut a small hole in the coir liner and tease it open. Remove the first plant from its pot and gently shake away the excess compost. Squeeze the root ball in your hand and insert it into the hole.

5 Firm the coir fibre back around the plant, then secure it with a florist's pin. Repeat steps 4–5 with the remaining plants, positioning them evenly around the globe with enough room between them to allow for growth.

6 When most of the globe is covered, invert it and hang it up from a secure point. Carefully plant up any empty areas on what was the underside. Once the whole globe is covered with plants, pin decorative moss onto any exposed areas of coir.

HOW TO MAINTAIN

TEMPERATURE 10–25°C (50–77°F)
LIGHT Full sun; some shade in summer
HUMIDITY Low

WATERING Place a deep tray under the hanging globe to catch any drips. Standing on a stepladder if necessary, carefully insert a funnel into the coir lining at the top of the globe and pour water into the funnel to saturate the compost within. Let all excess water drain away before removing the tray. Allow the compost to dry out fully in between waterings; you will be able to tell from the weight of the globe when it needs to be watered again.

MAINTENANCE AND CARE Display the globe in bright, indirect light, turning it in between waterings to ensure all the plants get plenty of sun. The globe will be heavy, especially after watering, so make sure to hang it from a secure point able to take the full weight of the display when saturated.

AIR PLANT STAND

Rootless air plants do not need soil to survive, and in the wild they are found clinging to rocky surfaces and hanging from the branches of trees. Echo their natural habitat by growing them on a wooden stand, which can comfortably display a small collection of air plants without using any glue or wire to hold them in place.

WHAT YOU WILL NEED

PLANTS
- Sustainably sourced decorative mosses and lichen
- Selection of air plants in a variety of shapes, colours, and sizes (see pp300-301)

OTHER MATERIALS
- Untreated, rugged piece of wood with plenty of crevices and hollows, such as driftwood, grapewood, cork bark, or tree fern
- Small branch
- Florist's wire

TOOLS
- Large bowl, for soaking
- Wire cutters
- Hot glue gun (optional)

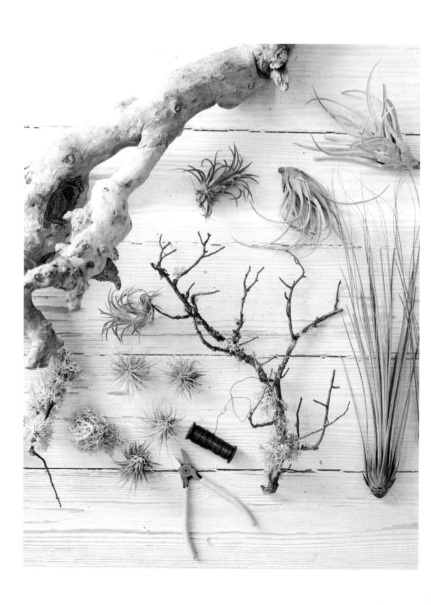

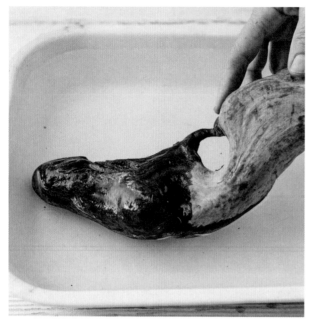

1 If using ocean driftwood, make sure it has been pre-soaked to remove all salt residue. To desalinate your own driftwood, soak it in freshwater for several weeks, replenishing the water a few times during this period.

2 Thread small pieces of moss onto the small branch and place it on top of the larger piece of wood. This will double up as both a decorative feature and an additional platform upon which to arrange your smaller air plants.

3 Fasten the branch to the wood with wire, wrapping it around at least a couple of times to ensure it is secure.

4 Attach bunches of moss and lichen to the larger piece of wood, using the wire or hot glue to secure them in place. If using glue, allow it to cool and solidify completely before adding your air plants to the display.

5 Gently arrange your air plants in the wood's natural crevices. Lighter, more delicate air plants can be placed along the attached branch. Do not glue the air plants in place (see right).

HOW TO MAINTAIN

TEMPERATURE 15-24°C (60-75°F)
LIGHT Filtered sun
HUMIDITY High
CARE Easy

WATERING Water your air plants with rainwater or distilled water once a week (see p313). Make sure the water is at lukewarm or at room temperature; cold water will shock the plants. Place them on a soft dishcloth and let them dry out completely before returning them to the stand. You can mist them 2-3 times a week.

MAINTENANCE AND CARE Place the stand in filtered sun. Make sure young plants have room to grow; if they become too large for their current spot, move them to a roomier, more stable part of the stand.

Never use glue or wire to attach airplants to a display. Not only would this make it very difficult to soak the plants, but the chemicals in glue may seriously harm the plants.

INDOOR WINDOW BOX

An indoor window box lets you take advantage of the brightest location in your home and offers the ideal conditions for your cacti and succulents to grow. By building your own box out of timber or reclaimed wood, you can make a display that will perfectly fill the length of your windowsill.

WHAT YOU WILL NEED

PLANTS
- Selection of mid-sized cacti and succulents

OTHER MATERIALS
- New or reclaimed timber boards
- Screws or nails
- Wood paint or stain (optional)
- Recycled or repurposed plastic sheeting
- 4mm grit or fine gravel
- Peat-free cactus compost
- Small pebbles

TOOLS
- Tape measure
- Saw
- Screwdriver or hammer
- Large paintbrush, for painting
- Staple gun
- Trowel
- Dibber
- Cactus gloves
- Spoon
- Soft-bristled paintbrush, for dusting
- Watering can with narrow spout

1 Measure the length of your chosen windowsill (see How to Maintain, opposite). Saw 3 equal lengths of timber slightly smaller than the sill (to form the base and sides), followed by 2 short lengths for the ends. Screw or hammer the sides to the base, then secure the end pieces in place.

2 If you wish, apply 1–2 coats of wood paint or stain to the outside of the box, following the instructions provided on the tin. Allow to dry completely.

3 When the box is fully dry, line the inside with plastic sheeting and staple it securely in place, to make it as watertight as possible.

4 Pour a layer of 4mm grit, about 2cm (¾in) deep, into the bottom of the box. Then fill it with a loose layer of cactus compost until it reaches up to 5cm (2in) from the top.

5 Select the first plant. Use the dibber to make a hole in the compost large enough to fit the plant's root ball. Wearing cactus gloves, remove the plant from its pot and loosen its roots, then gently place it into the hole. Firm down the compost around the plant.

6 Repeat with the remaining plants, placing them at regular intervals along the box. Leave some space between the plants to allow for growth and good air circulation, which reduces the risk of rot.

HOW TO MAINTAIN

TEMPERATURE 10–25°C (50–77°F)
LIGHT Filtered sun
HUMIDITY Low

WATERING Using a watering can with a narrow spout, water around the plants when the compost is completely dry. Take care not to overwater. Reduce watering between late autumn and early spring.

MAINTENANCE AND CARE Choose a windowsill that receives filtered or indirect sunlight; direct sunlight could scorch the plants in summer. Avoid draughty windowsills too, as well as those with radiators beneath them, as the heat may dry out the plants.

7 Once all the plants are in place, place decorative gravel on top of the compost, then gently brush off any compost with a soft-bristled paintbrush.

MACRAMÉ HANGER

Macramé, the art of decoratively knotting cords and rope, can be used to create a simple hanger in which to display your favourite house plants. Use wooden beads and cotton cord to create the simple, modern look shown here, or try different materials, such as metallic beads or unbleached rope, to design a unique macramé hanger of your own.

WHAT YOU WILL NEED

PLANT
- Suitable plant in a 15cm (6in) pot, such as a delta maidenhair fern

OTHER MATERIALS
- 10m (32ft) strong, non-stretch cord or string, such as cotton cord
- Wooden ring
- S-hook
- 8 wooden beads (4 small and 4 large)
- Decorative pot sleeve suitable for a 15cm (6in) plant

TOOLS
- Ruler or tape measure
- Scissors

1 Cut 4 lengths of cotton cord measuring 220cm (7¼ft), and 2 lengths measuring 50cm (20in). Thread the 4 long cords through the wooden ring, folding them in half over the edge. Hold the cords together in one hand just below the ring, leaving the lengths trailing below.

2 Take one of the shorter cords and make a loop at one end. Pinch the loop in place on top of the trailing cords in your right hand, leaving both the long and short tails of the loop above the wooden ring.

3 Tightly wrap the long tail around the loop and trailing cords 5 times, moving further away from the wooden ring. After 5 turns, thread the remainder of the long tail through the loop hole.

4 Pull the short tail so that the loop slides inside the 5 turns. Cut off both ends close to the binding and tuck inside to complete the knot. This technique is known as a "wrapping knot".

5 Using the S-hook, hang the ring up and check that you have 8 equal lengths of cord hanging down. Separate the cords into 4 pairs. Thread 1 small and 1 large wooden bead onto each pair of cords, approximately 30cm (12in) down from the ring.

6 Take 1 cord from 2 adjacent pairs and tie them together in a knot about 8cm (3in) down from the beads. Repeat this 3 times until all the cords are tied together. Repeat this process about 6cm (2in) below these knots (again taking 2 cords from adjacent pairs) to make another set of knots. The cords should now resemble a net.

7 Gather all the cords about 6cm (2in) below these knots. Using the second short length of cord, tie them together in another wrapping knot (see steps 2–4). Ensure this knot is as tight as possible, then trim any excess cord to the desired length.

8 Finally, fit your decorative pot sleeve securely into the hanger, then gently place your choice of plant inside the pot.

HOW TO MAINTAIN

WATERING When the plant needs watering, carefully remove it (and the pot) from the macramé hanger to prevent the cord from staining and rotting.

MAINTENANCE AND CARE Before displaying your plant, test its weight in the macramé hanger by gently lifting it up by the S-hook. The wrapping knots should hold firm; if the pot feels insecure within the hanger, remove it and retie the knots until you are confident that they will hold.

As the plant grows, it will cascade beautifully over the sides of the hanger. If it becomes too large and needs repotting, replace it with another 15cm (6in) plant rather than squeezing it back into the hanger in its larger pot.

BROKEN POT PLANTER

Give new life to broken clay plant pots by reworking them
into a tiered display for eye-catching succulents. The open side
of one big pot can make a window for smaller broken pot pieces
and, with careful planting, will create an impressive layered effect.
Take care when handling broken pots as the edges may be sharp.

WHAT YOU WILL NEED

PLANTS
- Selection of succulent plants of differing sizes, colours, and textures, such as *Aeonium*, *Crassula*, *Sedum*, and *Echeveria*

OTHER MATERIALS
- One large broken clay pot with a drainage hole in the base, with matching saucer
- Peat-free cactus compost
- 2-3 smaller clay pots, broken or whole
- A selection of broken pot pieces
- Small pebbles

TOOLS
- Trowel
- Dibber
- Soft-bristled paintbrush, for dusting
- Spoon
- Watering can with narrow spout

1 Fill one-third of the large pot with compost and firm it down. Arrange the smaller pots within the larger pot at irregular angles, filling them with compost as you go.

2 Fill the spaces around the smaller pots with compost. Use broken pot pieces to wedge everything in place, if necessary. Make sure that the composition leaves plenty of exposed compost and space for planting.

3 Remove the first plant from its pot and gently loosen the roots. Make a hole in the compost the same size as the root ball and place the plant in it. Use the dibber to firm the compost around the base of the plant.

4 Repeat this process with the smaller plants, allowing some space between them for growth. If necessary, use broken pot pieces to support the plants.

5 Fill narrower spaces by gently prizing apart the roots of compact plants to make 2-3 smaller plants. Carefully bed these plants into the gaps.

6 When you are happy with the arrangement, brush any remaining compost from the surface of the plants and cover any exposed compost with the small pebbles.

HOW TO MAINTAIN

TEMPERATURE 10-25°C (50-77°F)
LIGHT Filtered sun
HUMIDITY Low

WATERING Use a watering can with a narrow spout to water around the plants, ensuring that all the separate areas receive enough water. Wait until the compost has dried out completely before watering again.

MAINTENANCE AND CARE Stand in bright indirect light, turning the display occasionally to ensure all the plants receive enough sun.

OPEN BOTTLE TERRARIUM

A terrarium is a semi-enclosed glass container that creates a warm, humid microclimate for the plants that grow within. For this open bottle terrarium, choose a selection of foliage plants that showcase a variety of leaf shapes and colours. Pick one large "feature" plant that will stand out from the rest, taking care not to overcrowd the bottle so that they all have room to grow.

WHAT YOU WILL NEED

PLANTS
- Selection of humidity-loving foliage plants (including 1 larger focal plant), such as small ferns, peperomias, and fittonias
- Decorative mosses (optional)

OTHER MATERIALS
- Wide, open-topped, heavy glass bottle or jar
- Fine-grade gravel
- Activated charcoal
- Peat-free multipurpose compost
- Decorative pebbles (optional)

EQUIPMENT
- Dibber
- Small watering can with a rose attachment

1 Pour a layer of gravel, approximately 2.5cm (1in) deep, into the base of the bottle for drainage. Mix in a few spoonfuls of activated charcoal to prevent the growth of fungi.

2 Add an even layer of compost, 5–7.5cm (2–4in) deep, over the gravel-charcoal mixture. Make a hole in the compost the same size as the focal plant's root ball.

3 Remove the focal plant from its pot and loosen the roots to encourage healthy growth. Gently place the plant in the hole.

4 Firm the compost around the base of the plant using the dibber. Repeat steps 3–4 with your remaining plants.

5 If you wish, cover the surface of the compost with decorative mosses or pebbles. Carefully wipe the inside of the vase clean.

HOW TO MAINTAIN

WATERING Use a small watering can fitted with a rose attachment to water the plants. The grouped plants and semi-enclosed space create a humid environment that traps moisture, so take care not to overwater. Only water the plants when the compost dries out.

MAINTENANCE AND CARE Place the terrarium in a bright spot, but out of direct sunlight, which may scorch the leaves through the glass.

WILLOW CLIMBING FRAME

This simple support for climbing plants is quick and easy to assemble, and makes an attractive feature even before it is hidden by leafy plant growth. Once you've mastered this basic frame, you can apply the technique to more ambitious climbing projects by training the plant's stems onto a trellis room divider or staircase, or fanning them out across a wall.

WHAT YOU WILL NEED

PLANTS
- Climbing plant, such as a philodendron, hoya, jasmine, or stephanotis

OTHER MATERIALS
- Heavy-based pot with drainage holes
- House plant or multipurpose compost
- 7 pliable willow poles, each at least 1m (3ft) in length
- Garden twine

TOOLS
- Secateurs

1 Fill your pot with compost. Insert 6 evenly spaced willow poles around the edge of the pot.

2 Gather the poles together at a comfortable height directly above the centre of the pot, and tie together securely with a length of twine. Trim away any excess length from the tops of the poles using secateurs.

3 Weave the final length of willow through the poles, roughly one-third of the way up the stand. Secure in place with twine to prevent it from slipping, then remove the entire frame from the pot and place it to one side.

4 Make a hole in the compost the size of the root ball and lower the plant in, ensuring it sits at the same level that it rested at in its original pot. Fill in any gaps with new compost, firming it down gently.

6 One by one, wrap and weave the long stems of the plant around the poles. Thicker or heavier stems may need to be tied in with the twine; take care not to tie it too tightly.

HOW TO MAINTAIN

WATERING Keep the compost moist from spring to autumn; reduce in winter, watering when the top of the compost feels dry. Mist every few days in summer, or when necessary.

MAINTENANCE AND CARE As the plant grows, continue to weave the stems around the willow poles, tying them in with twine where necessary. If the plant climbs higher than the frame, most can be pruned to keep the size in check and the plant compact.

5 Spread the untangled stems of the climber out in a fan around the base of the pot. Insert the willow frame back into the compost, over the stems.

Alternatively, position the overgrown plant next to a trellis and weave the longer stems onto the frame, training it over time and securing with garden twine.

SAND TERRARIUM

This terrarium provides the perfect environment for an assortment of desert-loving cacti and succulents to grow together. The plants will seem at home nestled in the layered sand, which is cleverly kept separate from the cactus compost by placing a second smaller container within the outer vase.

WHAT YOU WILL NEED

PLANTS
- A selection of desert-loving cacti and succulents with a variety of shapes and textures

OTHER MATERIALS
- Small pebbles or gravel
- 17cm (7in) glass vase
- Peat-free cactus compost
- 20cm (8in) glass vase
- Decorative sand in 2–3 contrasting colours

TOOLS
- Trowel
- Dibber
- Cactus gloves
- Piece of stiff card or paper
- Small paintbrush, for dusting
- Watering can with narrow spout
- Moisture metre

1 Pour a 5cm (2in) layer of small pebbles or gravel into the smaller vase, then fill it almost to the top with the compost.

2 Choose an eye-catching focal plant. Remove the plant from its pot and gently loosen the roots. Using the dibber, make a hole in the compost large enough to fit the plant's root ball. Place the plant in the hole.

3 Firm the compost around the plant with the dibber. Repeat with the remaining plants, taking care and wearing gloves when handling the cacti.

4 Pour a layer of pebbles or gravel into the larger vase. Place the planted vase inside the larger vase, ensuring that the rims of the two vases are level with each other.

5 Use the stiff card to funnel the first layer of sand between the two vases, allowing it to settle in uneven waves. Continue to layer different colours of sand until the space is filled and the inner vase is entirely hidden.

6 Brush off any compost or sand from the plants' foliage before displaying the terrarium.

HOW TO MAINTAIN

TEMPERATURE 10-25°C (50-77°F)
LIGHT Filtered sun
HUMIDITY Low

WATERING Use a narrow-spouted watering can to pour a small amount of water onto the compost around the plants. As this terrarium does not have drainage holes, take extra care to avoid overwatering your plants. You may wish to insert a moisture metre into the soil now and then to help you judge if you are using the correct amount of water; cacti and succulents prefer to be kept in soil at the red end of the metre.

MAINTENANCE AND CARE Choose a bright and sunny spot for the terrarium. Move the display a little away from the window in summer months, as direct light may scorch the plants.

HYPERTUFA POT

Combining just three ingredients with water creates hypertufa, a clay-like mixture that can be used to make your own plant pot. Not only do hypertufa pots make great statement containers (see pp18–19), but they are also porous and lightweight, making them ideal for planting up desert cacti and succulents. This project takes around a month to complete, but it's well worth the wait.

WHAT YOU WILL NEED

MATERIALS
- Portland cement
- Coir fibre
- Perlite or vermiculite

TOOLS
- Cardboard or plastic sheeting, to protect surfaces (optional)
- Rubber gloves
- Bucket, for mixing
- Cooking oil spray
- 2 plastic containers, 1 larger than the other, to be used as moulds
- Rubber mallet
- Large plastic bag
- Stiff wire brush
- Plastic tray

1 Cover your work surface. In a bucket, combine equal parts cement, coir fibre, and perlite, bearing in mind the size of the pot you will be making. Put on rubber gloves, then stir the mixture together while gradually adding 1 part water until it resembles thick porridge. Allow to sit for 5–10 minutes.

2 Spray the inside of the larger container and the outside of the smaller container with oil. Press some of the mixture into the bottom of the larger container, firming it down into the corners. Gradually add more mixture, applying a thick, even layer to the sides.

3 Insert the smaller container into the mixture-lined larger container, pressing it firmly onto the bottom and around the sides. Continue packing more mixture between the containers until it feels firm. Ensure that at least 2.5cm (1in) of plastic remains exposed at the top of each container.

4 Tap around the outside of the container with a rubber mallet to encourage any large bubbles to move to the surface. Use your fingers to smooth any lumps around the top edge. Place inside a large plastic bag, seal it securely, then leave to dry and harden for 24–36 hours.

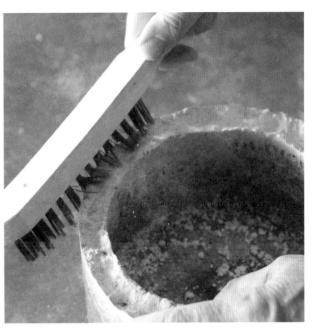

5 Remove the pot from the bag. Scratch the exposed rim with a fingernail to see if it has hardened. If it is still soft, leave it for a few more hours before retesting. When only a screwdriver can scratch the surface, remove the containers. If they are hard to move, gently tap the sides with the mallet to loosen them.

6 Leave in a dry place for 2-3 weeks to finish drying. The pot will turn light gray and will feel significantly lighter. Scrub the top edge of the pot with a wire brush to smooth away any sharp edges. Do not scrub too much; the pot should still look rustic.

7 Place the pot in a plastic tray then fill both with water. Leave to soak for a day, then pour away the water and repeat. This will leach away any alkaline compounds in the hypertufa mixture that could otherwise cause your plants to suffer. After 10 days, pour away the water and leave to dry thoroughly. The pot is now ready to be planted up.

HOW TO MAINTAIN

MAINTENANCE AND CARE To avoid scratches to floors and furniture, you may wish to glue felt to the underside of the pot. As hypertufa is relatively porous, plants can be potted up directly into the pot, without the need for a plastic container. However, as always, you should still take care to avoid overwatering.

SUCCULENT WREATH

Plant an assortment of small succulent plants into a ring of carpet
moss to create a beautiful and unique decorative wreath that will require
minimal care when kept in the right conditions. Pair a variety of succulents
with several different types of fluffy moss to add interest and
character to your display.

WHAT YOU WILL NEED

PLANTS
- Sustainably sourced carpet moss
- Selection of approximately
  12 mini succulent plants, each
  with a 5cm (2in) pot size, such
  as echeverias, sempervivums,
  aeoniums, and crassulas
- Reindeer moss

OTHER MATERIALS
- Florist's wire wreath frame,
  30cm (12in) in diameter
- Peat-free compost
- Florist's mossing pins
- Florist's wire

TOOLS
- Tray, for soaking
- Wire cutters
- Mister spray (optional)

1 Soak the pieces of carpet moss in a tray of water, to make them easier to work with.

2 Line the wire wreath frame with the carpet moss. Make sure that the bottom and sides of the frame are covered, and that you have enough moss to fold over the root balls of the plants.

3 Remove the plants from their pots and loosen their roots. Fold back the moss and bed the plants into the frame, allowing plenty of room for the plants to grow. Fill in the empty spaces between the plants with compost.

4 Fold the carpet moss back into place, over and around the bases of the plants and compost.

5 Use the mossing pins to secure the moss firmly around the base of the plants. Push the pins all the way down into the soil, so the moss holds tightly in place.

6 For extra security, wrap florist's wire around your wreath to stop the moss unravelling as it beds down.

7 Finally, cover any exposed areas of soil or wire with pieces of reindeer moss, firmly pinning them in place.

HOW TO MAINTAIN

WATERING Depending on the heat and the humidity of the room, water the display approximately once a week by submerging the mossy base in a sink full of water. Let the wreath fully dry out before soaking it again. If the air is very dry, mist the plants occasionally.

MAINTENANCE AND CARE Place your wreath out of direct sunlight and heat. Keep it laid flat for 1–2 months as the roots settle in. After this period, it will be safe to hang your wreath upright if you wish.

KOKEDAMA FERN

A type of bonsai, "kokedama" is the practice of suspending the roots of a plant in a mud ball coated with soft green moss. It is a great way to make a beautiful, hanging, sculptural object with a live plant. Arranging many kokedama plants together forms what is known as a "string garden".

WHAT YOU WILL NEED

PLANTS
- Mature fern, such as a Cretan brake, asparagus, or staghorn fern
- Sheet of sustainably sourced carpet moss

OTHER MATERIALS
- Peat-free potting compost
- Akadama (clay-like mineral used in bonsai)
- Garden twine

TOOLS
- Bucket
- Scissors
- Mister spray

82

1 Create a 2:1 mixture of potting compost and akadama in a bucket, adding a little water until it reaches a sticky, wet consistency. The akadama turns the compost into a "mud-cake" that will mould around the plant's roots.

2 Take the fern from its pot and gently shake loose some of the original compost from its roots.

3 Encase the fern roots in a layer of the damp compost-akadama mixture, approximately 2.5cm (1in) thick. Aim to create a ball of about the same volume as the original pot.

4 Envelope the root ball in a sheet of carpet moss, gathering the moss around the stem.

5 Trim the excess moss with a pair of scissors, leaving some behind at the neck of the root ball.

6 Wrap twine around the neck of the moss ball to secure the moss in place. Knot the twine firmly. To hang the fern up, attach a second length of string around the neck of the kokedama to form a loop.

HOW TO MAINTAIN

TEMPERATURE 13-24°C (55-75°F)
LIGHT Filtered sun/Light shade
HUMIDITY Moderate
CARE Fairly easy

WATERING Check if your plant needs to be watered by testing the weight of the moss ball. When it feels light, submerge the kokedama ball in water, keeping the foliage dry. Allow it to soak for 10-25 minutes, or until it is fully saturated. Remove the kokedama from the bucket, and gently squeeze the ball to drain any excess water.

MAINTENANCE AND CARE Place your kokedama in a humid spot with indirect light. Mist regularly using a spray bottle.

BARK SUCCULENT PLANTER

Create a contrast of colour and texture by planting a varied collection of succulents into a piece of bark or driftwood. Low-growing succulents are perfect for this project as they are shallow-rooted and therefore require little planting space. If using ocean driftwood, soak it in soapy water for 2 weeks to desalinate it and make it safe for planting.

WHAT YOU WILL NEED

PLANTS
- A selection of low-growing succulents of different shapes, colours, and textures, such as sempervivums and echeverias

OTHER MATERIALS
- Piece of freestanding bark or desalinated driftwood
- Sustainably sourced moss
- Peat-free cactus compost

TOOLS
- Power drill with spade bit (optional)
- Stiff-bristled paintbrush
- Florist's wire
- Wire cutters
- Soft-bristled paintbrush, for dusting
- Spoon
- Watering can with narrow spout

1 Use a power drill fitted with a spade bit to create extra planting holes along the piece of wood if needed. Carefully remove unwanted dirt and debris from the surface of the wood with a stiff-bristled paintbrush.

2 Line the crevices and holes in the base of the bark with a small amount of sphagnum moss, then top with compost.

3 Loosen the roots of the first plant. Push it firmly into the compost, right up alongside the edge of one of the planting holes, making sure that the roots are fully buried in the compost.

4 Repeat step 3 with the remaining plants, nestling them quite tightly together to mimic the way they would grow naturally. Pack moss around any exposed compost to hold the plants firmly in place.

5 If the planting hole is quite shallow, secure the plants and moss with florist's wire until the roots take hold.

6 Use the soft-bristled paintbrush to gently brush off any loose compost or moss from the plants.

HOW TO MAINTAIN

TEMPERATURE 10–25°C (50–77°F)
LIGHT Filtered sun
HUMIDITY Low

WATERING Water around the base of the plants to encourage the roots to grow and spread, enabling the plants to settle in. Allow the compost to dry out fully before watering again. Reduce watering in the winter months.

MAINTENANCE AND CARE Place the display in bright, filtered light. If one of the plants eventually outgrows the bark, you can divide it: gently remove it from the compost and separate it into 2–3 smaller pieces. Replant one of the pieces in the vacant space and plant the remaining piece(s) in another pot.

MOSS PICTURE FRAME

Living walls and vertical gardens have become increasingly popular in
urban homes across the world. You can easily make one at home using
a selection of mosses and moss-like plants, or alternatively with air
plants. Creating a moss arrangement is all about combining various
textures and colours to mimic a landscape.

WHAT YOU WILL NEED

PLANTS
- Variety of sustainably sourced
  mosses, such as bun moss to
  create hills and dips, and more
  decorative types like reindeer
  moss or trailing Spanish moss
- Moss-like plants, such as
  mind-your-own-business (see p172)

OTHER MATERIALS
- Repurposed shallow wooden
  container, such as a wine crate
  or old chitting tray, with a depth
  of approximately 10cm (4in)
- Recycled or repurposed
  plastic sheeting
- Florist's mossing pins
- Decorative branches, such as twigs
  with lichens growing on them and
  small pieces of driftwood
- Florist's wire

TOOLS
- Stapler or staple gun
- Wire cutters
- Watering can with a rose attachment
  or mister spray

1 Line the back of the wooden container with plastic sheeting, stapling it into place. This will help retain moisture within the frame.

2 Working on a flat surface, staple or pin a thin layer of sphagnum moss to the back of the container to completely cover the plastic.

3 Arrange pieces of bun moss in the container to add texture and interest. Pin to the sphagnum moss using mossing pins. Begin adding pieces of decorative mosses to the display as desired.

4 Remove your moss-like plants from their pots and loosen the roots. Bed the plants down between mounds of bun moss.

5 For extra interest, attach pieces of decorative moss to twigs and small branches using wire, then place them into the display by wedging them securely into the lower corners of the frame.

6 Add a few final pieces of decorative mosses to the display as desired, combining different colours and textures to mimic a landscape. Secure them discreetly to the twigs using wire.

HOW TO MAINTAIN

WATERING Lightly water or mist the moss frame every few days. If dry air or central heating dries the plant out, you can also completely soak the moss to revive it.

MAINTENANCE AND CARE Keep the frame laid flat for 1–2 months, to allow the moss and rooted plants to settle into place. After that time, you can prop up the display or hang it upright if you wish.

As with all photosynthetic organisms, your moss wall will prefer high humidity and indirect light; a bathroom would be ideal.

FLOATING TERRARIUM GARDEN

Maximize your space by displaying your own hanging terrarium garden across a window that receives plenty of bright, filtered light. Globe terrariums with large openings are best for this project, as they will provide the plants with plenty of air circulation.

WHAT YOU WILL NEED

PLANTS
- A selection of small and low-growing cacti and succulents, such as echeverias, crassulas, kalanchoes, and mammillarias

OTHER MATERIALS
- Wooden branch or pole (optional)
- 2 curtain brackets (optional)
- Screws (optional)
- 4mm grit or gravel
- A selection of small- and medium-sized hanging globe terrariums
- Peat-free cactus compost
- Small pebbles
- Twine or clear plastic wire

TOOLS
- Screwdriver (optional)
- Spirit level (optional)
- Spoon or small trowel
- Dibber
- Watering can with narrow spout

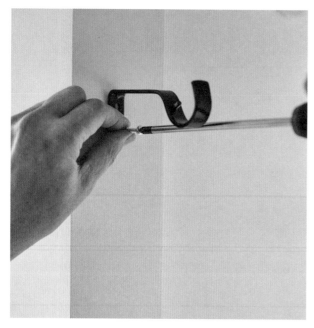

1 If you are putting up a new branch or pole, position a curtain bracket to one side of your chosen window and screw it in place. Repeat on the other side of the window, ensuring the brackets are level, then add the branch or pole.

2 Select your first terrarium. Spoon a layer of grit or gravel into the bottom. Top with a loose layer of compost approximately 2.5cm (1in) deep.

3 Remove your first plant from its pot and gently loosen the roots. Make a hole in the compost at the back of the terrarium and place the plant in it. Use a dibber to gently firm the compost around the base of the plant.

4 Repeat the process with 1-2 additional plants, ensuring that there is sufficient space between them for air circulation and growth. Place any trailing plants nearest the front, so that the stems can emerge from the opening.

5 Scatter decorative pebbles on top of any exposed compost. Repeat steps 2-5 for the remaining terrariums.

6 Thread a piece of twine through each terrarium's loop. Tie the ends securely around the loops at the top of the branch or pole. Vary the length of each piece of twine so that the terrariums "float" at different levels across the window.

HOW TO MAINTAIN

TEMPERATURE 8-25°C (46-77°F)
LIGHT Filtered sun
HUMIDITY Low

WATERING Use a watering can with a narrow spout to water the plants. Because they lack drainage and are partially covered, plants displayed in terraria retain moisture for longer than usual, making them more susceptible to overwatering and rot. Therefore, take care to water them only very occasionally, once the compost has completely dried out.

MAINTENANCE AND CARE These terrariums are best displayed beside a window that receives filtered light for a few hours a day; too much bright, full sunlight could scorch the plants through the terrarium glass.

DRY TERRARIUM

Unlike the humidity-loving plants displayed in the bottle terrarium
(see pp60–63), the plants in this display prefer drier, desert-like conditions.
Choose a selection of succulents and cacti that vary in height and shape
to create a more interesting display. This open terrarium does
not self-irrigate, and so must be watered occasionally.

WHAT YOU WILL NEED

PLANTS
- Selection of plants (including 1 larger focal plant), such as *Crassula*, *Haworthia*, and *Echeveria*

OTHER MATERIALS
- Glass terrarium with an opening of at least 18cm (7in)
- Gravel or small pebbles
- Activated charcoal
- Peat-free cactus compost
- Decorative pebbles

TOOLS
- Small trowel or spoon
- Dibber
- Watering can

1 Pour a shallow layer of gravel, with a depth of approximately 2.5cm (1in), over the base of the terrarium. Mix a small handful of activated charcoal into the gravel.

2 Add a layer of cactus compost, approximately 5–7.5cm (2–4in) deep, on top of the gravel-charcoal mixture.

3 Select your focal plant and remove it from its pot. Gently loosen the roots to encourage growth.

4 Make a hole in the compost the same size as the root ball and gently place the plant in it. Use the dibber to firm the compost around the base of the plant.

5 Repeat this process with 2-3 smaller plants. Leave space between the plants to allow for both growth and good air flow. This will prevent a build up of humidity between the plants, which could lead to rot.

6 Once the plants are firmly in place, carefully place decorative pebbles on top of the compost using a spoon.

HOW TO MAINTAIN

WATERING Only water your display occasionally, when the compost completely dries out. The semi-enclosed space of the terrarium will retain moisture and create humidity, so take care not to overwater, as this may cause rot.

MAINTENANCE AND CARE Place your terrarium in indirect light; bright light could magnify within the glass container and cause the plants to overheat and dry out.

POTTED PLANT WREATH

An assortment of new and recycled terracotta pots in different sizes not only put an eye-catching spin on a classic wreath, but also allow you to display living plants rather than cuttings. The plants in this arrangement create a warm colour palette to match the pots (see pp14–15), but you could also try combining white pots with blue-tinted plants for a more cool look.

WHAT YOU WILL NEED

PLANTS
- A selection of low-growing succulents, such as *Crassula*, *Echeveria*, *Sedum*, and *Sempervivum*
- Sustainably sourced decorative moss

OTHER MATERIALS
- Florist's wire
- A selection of 6cm (2½in) and 12cm (5in) terracotta pots with drainage holes
- Willow or wire wreath frame
- Peat-free cactus compost
- Strong twine or string

TOOLS
- Wire cutters
- Hot glue gun
- Spoon or small trowel
- Watering can with narrow spout
- Wide tray, for watering

1 Run a length of florist's wire through the drainage hole of one of the larger pots. Bring the ends of the wire together on the outside of the pot and twist together, as shown.

2 Position the pot at an angle beside the wreath frame. Wrap the wire ends around the frame and twist to secure. Repeat this process for the remaining large pots, spacing them equally around the frame.

3 Add the smaller pots to the frame using the method described in steps 1–2, filling in the gaps between the larger pots, alternating the angles of the pots as you go.

4 Once you are happy with the overall composition of the pots on the frame, secure them in place with a hot glue gun. Add compost to the base of each pot.

5 Add a plant to each pot, firming it down into the compost. If the plant will be upside-down once the wreath is hung up, run 1-2 pieces of wire across the lip of the pot between the compost and the plant's foliage and secure it to the frame.

6 Pack some moss around the surface of the compost and around the frame, securing it discreetly in place with florist's wire.

7 Leave the wreath to lie flat for up to 1 month to allow the plants to settle into their pots. To hang the wreath up, loop a piece of strong twine around the frame and secure with a firm knot.

HOW TO MAINTAIN

TEMPERATURE 5–25°C (41–77°F)
LIGHT Filtered sun
HUMIDITY Low

WATERING Place the wreath flat in a wide tray, then water each of the plants in turn using a watering can with a narrow spout. Leave the wreath lying down to drain before re-hanging. Allow the compost in the pots to dry out completely between waterings.

MAINTAINENCE AND CARE Display the wreath in bright indirect light. If any of the succulents start to outgrow their pots, take the wreath down and replant the pot with a new, small plant.

HANGING BASKET

Add vertical interest to your room with a hanging succulent planter. Trailing cacti such as *Rhipsalis* and *Epiphyllum* are epiphytic, meaning that they grow naturally from the surface of trees in the canopy of the rainforest. Suspended from a moss-lined basket, with some plants emerging from holes in the basket's sides, these plants will drape beautifully.

WHAT YOU WILL NEED

PLANTS
- 3 or 5 trailing cacti and succulents, such as *Ceropegia*, *Epiphyllum*, and *Rhipsalis*

OTHER MATERIALS
- 2m (6½ft) strong twine or rope
- Wire basket
- S-hooks
- Sheet of sustainably sourced moss, around 1.5cm (½in) thick
- Peat-free orchid compost (see pp318–19)

TOOLS
- Trowel
- Wire cutters
- Scissors
- Small sharp knife
- Watering can with narrow spout
- Tray, for watering

1 Cut the twine into four equal lengths around 50cm (1½ft) long. Knot the first piece around the edge of the basket so that it has two tails of equal length. Repeat with the other pieces at equal points around the basket.

2 Place the spaghnum moss around the inside and on the bottom of the basket. This will provide a lining for the compost, so it is important to ensure that there are no gaps.

3 Add compost to the moss-lined basket until it is three-quarters full. Gather the pieces of string above the frame and knot them together to make a secure loop.

4 Using the wire cutters, make 2-3 evenly distributed holes in the side of the basket frame to create space to display some of your trailing plants.

5 Select your first plant. Compress its root ball in your fingers and carefully push it into one of the holes and through the moss. Repeat to fill the remaining holes.

6 Plant up the top of the basket with any remaining cacti and succulents, firming the compost around each plant so that they sit snugly in place.

HOW TO MAINTAIN

TEMPERATURE 10–25°C (50–77°F)
LIGHT Light shade
HUMIDITY Medium

WATERING Lift the basket to judge if it needs water; the lighter the basket, the drier the soil. The size of the basket is directly related to the amount of water your hanging plants can retain, meaning that a smaller basket will need to be watered more often than a larger one. Place a tray under the basket before watering to catch the drips, then use a watering can to soak any exposed compost. Mist the basket occasionally, as these plants prefer humid conditions.

MAINTENANCE AND CARE Hang the basket in a bright area out of direct sun.

WOOD-MOUNTED ORCHID

Mounting an orchid on decorative wood makes a beautiful display and can be beneficial to your orchid's health. It mimics how the orchid would grow naturally and allows for good drainage and ventilation to the roots, which will help your plant to thrive and prevent disease.

WHAT YOU WILL NEED

PLANTS
- Small orchid, such as a moth orchid or nobile dendrobium
- Sustainably sourced bun mosses

OTHER MATERIALS
- Decorative piece of wood, such as driftwood, tree bark, cork bark, or birch pole
- Florist's wire

TOOLS
- Wire cutters

1 Remove the orchid from its pot and carefully tease the potting medium from its roots.

2 Pack sphagnum moss evenly in and around the roots of the orchid, leaving some outer roots partially exposed. Gently secure in place with a little wire.

3 Position the orchid on the piece of wood with the plant's crown angled downward. Wrap the wire around the base and roots of the orchid to secure it to the wood.

4 Take care not to wrap the wire around the orchid too tightly, as this could damage it. When the plant feels comfortably secure, twist the two ends of wire together and cut away the excess with wire cutters.

5 Decorate the rest of the piece of wood with additional handfuls of moss, using wire to secure them in place.

HOW TO MAINTAIN

TEMPERATURE 16-27°C (61-80°F)
LIGHT Filtered sun/Light shade
HUMIDITY Moderate/High
CARE Easy

WATERING Orchids attached to mounts tend to dry out fairly quickly, so water at least three times a week. To water the plant, submerge the entire mount in a large, deep bowl for 20 minutes until completely saturated.

MAINTENANCE AND CARE Place in a humid area and mist daily. Leave the wire intact while the orchid's roots find secure purchase on the wood. The root moss will eventually fall away as the plant grows new roots and explores the wood's surface. Over time, the plant will develop the elegant, flattened shape characteristic of orchids found in the wild.

PLANTED CANDLE HOLDER

Simple to make, this beautiful table centrepiece looks great all year round. If you like, you can easily switch the candle for one of a different colour to match the season or change the mood. Choose a slow-burning, dripless candle that will sit at least 10cm (4in) above the plants to avoid dripping hot wax onto the foliage.

WHAT YOU WILL NEED

PLANTS
- A selection of low growing succulents, such as *Sedum*, *Echeveria*, and *Crassula*
- A trailing plant, such as *Curio rowleyanus*
- Sustainably sourced decorative moss

OTHER MATERIALS
- Fine-grade gravel
- Terracotta pot, 20cm (8in) wide
- Terracotta pot, 12cm (5in) wide
- Peat-free cactus compost
- 16cm (6in) pillar candle, dripless if possible

TOOLS
- Trowel
- Dibber
- Spoon
- Soft-bristled paintbrush, for dusting
- Watering can with narrow spout

1 Pour a layer of gravel into the bottom of the larger pot. Place the smaller pot into the centre of the larger one, ensuring that the outer rims of both pots are level.

2 Fill the space between the two pots with compost, but leave a 2cm (1in) gap at the top. Pack the compost down firmly to secure the small pot in the centre.

3 Remove the first plant from its pot and gently loosen its roots. Using the dibber, make a hole in the compost and place the plant in it, firmly packing down the compost around the plant.

4 Repeat step 3 with the remaining plants. As the area between the two pots is quite narrow, you may need to divide the plants following the instructions on p59.

HOW TO MAINTAIN

TEMPERATURE 10–25°C (50–77°F)
LIGHT Filtered sun
HUMIDITY Low

WATERING Use a watering can with a narrow spout to direct the water onto the compost between the two pots. The gravel in the pot and hole at the base will stop the plants becoming waterlogged. Allow the compost to dry out fully before watering again.

MAINTENANCE AND CARE Keep in bright, indirect light. When the candle has burned low, replace it with a new one, packing it in place with fresh moss.

5 Place the candle in the smaller pot. Pack moss around the candle to secure it in place. Use the paintbrush to remove any remaining moss or debris from the plants.

LIVING SPACE DIVIDER

A moveable trailing plant space divider can be used to create a beautiful temporary wall or living screen between different parts of your indoor space. Choose bushier plants to fill out the divider more completely, or show off a selection of decorative containers using macramé hangers (see pp52–55).

WHAT YOU WILL NEED

PLANTS
- Selection of trailing plants that prefer bright, indirect sun, such as string of pearls, string of hearts, and mistletoe cacti
- Selection of tall, mid-sized foliage plants with similar requirements, such as fiddle-leaved figs, spider plant, and most ferns

OTHER MATERIALS
- Free-standing clothes rail, ideally with a lower shelf
- String
- S-hooks
- Decorative pot sleeves of appropriate sizes
- Macrame hangers
- Large pot or bucket

TOOLS
- Scissors
- Watering can

1 Select your first trailing plant. If its plastic pot is hidden by foliage, make 3 evenly spaced holes through the rim of the pot with a pair of scissors. Thread a length of string through each hole, securing each in place with a firm knot.

2 Gather the three strings together directly above the centre of the plant at the length from which you want the plant to hang from the rail. Tie a secure knot, leaving a short length of string above.

3 Form a small loop with the excess string, and tie it to the existing knot as tightly and neatly as possible. Trim any remaining string with scissors.

4 Slip the bottom curve of an S-hook through the loop and slowly lift the plant, checking that all the knots are secure. Clip the top curve of the S-hook over the bar of the clothes rail. Repeat for all the plants you wish to hang.

5 If you wish to hide a plastic pot from view, place the plant in a decorative sleeve and nestle it securely into a macramé hanger. Tie the hanger securely onto the rail, or use an S-hook to hold it in place.

6 Once the rail is full, fill the gaps beneath by arranging a second selection of plants on the shelf beneath. Try out different combinations of plants and decorative pots until you are happy with the final appearance of your living frame.

HOW TO MAINTAIN

WATERING Water and mist all plants as required. Remove plants from macramé hangers when watering them, to prevent saturating the decorative cord or rope (which could lead to rot over time).

MAINTENANCE AND CARE Wherever you position your room divider, ensure that the space is draught free. Prune plants as needed; swap them out if they grow too large for the display.

INDOOR ROCKERY

In their native South Africa, *Lithops* (also known as living stones) avoid being eaten by camouflaging themselves to look like the surrounding rocks. Make the most of this feature by nestling them with other low-growing succulents amongst a mini-landscape of rocks and pebbles. As these plants prefer their roots to be restricted, keep them in their individual pots when you plant them.

WHAT YOU WILL NEED

PLANTS
- Pebble-like plants such as *Lithops* and *Pachyphytum*

OTHER MATERIALS
- 4mm grit or fine gravel
- Shallow decorative container, preferably with drainage holes
- Peat-free cactus compost
- Decorative rocks and pebbles

TOOLS
- Spoons or small trowels
- Dibber
- Soft-bristled paintbrush, for dusting
- Watering can with narrow spout

1 Pour a layer of gravel, about 2.5cm (1in) deep, into the bottom of the container. Cover the gravel with an even layer of compost of a similar thickness.

2 Arrange the plants (still in their original plastic pots) on top of the compost. Leave some space between the plants for the rocks and stones to be added later.

3 Fill in the space between the plastic pots with the compost until the pot rims are no longer visible. Firm the compost down with a spoon or dibber.

4 Cover the surface of the compost with a mix of decorative rocks and pebbles until the compost is no longer visible.

5 Use a small paintbrush to gently remove any stray compost from the plants.

HOW TO MAINTAIN

TEMPERATURE 5–25°C (41–77°F)
LIGHT Full sun; some shade in summer
HUMIDITY Low

WATERING From spring to early autumn, after the *Lithops*' old leaves have withered, water when the top of the compost is dry. From late autumn to late winter, keep the compost almost dry, watering around the *Pachyphytum* occasionally to prevent their leaves from shrivelling. Take care not to overwater; the plants may rot in wet compost, and the *Lithops* could split open.

MAINTENANCE AND CARE Place the rockery in a bright spot near a window. Provide light shade in midsummer to avoid scorching the plants.

PROPAGATION SHELF

Rooting plants in water in pretty glass vessels makes a great display on a shelf or side table. You can make a temporary display while propagating offcuts to plant up later (see p340), or leave them as they are to create a permanent "water garden". This method is very simple, but not suited to all plants so choose your cuttings carefully.

WHAT YOU WILL NEED

PLANTS
- Cuttings from mature, healthy plants, such as *Tradescantia*, *Philodendron*, *Crassula*, *Pilea*, and *Chlorophytum*

OTHER MATERIALS
- Glass bottles or vases of different heights and shapes; flask-like vessels with narrow necks and large bodies work best
- Spring water, mineral water, or rainwater

TOOLS
- Small pair of pruning shears or scissors

HOW TO MAINTAIN

WATERING Top up the bottles and vases with more water as and when needed.

MAINTENANCE AND CARE After just a few weeks, your cuttings will begin to sprout roots. At this stage, if you want to plant your propagated cuttings, follow the instructions on p340.

You can also keep the cuttings permanently in water. If you choose to do so, remember to change the water or trim back the roots after a year or so.

1 Select your first cutting. Measure it against the bottle in which you wish to display it, then remove any leaves from the portion of the stem that will be submerged in water.

2 If taking a cutting of a plant's offset, such as a "baby spider" from a spider plant (see p167), make the cut at the base of the offset's individual stem. This is where the rooting hormone is most concentrated in the plant.

3 Half-fill your bottle with rainwater or distilled water (do not use tap water). Make sure to use a glass bottle with plenty of room, so that the roots receive plenty of light and have space to grow.

4 Place the cutting in the vase and leave it, undisturbed, on your chosen propagation shelf. Repeat this process with your remaining cuttings, each matched to a proportionally sized glass bottle or vase, until your display is complete.

LEAF PROPAGATION DISPLAY

Leaf propagation (see pp330–31) is one of the simplest ways to expand your plant collection. While you wait for your new plants to grow, create a work of living art by arranging your leaves in an eye-catching design. It's best to try this project in the spring or summer when the leaves will propagate more readily.

WHAT YOU WILL NEED

PLANTS
- A variety of succulents with leaves of different sizes and colours, such as *Echeveria*, *Sedum*, and *Crassula*

OTHER MATERIALS
- 4mm grit or gravel
- Wide and shallow decorative dish, ideally with drainage holes
- Peat-free cactus compost

TOOLS
- Shallow dishes, for drying
- Trowel
- Tray, for sorting
- Mister or watering can with rose attachment

1 Remove the leaves from the succulents, using the method described on p330. Make sure to remove the whole leaf as the young plant will sprout from the base.

2 Put the leaves in shallow dishes and set aside in a dry place out of direct sunlight for a few days to allow each leaf base to callus over.

3 Pour a layer of gravel, about 2.5cm (1in) deep, into the bottom of the decorative dish. Cover the gravel with an even layer of cactus compost of the same thickness.

4 Arrange the leaves on a tray so that you can clearly group them together, sorting them by size and colour. Starting with the largest leaves, place them around the edge of the dish, ensuring that the callused bases only rest on surface of the compost (do not bury them).

5 Continue to arrange the leaves in rings around the dish. Experiment with different repeating patterns of colour and leaf type, but try to alternate the direction of the leaves, so that no two leaf bases are directly beside one another; this will maximize the amount of rooting space each leaf will have.

6 If you wish, finish the design by inserting a stem cutting from one of the stripped plants (see p339) into the centre. As with the leaves, ensure that the stem is callused over, then gently insert it into the exposed compost.

HOW TO MAINTAIN

TEMPERATURE 10–25°C (50–77°F)
LIGHT Filtered sun
HUMIDITY Low

WATERING Do not water the display for a few weeks, until roots begin to form. Once the leaves begin to propagate, occasionally mist the display or lightly water it using a watering can with a rose attachment.

MAINTAIN Place the dish in a bright, dry spot out of direct sunlight. This project mimics step 1 of the leaf propagation process on pp332–35, with the compost-filled dish standing in as a decorative alternative to placing the leaves on kitchen towel. Once the leaves begin to propagate, you can either pot them on in separate containers, or push them gently into the soil of the dish to continue growing. If any leaves dry up without propagating, remove them and replace them with fresh leaves.

HOUSE PLANT
PROFILES

BROMELIADS

AMAZONIAN ZEBRA PLANT
Aechmea chantinii

These colourful plants bloom for many months and add a hint of the tropics to any bright room. They grow on trees in their native habitat, deriving moisture and nutrients from the air rather than soil, but they do not require exceptionally high humidity levels and are quite easy to care for. After blooming, the plants die back, but most bromeliads produce "baby" offsets (see pp342–43) next to the base of the old leaves, which then grow into new plants.

TEMPERATURE 15–27°C (59–80°F)
LIGHT Filtered sun/Light shade
HUMIDITY Moderate
CARE Fairly easy
HEIGHT & SPREAD 60 x 60cm (2 x 2ft)

This dramatic plant's dark green and silver striped leaves and tall flower spikes appear from late spring to autumn. The blooms are composed of red, orange, and yellow bracts (petal-like modified leaves) and small red flowers.

WATERING Fill the cup-like well in the centre of the leaf rosette with rainwater or distilled water; replenish every 4–8 weeks. Keep the compost moist, but allow it to dry out between waterings in winter. Mist the plant every day or two in hot weather.

FEEDING From spring to late summer, apply a half-strength balanced liquid feed every 2 weeks in the leaf well.

PLANTING AND CARE Grow in an equal mix of orchid compost, horticultural grit, and coir fibre (or a 50:50 mix of orchid and multipurpose compost) in a 12.5–15cm (5–6in) pot. Repot young plants in a container one size larger.

SILVER VASE PLANT
Aechmea fasciata AGM

TEMPERATURE 15-27°C (59-80°F)
LIGHT Filtered sun/Light shade
HUMIDITY Moderate
CARE Fairly easy
HEIGHT & SPREAD
60 x 60cm (2 x 2ft)

The elegant arching silver and green leaves offer reason enough to grow this beautiful plant. In summer, a tall flower spike appears, topped with delicate pink bracts and small purple flowers that add to its star quality.

WATERING Fill the well in the centre of the leaf rosette with rain or distilled water; replenish every 4-8 weeks. Keep the compost moist; allow it to dry out between waterings in winter. Mist plants every day or two in hot weather.

FEEDING From spring to late summer, apply a half-strength balanced liquid fertilizer every 2 weeks to the leafy well.

PLANTING AND CARE Grow in a 12.5-15cm (5-6in) pot in an equal mix of orchid compost, horticultural grit, and coir fibre (or a 50:50 mix of orchid and multipurpose compost). Repot young plants in a container one size larger.

VARIEGATED PINEAPPLE
Ananas comosus var. *variegatus*

TEMPERATURE 16-29°C (60-85°F)
LIGHT Sun
HUMIDITY Moderate
CARE Fairly easy
HEIGHT & SPREAD At least 60 x 90cm (2 x 3ft)

Show-stopping, spiny-edged, green, and cream foliage and pretty yellow and purple flowers make up for the fact that this pineapple's red fruits are bitter and inedible. It will make a feature in any sunny room, but check that you have space for its wide, arching leaves.

WATERING Water frequently in spring and summer, but keep the compost just moist in winter. Mist daily or set on a tray of damp pebbles.

FEEDING Apply a half-strength balanced liquid fertilizer every 2 weeks from spring to autumn and once a month in winter.

PLANTING AND CARE Plant in an equal mix of fine composted bark or orchid compost, horticultural grit, and coir fibre (or a 50:50 mix of orchid and multipurpose compost is ideal). A heavy 12.5-15cm (5-6in) pot will restrict the plant's size. Repot young plants in early spring.

FRIENDSHIP PLANT
Billbergia nutans

TEMPERATURE 16–27°C (60–80°F)
LIGHT Filtered sun/Light shade
HUMIDITY High
CARE Fairly easy
HEIGHT & SPREAD 60 x 60cm (2 x 2ft)

Set this bromeliad on a stand or in a hanging basket so that the graceful flowers can flow down over the edges. The plant's pink bracts (petal-like modified leaves) and small pink and purple blooms appear from late spring to summer among a fountain of grey-green strappy leaves.

WATERING Use rainwater or distilled water to keep the compost moist. In winter, allow the top of the compost to dry out between waterings. Mist daily in summer; reduce to every few days in winter.

FEEDING In early spring, add a teaspoon of Epsom salts diluted in distilled or rain water to encourage flowering. Apply a half-strength balanced liquid fertilizer every month in spring and summer.

PLANTING AND CARE Plant in an equal mix of orchid compost, horticultural grit, and coir fibre (or a 50:50 mix of orchid and multipurpose compost) in a 12.5–15cm (5–6in) pot. Repot young plants in early spring in a container one size larger.

EARTH STAR
Cryptanthus bivittatus AGM

TEMPERATURE 16–27°C (60–80°F)
LIGHT Sun/Filtered sun
HUMIDITY Moderate
CARE Fairly easy
HEIGHT & SPREAD 15 x 15cm (6 x 6in)

This dainty bromeliad is grown for its wavy, tooth-edged leaves, which form a flat star-shaped rosette. Ideal for decorating a sunny windowsill in a small room, the colourful foliage, which can be red, orange, purple, pink, or green, makes a sparkling feature.

WATERING In spring and summer, use rain or distilled water to keep the compost moist, but not wet. In winter, keep it just moist. Mist the plant regularly with tepid rain or distilled water.

FEEDING Apply a half-strength balanced liquid fertilizer every 2–3 months from spring to late summer.

PLANTING AND CARE Plant in a small 10cm (4in) pot in an equal mix of orchid compost, horticultural grit, and coir fibre (or a 50:50 mix of orchid and multipurpose compost). Set in sun or filtered sun, and repot every 2–3 years in the spring.

ZEBRA PLANT
Cryptanthus zonatus

TEMPERATURE 16–27°C (60–80°F)
LIGHT Sun/Filtered sun
HUMIDITY Moderate
CARE Fairly easy
HEIGHT & SPREAD Up to 25 x 40cm (10 x 16in)

Prized for its striped, spidery-looking, burgundy and cream leaves, the zebra plant makes a dramatic focal point when set alongside other small leafy plants that like similar conditions. Small white flowers may appear in summer on mature plants.

WATERING From spring to early autumn, keep the compost moist with rain or distilled water. The compost should be just moist in winter. Mist with tepid rainwater or distilled water every few days.

FEEDING Apply a half-strength balanced liquid fertilizer every 2–3 months from spring to late summer.

PLANTING AND CARE Plant in an equal mix of orchid compost, horticultural grit, and coir fibre (or a 50:50 mix of orchid and multipurpose compost) in a small 10–12.5cm (4–5in) pot. Set in sun or bright filtered light; the plant may lose its variegations in shady conditions. Repot zebra plants every 2–3 years in spring.

SCARLET STAR
Guzmania lingulata

TEMPERATURE 18-27°C (65-80°F)
LIGHT Filtered sun
HUMIDITY High
CARE Challenging
HEIGHT & SPREAD 45 x 45cm
(18 x 18in)

The eye-catching flower spike of this compact bromeliad shoots up from the glossy green leaves like a firework. Its small white or yellow blooms are protected by long-lasting bright orange or red bracts.

WATERING Allow the compost to dry out between waterings, and fill the leafy cup in the centre of the plant with distilled or rainwater, replenishing it every 4-7 days. Mist the leaves, flowers and aerial roots daily with distilled or rainwater.

FEEDING Apply a half-strength balanced fertilizer to the central cup once a month. Pour this out after 4-5 days and replace with rain water. When not in flower, mist the leaves once a month with the same fertilizer, diluted to one-quarter strength.

PLANTING AND CARE Use an equal mix of orchid compost, horticultural grit, and coir fibre (or a 50:50 mix of multipurpose and orchid compost) in a 10-12.5cm (4-5in) pot. Repot young plants each spring in fresh compost.

BLUSHING BROMELIAD
Neoregelia carolinae f. tricolor

TEMPERATURE 18-27°C (65-80°F)
LIGHT Filtered sun
HUMIDITY Moderate to high
CARE Fairly easy
HEIGHT & SPREAD 30 x 60cm
(12 x 24in)

Like a blushing bride, this plant's leafy rosette of green and yellow striped leaves is suffused with red at the centre. In summer, violet flowers and bright red bracts appear.

WATERING Fill the central well formed by the leaves with distilled or rainwater; replenish every 4-6 weeks. Keep the compost moist, but not wet, and mist the leaves every few days.

FEEDING Mist leaves monthly with a half-strength balanced liquid fertilizer. Overfeeding reduces the leaf colour.

PLANTING AND CARE Plant in a small 10-12.5cm (4-5in) pot using an equal mix of orchid compost, horticultural grit, and coir fibre (or a 50:50 mix of orchid and multipurpose compost). Repot every year in fresh compost.

FLAMING SWORD
Vriesea splendens AGM

TEMPERATURE 18-26°C (64-79°F)
LIGHT Filtered sun
HUMIDITY Moderate
CARE Fairly easy
HEIGHT & SPREAD 60 x 45cm (24 x 18in)

This plant's dark green and reddish brown striped leaves and long-lasting sword-like flowers make a striking partnership. The scarlet bracts envelop small yellow flowers, and can appear at any time of year. This is a relatively easy bromeliad for beginners to try.

WATERING Top up the central well formed by the leaves with rainwater or distilled water; replish every 2-3 weeks. Water when the top of the compost feels dry; keep it just moist in winter. Mist every few days with rainwater or distilled water.

FEEDING Dilute a foliar fertilizer to a quarter strength and use to spray the leaves monthly from spring to autumn.

PLANTING AND CARE Plant in a 12.5-15cm (5-6in) pot in an equal mix of fine composted bark or orchid compost, horticultural grit, and coir fibre (or a 50:50 mix of orchid and multipurpose compost). Repot young plants into containers one size larger in early spring.

BULBOUS PLANTS

From tropical woodland plants to classic spring garden favourites, these flowers inject splashes of seasonal colour and scent into indoor displays. Although bulbs are often associated with spring, many bloom at other times of the year – even in winter – so, with a little planning, you can enjoy flowers in your home in every season. Just remember to plant the bulbs a few months before you want them to bloom.

NATAL LILY
Clivia miniata AGM

TEMPERATURE 10–23°C (50–73°F)
LIGHT Filtered sun
HUMIDITY Low to moderate
CARE Fairly easy
HEIGHT & SPREAD 45 x 30cm (18 x 12in)
WARNING! Bulbs are toxic

Brighten up your home in spring with the natal lily's sunny orange, yellow, or apricot flowers. The clusters of trumpet-shaped blooms last until summer, and these pretty woodland plants will thrive in a cool, bright room.

WATERING Allow the top of the compost to dry out between waterings from spring until autumn. Plants need a rest from late autumn to midwinter, when the compost should be kept almost dry.

FEEDING Feed with a half-strength balanced liquid fertilizer once a month from spring to early autumn.

PLANTING AND CARE In autumn, plant in a 50:50 mix of soil-based and multipurpose composts in a 20cm (8in) pot, with the neck of the bulbs above the surface. Plants need a cool rest at 10°C (50°F) from mid-autumn to late winter, then move to a well-lit room at 16°C (60°F) to bloom. Do not repot; it flowers best when cramped, so just replace the top layer of compost in spring.

SIAM TULIP
Curcuma alismatifolia

TEMPERATURE 18-24°C (65-75°F)
LIGHT Filtered sun
HUMIDITY Moderate to high
CARE Fairly easy
HEIGHT & SPREAD 60 x 60cm (2 x 2ft)

This beauty from Thailand brings a touch of the tropics to your home in summer, when its tulip-shaped pink and violet flowers appear on tall stems between dark green leaves. It will thrive in a warm room with high humidity levels, such as a bathroom or kitchen.

WATERING From late spring to late summer, keep the compost moist, and mist the plant regularly or set on a tray of damp pebbles. From mid-autumn to early spring, the plant becomes dormant (the leaves will die off), and the compost should be almost dry.

FEEDING Feed with a balanced liquid fertilizer every 2 weeks from mid-spring to late summer.

PLANTING AND CARE In spring, add a layer of gravel to a medium-sized 15cm (6in) pot, and top with a layer of bulb compost. Then plant the bulbs 7.5cm (3in) below the compost surface. Place in a bright area out of direct sun. Cut off old flower stems and dying leaves in autumn. Repot annually in spring in fresh compost.

LILY OF THE VALLEY
Convallaria majalis AGM

TEMPERATURE -20-24°C (-4-75°F)
LIGHT Filtered sun/Light shade
HUMIDITY Low
CARE Fairly easy
HEIGHT & SPREAD Up to 25 x 20cm (10 x 8in)
WARNING! All parts are toxic

This dainty bulb's white bell-shaped flowers will fill your home with sweet perfume when they appear in spring. The blooms are set off by bright green spear-shaped leaves.

WATERING Keep the compost moist from late winter to early summer; when dormant from late summer to early winter, allow the compost to dry out.

FEEDING Feed monthly with a half-strength balanced liquid fertilizer from late winter to early summer.

PLANTING AND CARE Plant the bulbs, with the roots down, in a deep 15-20cm (6-8in) pot of soil-based compost, so they are just covered. See p199 to force them to flower indoors. When in bud, set in a cool room at 16-21°C (60-70°F) to bloom. After the leaves die down, plant in shade outside; they need a cold period to reflower.

AMARYLLIS
Hippeastrum hybrids

TEMPERATURE 13-21°C (55-70°F)
LIGHT Filtered sun
HUMIDITY Low
CARE Fairly easy
HEIGHT & SPREAD 60 x 30cm (2 x 1ft)
WARNING! Bulbs are toxic

Give this striking plant pride of place when its trumpet-shaped flowers appear from winter to spring. Choose from white, pink, red, and orange blooms, or varieties with bicoloured or patterned petals.

WATERING Water sparingly from early winter until the new leaves develop, then keep the compost moist while in bloom. Do not water when the plant is resting from late summer to late autumn.

FEEDING After flowering, apply a balanced liquid fertilizer until the foliage dies down in late summer or autumn.

PLANTING AND CARE In late autumn or winter, plant in multipurpose compost in a pot slightly larger than the bulb, with one-third of the bulb above the surface. Set in a bright, warm spot. Leaves, then flowers, appear 6-8 weeks later. Move to a cooler area when buds appear to prolong the flowering period. In late summer, let the bulbs dry out, repot, and set in a frost-free shed or garage for 2 months, then bring back indoors and resume watering.

HYACINTH
Hyacinthus orientalis

TEMPERATURE -15–20°C (5–68°F)
LIGHT Filtered sun
HUMIDITY Low
CARE Fairly easy
HEIGHT & SPREAD 25 x 20cm
(10 x 8in)
WARNING! All parts are toxic

The intense perfume and rich colours
of this classic spring-flowering bulb
make it a favourite for indoor displays.
Plant prepared hyacinth bulbs in autumn
to enjoy the spikes of blue, purple,
white, pink, or red blooms when they
open a few months later.

WATERING After planting the bulbs,
water the compost and leave to drain.
Keep just moist throughout winter, and
then consistently moist when the shoots
and flowers appear.

FEEDING Apply a liquid seaweed feed
every 2 weeks when the leaves are dying
down, if you want to keep the bulbs.

PLANTING AND CARE Plant bulbs
in pots of bulb fibre (or a 2:1 mix of
soil-based compost and sharp grit) in
early autumn, with the pointed ends
up and just showing above the surface.
Leave outside on a balcony, or in the
garden until ready to flower in mid-
spring. To force bulbs, see pp328–29.

GRAPE HYACINTH
Muscari species

TEMPERATURE -15–20°C (5–68°F)
LIGHT Filtered sun
HUMIDITY Low
CARE Fairly easy
HEIGHT & SPREAD 20 x 10cm (8 x 4in)

This easy-to-grow bulb is a top choice
for spring colour, with its dainty little
cones of lightly fragrant blue, purple,
or white flowers and grassy foliage.
These bulbs can be forced for early-
season displays indoors.

WATERING Water bulbs after planting,
and keep the compost almost dry in
winter. The compost should be moist
when the shoots and flowers appear.

FEEDING Apply a balanced liquid
fertilizer every 2 weeks after flowering,
while the leaves are dying down.

PLANTING AND CARE Fill a pot at
least 15cm (6in) wide and deep with
multipurpose compost. Plant the bulbs,
pointed ends up, close together but not
touching, and leave the tips just exposed.
Set outside on a balcony or in a sheltered
area until ready to flower, or force the
bulbs for earlier display (see pp328–29).
After blooming, set outside in shade;
they will then reflower the following year.

DAFFODIL
Narcissus species

TEMPERATURE -15–20°C (5–68°F)
LIGHT Filtered sun
HUMIDITY Low
CARE Easy
HEIGHT & SPREAD 40 x 10cm
(16 x 4in)
WARNING! All parts are toxic

The most popular daffodil for indoor
gardens is the tender, scented
paperwhite, but other hardy
Narcissus, such as the perfumed
Tazetta varieties or popular
'Tête-à-tête', also flower
well inside. Plant the bulbs
in autumn for spring flowers.

WATERING Water bulbs after planting,
and keep the compost just moist
through winter. Water every few days
when the shoots and flowers appear.

FEEDING Apply a balanced liquid
fertilizer every 2 weeks after flowering,
while the leaves are dying down.

PLANTING AND CARE Add a layer
of gravel to the bottom of a wide pot,
and top up with bulb fibre (or a 2:1 mix
of soil-based compost and sharp grit).
Plant bulbs, with the pointed ends up
and the tips just below the surface. Set in
an unheated room on a sunny windowsill.

CALLA LILY
Zantedeschia species

TEMPERATURE 10-20°C (50-68°F)
LIGHT Filtered sun
HUMIDITY Moderate
CARE Fairly easy
HEIGHT & SPREAD up to 60 x 60cm
(2 x 2ft)
 WARNING! All parts are toxic

While the white arum lily (*Zantedeschia aethiopica*) is best grown outdoors, the smaller, often more colourful calla lilies, such as *Z. elliottiana* and *Z. rehmannii*, make beautiful house plants. They feature plain or spotted leaves and the flowers, which comprise yellow, pink, purple, dark red, or black spathes (petal-like sheathes) around a spike of tiny flowers, appear from spring to autumn.

WATERING Keep the compost moist from late spring to late summer; the compost should be almost dry in winter.

FEEDING Apply a balanced liquid fertilizer every 2 weeks from spring until the flowers have faded.

PLANTING AND CARE In late winter, plant in a wide pot in multipurpose compost, with the rhizomes (large, oval bulbs) just showing above the surface, and the eyes (dark bumps) uppermost. Set in a warm spot in filtered sun. Leave foliage to die down in autumn. Repot in winter, and store in a cool place.

FALSE SHAMROCK
Oxalis triangularis

TEMPERATURE 15-21°C (60-70°F)
LIGHT Light shade
HUMIDITY Low
CARE Easy
HEIGHT & SPREAD 30 x 30cm
(12 x 12in)
 WARNING! All parts are toxic to pets

The green, purple, or variegated leaves of this highly decorative plant resemble those of shamrock. The triangular leaves also perform a party trick, folding up at night and opening during the day. In addition to the foliage, sprays of small pink or white starry flowers appear over many weeks from spring to summer.

WATERING Allow the top of the compost to dry out between waterings. From autumn to winter, when the plant becomes dormant and the foliage starts to die off, refrain from watering. The plant may look dead, but if you then start watering again after 4-6 weeks, new leafy growth will soon reappear.

FEEDING Apply a balanced liquid fertilizer every month when the plant is in growth from spring to late summer. Stop feeding during dormancy.

PLANTING AND CARE Plant the bulbs in autumn in a 15-20cm (6-8in) pot in an equal mix of soil-based compost, multipurpose compost, and horticultural grit. The bulbs should be 5cm (2in) below the soil surface. False shamrock is also frequently sold in leaf as a pot plant. Set in a lightly shaded spot, out of direct sun, from spring to autumn, and then move to a cool room in winter.

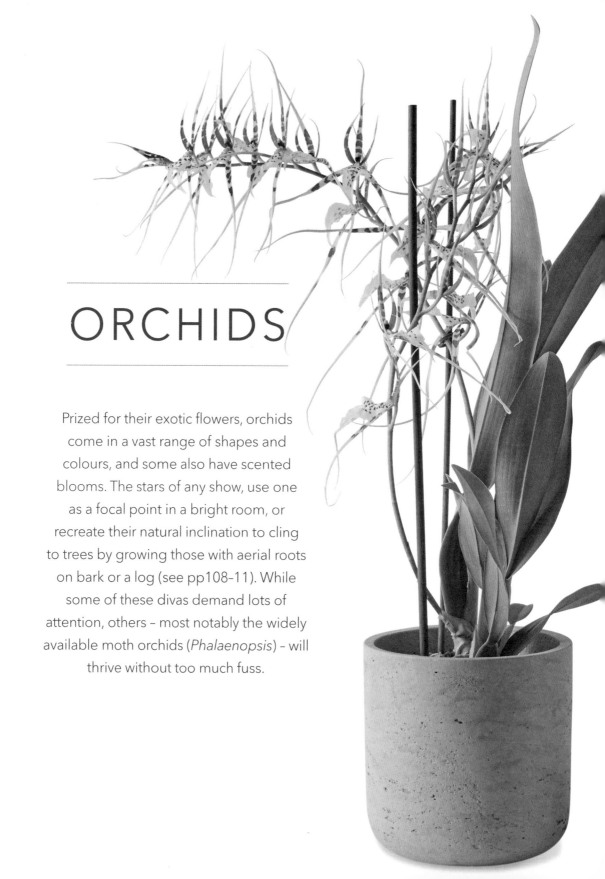

ORCHIDS

Prized for their exotic flowers, orchids come in a vast range of shapes and colours, and some also have scented blooms. The stars of any show, use one as a focal point in a bright room, or recreate their natural inclination to cling to trees by growing those with aerial roots on bark or a log (see pp108–11). While some of these divas demand lots of attention, others – most notably the widely available moth orchids (*Phalaenopsis*) – will thrive without too much fuss.

SPIDER ORCHID
Brassia species

TEMPERATURE 12-24°C (55-75°F)
LIGHT Filtered sun
HUMIDITY High
CARE Fairly easy
HEIGHT & SPREAD Up to 1 x 1m
(3 x 3ft)

Like colourful spiders crawling along arching stems, the unusual blooms of this orchid comprise long, thin, yellow or green petals, with brown or maroon stripes or spots, attached to a rounded central lip. The spidery flowers also have a delicious spicy scent and appear in late spring and summer, while the pseudobulbs (swellings at the base of the stems) each produce two or three long, strap-shaped green leaves.

WATERING Allow the top of the compost to dry out between waterings in spring and summer. Partly submerge the pot in a tray of rainwater or distilled water for half an hour, then leave to drain. In winter, the plant needs a rest and should be kept drier, watering just enough to prevent the pseudobulbs from shrinking. Mist the leaves daily from spring to late summer, and stand the pot on a tray of damp pebbles, or install a room humidifer.

FEEDING Apply a specialist orchid fertilizer with every other watering from midspring, when new growth emerges, to late summer.

PLANTING AND CARE Plant the spider orchid in a 10-20cm (4-8in) clear pot in specialist orchid compost (or a 6:1:1 mix of composted bark, perlite, and charcoal). Do not cover the aerial roots, which should be left exposed to the light. Set in a bright position, out of direct summer sun and away from draughts, and provide good ventilation. Cut the flower spike down to just above the first node (bump on stem) after blooming. The orchid likes to be cramped, so only repot when growth starts to suffer.

CYMBIDIUM
Cymbidium species and hybrids

TEMPERATURE 10-24°C (50-75°F)
LIGHT Filtered sun
HUMIDITY Moderate
CARE Fairly easy
HEIGHT & SPREAD 60 x 60cm (2 x 2ft) for miniatures, and 1.2 x 0.75m (4 x 2½ft) for standards

This free-flowering orchid will brighten up your home from late autumn to spring, when few other plants are at their best. The stems of large blooms emerge from between strap-shaped green leaves, creating an explosion of colour. The named hybrids are easier than the species, and there are two types to choose from: large "standards" that can grow up to 1.2m (4ft), and the smaller, more popular, "miniatures", which are ideal for a windowsill.

WATERING In spring and summer, allow the top of the compost to dry out between waterings, and water from above with rainwater or distilled water, making sure that any excess can drain away. Reduce watering to once every 2 weeks in winter. Place on a tray of damp pebbles or mist every few days.

FEEDING Apply a half-strength general liquid fertilizer with every third watering in spring, then switch to a specialist orchid fertilizer throughout summer.

PLANTING AND CARE Plant in a 15-20cm (6-8in) opaque pot in specialist orchid compost (or a 6:1:1 mix of composted bark, perlite, and charcoal). This ground dwelling orchid does not have aerial roots, and does not need a clear pot. Stand in filtered sunlight all year, out of direct summer sun. Ideally, set it on a part shaded patio outdoors in summer and early autumn (before the frosts), when plants need a distinct drop between day and night temperatures to form flower buds. In late autumn, keep in a cool room, ideally below 15°C (59°F); bring into a slightly warmer room to flower. Repot every year or two in spring.

Cymbidium hybrid

Cymbidium miniature

Named hybrids are the most widely available and easy to care for. Choose from the huge range of flower colours, many with patterned or spotted petals.

Miniature cymbidiums are compact hybrids, ranging in height from 30 to 60cm (12-24in). Like all cymbidiums, they need a cool room to flower well.

NOBILE DENDROBIUM
Dendrobium nobile hybrids

TEMPERATURE 5–24°C (40°–75°F)
LIGHT Filtered sun
HUMIDITY Moderate to high
CARE Challenging
HEIGHT & SPREAD 60 x 45cm
(24 x 18in)

Upright cane-like stems of scented flowers appear from autumn to early spring on this flamboyant orchid. Those with pink or white flowers are the most popular, but they come in a wide range of colours. Be prepared to pamper it, and do not worry if the plant loses some leaves in winter, as it is a semi-deciduous.

WATERING From spring to late summer, water once or twice a week in the morning using tepid rainwater or distilled water (see *Brassia* watering method on p143). Reduce watering to every 2 weeks in early autumn to stimulate flower buds to form; in winter, do not water but mist occasionally to prevent the pseudobulbs (swellings at the base of the plant) from shrivelling. Set on a tray of damp pebbles from early spring to late summer.

FEEDING Apply a half-strength balanced liquid feed every 2–3 weeks from spring to summer. In late summer, change to a half-strength high potash fertilizer for one month, then discontinue feeding until the following spring.

PLANTING AND CARE Plant this orchid in a 15–20cm (6–8in) clear pot in specialist orchid compost (or a 6:1:1 mix of composted bark, perlite, and charcoal). Grow in a bright spot, out of direct summer sun, and away from draughts. To bloom, this dendrobium needs a distinct difference between day and night temperatures, and it is best grown outside in semi-shade from summer to early autumn (before the frosts). In winter when blooming, keep it in an unheated room with a night-time temperature of about 10°C (50°F) or slightly lower. Repot every year in spring.

Dendrobium nobile 'Star Class Akatsuki'

This brighly coloured orchid produces spikes of dazzling fuchsia-pink flowers with white and yellow centres.

Dendrobium nobile 'Star Class Apollon'

One of the popular clear white forms of nobile dendrobium, it forms tall spikes of small, long-lasting blooms.

PANSY ORCHID
Miltoniopsis hybrids

TEMPERATURE 12–27°C (54–80°F)
LIGHT Filtered sun/Light shade
HUMIDITY High
CARE Fairly easy
HEIGHT & SPREAD 60 x 60cm (2 x 2ft)

Often labelled as Miltonia (hybrids of *Miltoniopsis*), this compact orchid produces large, fragrant blooms with distinctive pansy-like markings on the face, hence its common name. The flowers can appear in spring or autumn, depending on the hybrid.

WATERING In the summer, apply rainwater or distilled water every day or two from above, giving the plant a good soaking, and then leaving it to drain. In winter, reduce watering to once every 2–3 weeks. Set on a tray of damp pebbles and mist every few days.

FEEDING Apply a specialist orchid fertilizer every 2 weeks, but flush the plant with plenty of rainwater or distilled water once a month to prevent a build-up of salts.

PLANTING AND CARE Plant in a 15–20cm (6–8in) clear pot in specialist orchid compost (or a 6:1:1 mix of composted bark, perlite, and charcoal). The pansy orchid will be happy in light shade in summer; move closer to the window in winter. Avoid direct sun and draughts, and repot annually in spring.

NELLY ISLER
× Oncidopsis Nelly Isler gx

TEMPERATURE 16-24°C (60-75°F)
LIGHT Filtered sun/Light shade
HUMIDITY High
CARE Challenging
HEIGHT & SPREAD Up to 50 x 50cm
(20 x 20in)

This orchid hybrid is prized for its tall stems of bright red flowers with white spotted lips and a yellow eye. Blooms appear at any time of year, but most flower in autumn, and they have an intense lemony fragrance.

WATERING Using rainwater or distilled water, apply when the top of the compost is slightly dry (see watering method for *Brassia* on p143). In winter, reduce watering slightly. Set on a tray of damp pebbles and mist every day or two.

FEEDING Apply a half-strength orchid fertilizer every 2 weeks year round.

PLANTING AND CARE Grow in a 15-20cm (6-8in) clear pot in specialist orchid compost. Stand out of direct sun, in temperatures of 16-24°C (60-75°F). After flowering, trim the stems to just above the lowest node (bump on stem) to encourage a second flush. Repot every year or two in spring.

BUTTERFLY ORCHID
Oncidium hybrids

TEMPERATURE 13-25°C (55-77°F)
LIGHT Filtered sun
HUMIDITY Moderate
CARE Fairly easy
HEIGHT & SPREAD Up to 60 x 60cm
(2 x 2ft)

The stems of this dainty orchid hold dozens of small flowers that look like butterflies or dancing ladies, creating a spectacular effect, usually in autumn. The hybrids are relatively easy, and can be mounted on bark or slate.

WATERING Apply rainwater or distilled water when the top of the compost is slightly dry. In winter, water just once a month. Set on a tray of damp pebbles, and mist every day or two.

FEEDING Apply specialist orchid fertilizer, diluted to a quarter strength, with every second or third watering.

PLANTING AND CARE Grow on bark, or in a 12.5-15cm (5-6in) opaque pot in specialist orchid compost. It likes to be cramped, so repot only when the pot becomes too small for the new growth.

SLIPPER ORCHID
Paphiopedilum 'Maudiae Femma'

TEMPERATURE 17–25°C (63–77°F)
LIGHT Filtered sun/Light shade
HUMIDITY Moderate
CARE Fairly easy
HEIGHT & SPREAD 30 x 20cm
(12 x 8in)

This orchid has great allure, and features large showy flowers in a wide range of colours, with a distinctive slipper-like pouch that gives rise to its common name. The blooms generally appear for many weeks from winter to early summer, although some hybrids flower at other times too. The long green or mottled leaves form a fan shape, and provide interest while the plant is not in flower. Named hybrids are easier than the species to look after.

WATERING Using rainwater or distilled water, keep the compost moist from spring to autumn, applying water once or twice a week (see *Brassia* watering method on p143). Reduce watering in winter but do not let the compost dry out completely. Set on a tray of damp pebbles to raise humidity levels, but do not mist, as this may lead to rotting.

FEEDING Apply specialist orchid fertilizer every 2–3 weeks from spring to autumn; in winter apply it at half strength at the same frequency.

PLANTING AND CARE Grow the slipper orchid in a 15–20cm (5–8in) opaque pot in specialist orchid compost (or a 4:1 mix of finely composted bark and perlite). This ground-dwelling orchid does not need a clear pot, as it produces no aerial roots. Grow in light shade in summer, out of direct sun, and in full light in winter. The plain green-leaved like orchids like cool conditions; the more widely available mottle-leaved types need warmth, with a minimum of 17°C (64°F) at night. Repot annually after flowering in a slightly larger container, making sure new growth is not buried.

MOTH ORCHID
Phalaenopsis hybrids

TEMPERATURE 16–27°C (61–80°F)
LIGHT Filtered sun/Light shade
HUMIDITY Moderate
CARE Easy
HEIGHT & SPREAD Up to 90 x 60cm
(3 x 2ft)

One of the most widely available and easiest orchids to grow, the moth orchid produces long arching stems topped with large round blooms in a huge range of colours, some with delicate patterning. The flowers can appear at any time of the year. There are also miniature hybrids for small spaces and all types are happy in high daytime winter temperatures and will grow well in a centrally heated home.

WATERING Keep the compost moist at all times and apply water every 5–7 days in the morning (ideally use rainwater or distilled water in hard water areas). Reduce watering slightly in winter but do not let the compost dry out

Phalaenopsis hybrid

Many orchids are not named when you buy them, but the most widely available will be easy-care hybrids. Simply choose colours to suit your scheme, and team up matching hues.

completely. Set on a tray of damp pebbles; mist plants occasionally in the morning, which allows excess water to dry before the colder nights.

FEEDING Apply a specialist orchid fertilizer with each watering, but flush through the plant with plain water and no fertilizer once a month to remove excess salts. Reduce feeding to once a month in winter.

PLANTING AND CARE Plant in a 10-15cm (4-6in) clear pot in specialist orchid compost (or a 6:1:1 mix of composted bark, perlite, and charcoal). Do not bury the aerial roots, which need to be exposed. Set in light shade in summer; bring closer to a bright window in winter. Avoid draughts and major temperature fluctuations; these orchids prefer warmth year-round. After flowering, cut the stem just above the lowest node (bump on stem) to encourage a second flush. Repot every 2 years in a slightly larger container.

Phalaenopsis So Petit range

This group of miniature hyrbid moth orchids comes in a range of colours, including pink, peach, and white, and they fit neatly onto a windowsill.

VANDA ORCHID
Vanda hybrids

TEMPERATURE 16-32°C (61-90°F)
LIGHT Filtered sun
HUMIDITY High
CARE Challenging
HEIGHT & SPREAD 1.2 x 0.6m (4 x 2ft)

This tropical orchid is demanding, but its large colourful blooms, often patterned and up to 15cm (6in) in diameter, make the effort worthwhile when they appear in spring and summer. Vandas need very high levels of humidity, and they are commonly grown in a vase or an open wire basket without compost.

WATERING Water every morning by plunging the roots into a bucket of tepid rainwater or distilled water for 15 minutes until the roots go green, then drain; reduce to every 3-4 days in winter. Vandas demand high humidity and should be misted a few times a day; alternatively, install a humidifier.

FEEDING Mist the leaves and roots once a week with a ready mixed orchid fertilizer spray. Feed every 2 months in winter.

PLANTING AND CARE Grow in a slatted basket or in a large clear vase with no potting compost. Set in a bright spot, out of direct summer sun, but in good light in winter. A heated, well-ventilated conservatory or bathroom is ideal. Lower night-time temperatures in autumn encourage flower buds to form. To repot, soak the roots and gently pull them away from sides of the basket, then place the plant in its small basket into a larger basket; the roots will then grow on without disturbance.

CAMBRIA ORCHID
× *Vuylstekeara Cambria* gx 'Plush'

TEMPERATURE 10-24°C (50-75°F)
LIGHT Filtered sun
HUMIDITY High
CARE Challenging
HEIGHT & SPREAD Up to 50 x 35cm (20 x 14in)

While this beautiful hybrid orchid is not widely available, it is worth seeking out if you like a challenge. The rewards for your efforts are tall arched stems of large, dark red, fragrant flowers, with white spotted lips and a yellow eye. The long lasting blooms appear at any time of year, but mostly in winter or spring.

WATERING Apply rainwater or distilled water when the top of the compost is slightly dry (use the method described for *Brassia* on p143) and water every 5-7 days from spring to autumn, and every 7-10 days in winter. Set on a tray of damp pebbles and mist the leaves every day or two, or install a room humidifier.

FEEDING Apply a half-strength orchid fertilizer with every second or third watering year round.

PLANTING AND CARE Grow in a 10-20cm (4-8in) clear pot in specialist orchid compost. To promote flowering, make sure there is a 6°C (10°F) drop in temperature at night. After flowering, trim back the stems to just above the lowest node (bump on stem) to encourage a second flush of blooms. Repot only when the pseudobulbs (swellings at the base of the stems) fill the container completely.

FLOWERING MAPLE
Abutilon × hybridum

TEMPERATURE 12–24°C (54–75°F)
LIGHT Filtered sun
HUMIDITY Low
CARE Fairly easy
HEIGHT & SPREAD Up to 90 x 60cm (36 x 24in)

Dress up your home with this tall shrub's large bell-shaped flowers, which come in a variety of colours, including red, yellow, pink, and white. The maple-like green or variegated foliage provides a foil for long-lasting summer blooms.

WATERING Keep the compost moist from spring to autumn; in winter, allow the top of the compost to dry out between waterings.

FEEDING Apply a balanced liquid fertilizer every 2 weeks between spring and autumn, replacing it in summer with a high-potash feed.

PLANTING AND CARE Grow in an equal mix of multipurpose and soil-based composts in a 20–30cm (8–12in) pot. Set in a bright position, and move in winter to a cooler room with daytime temperatures of 16–20°C (61–68°F). Trim back stems and pinch out the tips in spring to create a bushier, compact plant. Prune again in autumn if necessary. Repot every 2 years.

OTHER FLOWERING PLANTS

While many house plants produce flowers, some are grown specifically for their beautiful blooms, and can be used to inject seasonal colour into a green leafy display. This selection includes plants that bloom at different times of the year, and some that even flower in the depths of winter.

TAIL FLOWER
Anthurium andraeanum AGM

TEMPERATURE 16–24°C (61–75°F)
LIGHT Filtered sun
HUMIDITY Moderate
CARE Fairly easy
HEIGHT & SPREAD 45 x 30cm
(18 x 12in)

This top-performing house plant sports dramatic, arrow-shaped, dark green leaves, and elegant waxy flowers which appear throughout the year. It is best displayed in simple, modern pot, and the blooms, which come in white, red, pink, and a fashionable dark burgundy, are made up of a tear-shaped spathe (leaf-like sheath) and a long spadix (spike of tiny flowers). As well as its stylish good looks and obvious charm, the tail flower, or flamingo flower as it is sometimes known, is also quite easy to grow.

WATERING Keep the compost moist throughout the year; avoid waterlogging, which may rot the roots. Mist every few days, or set on a tray of damp pebbles.

FEEDING Feed every 2 weeks from spring to summer with a half-strength, high-potash liquid fertilizer.

PLANTING AND CARE Plant with the top of the root ball just above the soil surface in a 12.5–20cm (5–8in) pot and an equal mix of multipurpose and soil-based composts. Cover the root ball with sustainably sourced moss to prevent it drying out. Stand in bright filtered light and keep at 20–24°C (68–75°F) all year round. Repot only when plant has become root-bound.

Anthurium andraeanum - white form

Most tail flower species produce bright red flowers, but the cooler, sophisticated white forms are also very popuar and widely available.

Anthurium andraeanum 'Black Queen'

The fashion for dark blooms has led breeders to produce flowers in a range of sultry single shades, from burgundy to near black, and moody bicolours.

ANGEL'S TRUMPET
Brugmansia × candida

TEMPERATURE 16–25°C (61–77°F)
LIGHT Sun/Filtered sun
HUMIDITY Moderate
CARE Fairly easy
HEIGHT & SPREAD 1.2 x 1m
(4 x 3ft)
 WARNING! All parts are toxic

The knock-out evening fragrance and large, showy, trumpet-shaped flowers of this tall plant make it a favourite for a conservatory or big, bright room. The blooms come in yellow, pink, white, or red, but the plant has one major vice – all parts are poisonous, so it is not a good choice for those with children or pets. You may also see it sold as *Datura*.

WATERING Keep the compost moist from spring to early autumn; reduce watering so that the compost is just moist in winter when temperatures are lower.

FEEDING Apply a balanced liquid fertilizer every month in spring; switch to a high-potash feed in summer.

PLANTING AND CARE Grow in a 20–30cm (8–12in) pot in soil-based compost. Set in a sunny spot and a cool room in winter. Wearing gloves, trim the stems after flowering to keep it compact, but do not prune too hard or you may lose the flowers. Repot every 2–3 years.

PRAIRIE GENTIAN
Eustoma grandiflorum

TEMPERATURE 12–24°C (54–75°F)
LIGHT Sun/Filtered sun
HUMIDITY Low
CARE Fairly easy
HEIGHT & SPREAD 30 x 45cm
(12 x 18in)

The cup-shaped blooms of this pretty annual are often used in floristry, but the plant can also be grown as a house plant, adding temporary colour to a mixed display in spring and summer. The flowers are available in a wide range of colours, including purple, pink, white, and bicolours. Look out for compact varieties, which are sometimes sold as garden bedding plants.

WATERING Keep the soil moist from spring to autumn, but avoid overwatering.

FEEDING Apply a high-potash fertilizer every 2 weeks from spring to autumn.

PLANTING AND CARE Plant prairie gentian in a container about 15–20cm (6–8in) wide in multipurpose compost. Young plants bought in spring will grow rapidly if set in a sunny position, protected from strong midday sun in summer. Pinch out the tips of the stems in spring to create a bushier plant with more flowers, and deadhead faded blooms regularly. Buy new plants each year.

PERSIAN VIOLET
Exacum affine AGM

TEMPERATURE 18–24°C (65–75°F)
LIGHT Filtered sun
HUMIDITY Moderate to high
CARE Fairly easy
HEIGHT & SPREAD 20 x 20cm (8 x 8in)

This plant may only perform for a few months, but its fragrant, violet-blue flowers with yellow centres, which appear over many weeks above a mound of glossy green leaves, make it well worth growing. It is a biennial, which means it produces leaves in the first year, and blooms in the second, but those you buy will flower the same year.

WATERING Keep the compost moist – the flowers fade quickly if the roots are dry. Mist with tepid water every day or two, or set on a tray of damp pebbles.

FEEDING Feed every 2 weeks from spring to late summer with a half-strength balanced liquid fertilizer.

PLANTING AND CARE You will probably not need to repot the plants, but if yours is root-bound (see pp320–21), transfer it to a slightly larger pot of multipurpose compost. Try growing it from seed in winter or early spring (see pp344–45).

CAPE JASMINE
Gardenia jasminoides AGM

TEMPERATURE 16–24°C (61–75°F)
LIGHT Filtered sun
HUMIDITY High
CARE Fairly easy
HEIGHT & SPREAD 60 x 60cm (2 x 2ft)
WARNING! All parts are toxic to pets

This shrub's main appeal is its large, round, sweetly scented white flowers, which appear in summer and autumn against a backdrop of glossy, dark green leaves. It can grow into a large plant in warm, frost-free climes but rarely reaches more than 60cm (2ft) tall when grown indoors in a pot.

WATERING From spring to autumn, water with tepid distilled or rainwater, keeping the compost moist. In winter, allow the top of the compost to dry out between waterings. Mist the leaves (not the flowers) regularly, or stand on a tray of damp pebbles.

FEEDING From spring to late summer, apply a half-strength fertilizer designed for acid-loving plants every 2 weeks.

PLANTING AND CARE Grow cape jasmine in a 20–30cm (8–12in) pot in ericaceous compost. Place in a bright spot, out of direct sun and draughts. To prevent the buds failing, it needs temperatures of 21–24°C (70–75°F) by day and 15–18°C (59–65°F) at night in summer. In winter, move to a sunny window. Repot every 2–3 years in spring.

AFRICAN DAISY
Gerbera jamesonii

TEMPERATURE 13–24°C (55–75°F)
LIGHT Sun/Filtered sun
HUMIDITY Low to moderate
CARE Fairly easy
HEIGHT & SPREAD Up to 60 x 60cm (2 x 2ft)

Often used in floral bouquets, African daisies make a statement with their tall flower stems topped by colourful daisy-like blooms and triangular, slightly lobed, bright green leaves. Flowers appear mainly in summer, but given a warm home and enough light, they can bloom intermittently all year round.

WATERING Keep the compost moist, but not wet, from spring to summer. Reduce watering in winter, allowing the top of the compost to dry out between waterings.

FEEDING Feed every 2 weeks from spring to late summer with a balanced liquid fertilizer.

PLANTING AND CARE Plant in a 12.5–15cm (5–6in) pot in an equal mix of multipurpose and soil-based composts. Set in a bright, cool, well-ventilated area, out of midday sun in summer. If night-time temperatures do not drop below 10°C (50°F), gerberas will often flower all year round. Repot when root-bound.

ROSE OF CHINA
Hibiscus rosa-sinensis

TEMPERATURE 10–26°C (50–79°F)
LIGHT Sun/Filtered sun
HUMIDITY Moderate
CARE Easy
HEIGHT & SPREAD 1 x 2m (3 x 6ft)

Large, trumpet-shaped flowers and lush green foliage create a colourful show in summer, when this vase-shaped shrub is at its best. In warm rooms with good light, flowers may open at other times of the year too. The blooms come in a range of colours, including white, red, yellow, or orange, most with a dark red throat in the centre of each bloom.

WATERING Keep the compost moist from spring to autumn; allow the top to dry out between waterings in winter. Mist regularly or stand on a tray of damp pebbles.

FEEDING Apply a balanced liquid feed every 2 weeks from spring to autumn.

PLANTING AND CARE Plant in a large 20–25cm (8–10in) pot in house plant compost (or an equal mix of soil-based and multipurpose composts). Place in bright light, but out of direct sun in summer, and away from draughts. Prune hard in spring to keep plants compact. Replace the top layer of compost each spring, and repot every 2–3 years.

MOP-HEAD HYDRANGEA
Hydrangea macrophylla

TEMPERATURE -10–21°C (14–70°F)
LIGHT Filtered sun/Light shade
HUMIDITY Moderate
CARE Fairly easy
HEIGHT & SPREAD 1 x 1m (3 x 3ft)
WARNING! All parts are toxic

Although this large shrub will not be happy long-term indoors, it will make a beautiful house plant for a couple of years, brightening up a dull interior with its apple-green deciduous leaves, and large flowerheads in summer.

WATERING Keep the compost moist from spring to autumn; use rainwater or distilled water for blue varieties. Keep the compost just moist in winter.

FEEDING In spring and summer, apply a half-strength balanced liquid fertilizer every 2 weeks.

PLANTING AND CARE Plant in a 20–25cm (8–10in) pot in ericaceous compost if you have a blue variety, or soil-based compost for other colours. Place in bright filtered light in a cool room or hallway. Move to a shed or garage over winter; bring indoors again in spring. Prune stems lightly in early spring. After a year or two, plant in the garden or in a large patio pot outside.

BUSY LIZZIE
Impatiens 'New Guinea' hybrids

TEMPERATURE 16–24 (60–75°F)
LIGHT Filtered sun/Light shade
HUMIDITY Moderate
CARE Easy
HEIGHT & SPREAD 20 x 30cm (8 x 12in)

Dark green or bronze-tinged foliage and a profusion of round flowers in shades of pink, lilac, red, white, or orange, make a beautiful combination in this exotic form of the more common busy lizzie. It can be grown outside in summer, but also makes a good house plant, injecting splashes of bright colour from late spring to autumn.

WATERING Keep the compost moist from spring to autumn; allow the top of the compost to dry out between waterings in winter.

FEEDING Apply a high-potash fertilizer every 2 weeks from spring to autumn.

PLANTING AND CARE Plant in a medium-sized 12.5–15cm (5–6in) pot in multipurpose compost; these plants like cramped conditions so do not choose an overly large container. Set in a bright position out of direct sunlight, and deadhead the flowers regularly to prolong the blooming period. Take stem cuttings in autumn, or sow seed or buy new plants each spring.

SHRIMP PLANT
Justicia brandegeeana AGM

TEMPERATURE 15–25°C (60–77°F)
LIGHT Sun/Filtered sun
HUMIDITY Low
CARE Easy
HEIGHT & SPREAD 60 x 60cm (2 x 2ft)

This unusual Mexican houseplant makes an intriguing talking point, with its coral and yellow flowers that resemble little shrimps, hence the name. The blooms comprise small white flowers wrapped in colourful bracts (modified petal-like leaves), and appear throughout the year between the spear-shaped leaves.

WATERING Ensure the compost is moist in spring and summer; in winter, allow the compost to dry out between waterings.

FEEDING Feed every 2 weeks from mid-spring to early autumn with a balanced liquid fertilizer.

PLANTING AND CARE Plant in a medium-sized 15–20cm (6–8in) pot in soil-based compost. Set in a bright position, but protect from the midday sun in summer. This plant benefits from a hard prune every spring, which keeps it compact and creates a bushier habit. Repot every 2–3 years in spring when root-bound.

YELLOW SAGE
Lantana camara

TEMPERATURE 10–25°C
(50–77°F)
LIGHT Sun/Filtered light
HUMIDITY Low
CARE Fairly easy
HEIGHT & SPREAD
Up to 1 x 1m (3 x 3ft) in a pot

Small round clusters of flowers adorn this potentially large shrub from spring to late autumn. It may remind you of holidays in the Mediterranean or California, where it is often grown in pots outside. The flowers come in a range of colours, including pink, red, yellow, and cream. Large plants can be trained into standards to keep them compact or you can buy a dwarf variety.

WATERING Keep the compost moist in the growing season from spring to autumn, and only just moist in winter.

FEEDING Feed monthly from spring to autumn with a balanced liquid fertilizer.

PLANTING AND CARE Grow in a large 20–30cm (8–12in) pot in 3:1 mix of soil-based compost and grit, and set in full sun. Prune the stems in winter if plants have outgrown their space, and repot root-bound plants every 2–3 years. Plants can also be grown from seed (see pp344–45).

ROSE GRAPE
Medinilla magnifica AGM

TEMPERATURE 17–25°C (63–77°F)
LIGHT Filtered sun
HUMIDITY Moderate to high
CARE Challenging
HEIGHT & SPREAD up to 1.2 x 1m
(4 x 3ft)

Native to the tropical forests of the Philippines, this spectacular plant will create a dazzling display when it flowers in summer. Long arching stems hold large pendent blooms made up of pink bracts and small, violet flowers and seeds. The wide-spreading, dark green, oval-shaped leaves with bold vein patterns add further interest. It is best grown in a tall pot or on a stand, so that the flowers can flow over the sides.

WATERING Water sparingly from below by placing the pot in a tray of tepid rainwater or distilled water for 20 minutes, then lifting it out to drain. Allow the top of the compost to dry out between waterings, and reduce watering in winter after blooming until new flower stems appear in early spring. Mist the plant every day or two, or set on a tray of damp pebbles.

FEEDING Apply a half-strength, high-potash liquid feed every 2 weeks from spring to late summer.

PLANTING AND CARE Plant the rose grape in a 20–25cm (8–10in) pot in orchid compost, and place in a bright area, out of direct sun. In winter, bring it closer to a sunny window. Remove the flower stems after blooming. Repot every 2–3 years.

GERANIUM
Pelargonium species and hybrids

TEMPERATURE 7-25°C (45-77°F)
LIGHT Sun/Filtered sun
HUMIDITY Low
CARE Easy
HEIGHT & SPREAD up to 40 x 25cm (16 x 10in)

While geraniums are often grown in pots in the garden in summer, some varieties also make pretty house plants, and will flower for longer indoors. Look out for regal *Pelargoniums*, with their clusters of large blooms, and zonal *Pelargoniums*, which have dark ringed leaf marks. Scented-leaved geraniums with smaller blooms are also prized, and release a lemon, mint, or rose fragrance when the foliage is touched.

WATERING Allow the top of the compost to dry out between waterings from spring to summer, ensuring you do not wet the leaves or flowers. In winter, keep the compost almost dry.

FEEDING Apply a balanced liquid fertilizer every 2 weeks in spring, and then switch to a high potash fertilizer, such as tomato feed, in summer.

PLANTING AND CARE Plant geraniums in a 12.5-20cm (5-8in) pot in either multipurpose or soil-based compost with some added grit. Set in a light area, out of midday summer sun, with good ventilation. Cut back stems in early spring before growth resumes. Repot annually in fresh compost and a slightly larger pot.

FLORIST'S CINERARIA
Pericallis × hybrida Senetti Series

TEMPERATURE 5-21°C (41-70°F)
LIGHT Filtered sun
HUMIDITY Low
CARE Easy
HEIGHT & SPREAD 40 x 25cm (14 x 10in)

Producing a blaze of colour with their bright magenta-pink, blue, violet, or bicoloured daisy-like flowers, florist's cineraria are hard to beat for spring to summer impact. The blooms appear above triangular, wavy-edged green foliage, and these cool-season annuals will also reflower later in the year if cut back in early summer.

WATERING Ensure the compost is moist but never wet, which may rot the roots.

FEEDING Feed monthly with a balanced liquid fertilizer from spring to autumn.

PLANTING AND CARE Plant cineraria in a medium-sized 15cm (6in) pot in multipurpose compost, and set in a cool, bright room, away from radiators and heaters. After the flowers have faded, trim the stems back to 10-15cm (4-6in) above the compost to encourage a second flush later in the year. Buy new plants each year.

POMEGRANATE
Punica granatum

TEMPERATURE -5-25°C (23-77°F)
LIGHT Sun/Filtered sun
HUMIDITY Low
CARE Fairly easy
HEIGHT & SPREAD 2 x 2m (6 x 6ft)

Pomegranates can grow into large shrubs outside in mild areas, but their size will be restricted when grown in a pot indoors. They produce deciduous, oval-shaped green leaves, bronze when young, and funnel-shaped red flowers in late summer, followed by edible round fruits. The dwarf form, *P. granatum* var. *nana*, is a good choice for small spaces, but its fruits are not edible.

WATERING Keep the compost moist from spring to autumn; allow the top of the compost to dry out between waterings through winter.

FEEDING Apply a balanced liquid fertilizer once a month from spring to summer, then switch to a high-potash fertilizer when the flower buds appear.

PLANTING AND CARE Plant in a large 20–30cm (8–12in) pot in a 3:1 mix of soil-based compost and grit. In spring, set in a sunny room, but move to a cooler spot in winter after it has lost its leaves. Fruits will only ripen if temperatures are at least 13–16°C (55–60°F). Prune in spring, and repot every 2–3 years.

INDIAN AZALEA
Rhododendron simsii

TEMPERATURE 10–24°C (50°–75°F)
LIGHT Light shade
HUMIDITY Low
CARE Fairly easy
HEIGHT & SPREAD 45 x 45cm (18 x 18in)
WARNING! All parts are toxic

The perfect pick me up in spring, the Indian azalea's blend of glossy, dark green leaves and early blooms will liven up any cool room at this time of year. Its clusters of single or double flowers, sometimes with ruffled petals, come in shades of pink, red, white, or bicolours. The buds are beautiful too, and the blooms last for many weeks.

WATERING Water with rainwater or distilled water and keep the compost moist from early spring to autumn; reduce watering just slightly over winter but never let the plant dry out.

FEEDING Apply a balanced liquid fertilizer designed for acid-loving plants once a month from spring to autumn.

PLANTING AND CARE Grow in a 15–20cm (6–8in) pot, depending on the size of the azalea, in ericaceous compost. Set in light shade and a cool room when in flower. Stand the plant outside in shade or in a cool room in summer. Repot every 2–3 years in spring when root-bound.

AFRICAN VIOLET
Saintpaulia cultivars

TEMPERATURE 16–24°C (61–75°F)
LIGHT Filtered sun
HUMIDITY Moderate
CARE Fairly easy
HEIGHT & SPREAD Up to 7.5 x 20cm (4 x 8in)

This classic house plant used to be found in almost every home, and it is now enjoying a renewed popularity. The small round flowers come in a wide variety of colours, including pink, red, purple, and white, and the petals may also be ruffled or frilly. African violets bloom throughout the year, the flowers appearing above soft round dark green leaves, which can be maroon beneath.

WATERING Water from below by placing the pot in a shallow tray of water for about 20 minutes, then leaving it to drain; soggy compost can lead to root rot. Allow the top of the compost to dry out between waterings. Set on a tray of damp pebbles to increase humidity.

FEEDING Apply a balanced liquid fertilizer once a month between spring and late summer.

PLANTING AND CARE Plant in a small 7.5–10cm (3–4in) pot in house plant compost (or a 2:1 mix of soil-based and multipurpose composts). Set in filtered light, out of draughts, but move to sunny windowsill in winter. Deadhead regularly. Repot only when tightly root-bound.

JERUSALEM CHERRY
Solanum pseudocapsicum

TEMPERATURE 10-21°C (50-70°F)
LIGHT Filtered sun
HUMIDITY Low
CARE Fairly easy
HEIGHT & SPREAD 45 x 60cm
(18 x 24in)
WARNING! All parts are toxic

Unremarkable for much of the year, this plant explodes with colour in autumn and winter when its red tomato-like fruits emerge, adding a colourful natural feature to winter festive decorations. The dark green wavy-edged leaves and starry white summer flowers provide interest at other times. Do not eat the poisonous fruits.

WATERING Keep the compost moist from late spring to midwinter. After the fruits have faded, allow the top of the compost to dry out between waterings.

FEEDING Feed with a balanced fertilizer once a month from late spring until the fruits appear. After fruiting, allow a few weeks without fertilizer.

PLANTING AND CARE Grow this plant in a 10–15cm (4–6in) pot, or larger, in an equal mix of soil-based and multipurpose composts. Set in bright spot from autumn to spring. Stand it outside after the frosts or place in a cool bright room in summer. When the fruits have shrivelled, cut the stems back by half to encourage bushy growth. Repot every 2-3 years in spring.

PEACE LILY
Spathiphyllum wallisii

TEMPERATURE 12-24°C (55-75°F)
LIGHT Filtered sun/Light shade
HUMIDITY Moderate
CARE Easy
HEIGHT & SPREAD 60 x 60cm
(24 x 24in)
WARNING! All parts are poisonous

The peace lily makes an elegant house plant with its glossy dark green leaves and large white flowers. The blooms are composed of a spike of small flowers, known as a spadix, and a tear-shaped spathe (petal-like sheath). The long-lasting blooms appear in spring and fade gradually from white to green. This plant also helps to reduce air pollutants.

WATERING From spring to autumn, keep the compost moist; allow the top of the compost to dry out between waterings in winter. Mist regularly or set on a tray of damp pebbles.

FEEDING Apply a balanced liquid fertilizer every 2 weeks from early spring to late autumn.

PLANTING AND CARE Grow a peace lily in a 15-20cm (6-8in) pot in an equal mix of multipurpose and soil-based compost. Stand in a bright spot or some shade, out of direct sun. Remove flower stems after blooming. Repot only when root-bound.

BIRD OF PARADISE
Strelitzia reginae AGM

TEMPERATURE 12-24°C (55-75°F)
LIGHT Sun/Filtered sun
HUMIDITY Moderate
CARE Challenging
HEIGHT & SPREAD 90 x 60cm (3 x 2ft)
WARNING! All parts are toxic

Large, blue-grey, paddle-shaped leaves provide a foil for this plant's sculptural flowers. The exotic blooms, which look like an exotic bird, take several months to appear on fully mature plants that are at least three years old.

WATERING Keep the compost moist in spring and summer; reduce in autumn and winter, allowing the top to dry out between waterings. Mist daily, set on a tray or damp pebbles, or use a humidifier.

FEEDING Apply a balanced liquid feed every 2 weeks from spring to autumn.

PLANTING AND CARE Grow in a 20-30cm (8-12in) pot in an 3:1 mix of soil-based compost and grit. Set in full sun and provide good ventilation in summer. Replace the top compost layer annually; repot every 2 years in spring.

CAPE PRIMROSE
Streptocarpus hybrids

TEMPERATURE 12-24°C (55-75°F)
LIGHT Filtered sun/Light shade
HUMIDITY Moderate
CARE Easy
HEIGHT & SPREAD 60 x 60cm
(24 x 24in)

These free-flowering plants come in a huge assortment of colours to suit any decor or display, from white, pink, and red, to blues and purples. Many are also bicoloured or have patterned petals. The blooms appear from spring to autumn on slim stems above a rosette of wrinkled, lance-shaped green leaves, although some types, such as Crystal varieties, flower in winter too. Cape primroses are quite easy to grow, and will decorate a windowsill or bright area of your home for many years.

WATERING Water either from above or below, by placing the pot in a tray of water for 20 minutes and then leaving the plant to drain. Allow the top of the compost to dry out between waterings from spring to autumn, and reduce so that the compost is almost dry in winter. Overwatering can cause root rot.

FEEDING Apply a high-potash fertilizer once a month from spring to autumn.

PLANTING AND CARE Plant in a small 10-15cm (4-6in) pot in multipurpose or house plant compost. Set in a partly shaded spot, such as near a window which receives direct sun for half the day. During winter, move it to a windowsill in a window that receives direct sunlight for most of the day. Cut off flower stems as blooms begin to fade and remove old leaves in spring when fresh growth appears. Repot into a slightly larger container each spring, but keep the plant a little root-bound.

Streptocarpus 'Polka Dot Purple' AGM

One of the more unusual varieties, 'Polka-Dot Purple' sports white blooms, decorated with a fine purple lacy pattern that makes them looks spotty from a distance.

Streptocarpus
'Falling Stars' AGM

This award-winning pale blue Cape primrose produces an abundance of small blooms from early spring, and continues to flower until autumn.

Streptocarpus 'Pink Leyla' AGM

The blooms of 'Pink Leyla' warrant close inspection to appreciate the clear white upper petals with delicate rose-pink brush strokes on the lower lips.

Streptocarpus 'Targa'

You may also find this Cape primrose under the name 'Stella', but either way, it is an excellent variety, producing a wealth of velvety-looking flowers with a slight sheen in two rich tones of purple.

FERNS

With their graceful, arching stems of finely divided or wavy-edged leaves, known as fronds, ferns make beautiful house plants for shady areas. Try using one as an elegant focal point on a table or stand, or group a few together to create a lush woodland effect. Ferns do not bear flowers or seeds, instead reproducing via spores held in small brown cases ("sporangia") on the undersides of the fronds.

DELTA MAIDENHAIR FERN
Adiantum raddianum AGM

TEMPERATURE 10–24°C (50–75°F)
LIGHT Filtered sun/Light shade
HUMIDITY Moderate to high
CARE Fairly easy
HEIGHT & SPREAD 50 x 80cm (20 x 32in)

This elegant fern's dark stems and small round leaves produce an airy, tree-like shape, and it makes a stand-out centre-piece on a table or plant stand. It is a good candidate for a terrarium, too, as it thrives in humid conditions.

WATERING Keep the compost moist, not wet, at all times, and set on a tray of damp pebbles or mist the foliage daily.

FEEDING Apply a balanced liquid fertilizer monthly from spring to autumn.

PLANTING AND CARE Plant this fern in a 15–20cm (6–8in) container in multipurpose compost. Stand in light shade, out of direct sun and draughts; a humid bathroom or kitchen would make a good home. Repot every 2 years in spring. If the plant starts to look tatty, cut off all the stems at the base in spring; it will soon regenerate healthy growth.

FOXTAIL FERN
Asparagus densiflorus

TEMPERATURE 13–24°C (55–75°F)
LIGHT Filtered sun/Light shade
HUMIDITY Low to moderate
CARE Easy
HEIGHT & SPREAD 60 x 60cm
(2 x 2ft)

Despite its delicate appearance, the foxtail fern is very easy to grow, and makes a handsome specimen in a hanging basket or tall pot where its feathery fronds will cascade over the sides. Although not a true fern, its finely divided foliage and general appearance means it is usually sold as one.

WATERING Keep the compost moist from spring to autumn; reduce in winter, allowing the top to dry out between waterings. It is tolerant of drier air than true ferns, but misting the foliage occasionally keeps it healthy.

FEEDING Apply a half-strength balanced liquid fertilizer once a month from spring to autumn.

PLANTING AND CARE Plant in a small to medium-sized 10–15cm (4–6in) pot in soil-based compost, and set in bright filtered sun or light shade. Remove brown or overly long stems in spring, and, if root-bound, repot into a container one size larger.

BIRD'S NEST FERN
Asplenium nidus AGM

TEMPERATURE 13–24°C
(55–75°F)
LIGHT Filtered sun/Light shade
HUMIDITY Moderate to high
CARE Fairly easy
HEIGHT & SPREAD Up to
60 x 40cm (24 x 16in)

Unlike many ferns, this one has wide strap-shaped, undivided, fronds. The handsome bright green foliage forms a compact vase shape, and some types, such as 'Crispy Wave', have crinkled, wavy-edged leaves that look like the ruffles on a flamenco skirt.

WATERING Keep the compost moist at all times, ensuring water does not drip into the frond rosette, which can lead to rotting. Mist with rainwater or distilled water every day or two, or set on a tray of damp pebbles.

FEEDING From spring to early autumn, apply a half-strength balanced liquid fertilizer every 2 weeks.

PLANTING AND CARE Plant in an equal mix of charcoal, loam-based compost, and multipurpose compost, in a 15–20cm (6–8in) pot. Set in a draught-free area, out of direct sunlight; a bathroom would be a good spot. Repot young plants every 2 years in spring.

RABBIT'S FOOT FERN
Humata tyermanii

TEMPERATURE 13–24°C (55–75°F)
LIGHT Light shade
HUMIDITY Moderate to high
CARE Fairly easy
HEIGHT & SPREAD 30 x 50cm
(12 x 20in)

Also known as the spider fern, its long, furry rhizomes (root-like structures) make an eye-catching feature when they trail over the sides of a pot. You can also show them off in kokedama displays (see pp80–83). The rich green lacy foliage adds to this plant's charms.

WATERING Keep the compost moist from spring to autumn; allow the top of the compost to dry out between waterings in winter. Mist regularly or place on a tray of damp pebbles.

FEEDING Apply a half-strength balanced liquid fertilizer every 2 weeks from spring to early autumn.

PLANTING AND CARE Plant in an equal mix of multipurpose and ericaceous composts in a 15–20cm (6–8in) pot or a hanging basket. Do not bury the furry rhizomes. Place in an area of high humidity, such as a bathroom, in light shade and a cool spot in summer. Repot in spring if the plant becomes root-bound.

CROCODILE FERN
Microsorum musifolium 'Crocodyllus'

TEMPERATURE 13–24°C (55–75°F)
LIGHT Light shade
HUMIDITY Moderate
CARE Fairly easy
HEIGHT & SPREAD
60 x 60cm (24 x 24in)

Display this remarkable-looking fern where its distinctive crocodile-skin leaf patterns can be admired up close – a hanging basket at eye-level would be ideal. This architectural plant demands high humidity and will thrive in a kitchen or bathroom where there is space for its wide-spreading fronds.

WATERING Water from spring to early autumn when the top of the compost is almost dry; in winter, allow the top to dry out between waterings. Set on a tray of damp pebbles, and mist the leaves every few days in spring and summer.

FEEDING Apply a half-strength balanced liquid fertilizer once a month from spring to early autumn.

PLANTING AND CARE In a 15–20cm (6–8in) pot, plant this fern in an equal mix of soil-based and multipurpose composts. Place out of direct sunlight in a lightly shaded spot; it may need to be moved closer to a window in winter. Repot every 2 years or when root-bound.

BOSTON FERN
Nephrolepis exaltata AGM

TEMPERATURE 12–24°C (54–75°F)
LIGHT Filtered sun/Light shade
HUMIDITY Moderate
CARE Fairly easy
HEIGHT & SPREAD 60 x 60cm
(24 x 24in)

This popular plant, also known as the sword fern, is loved for its fountain of arching, finely divided, green fronds, which look spectacular flowing from a pot on a stand or a hanging basket. Relatively easy to care for, just maintain a humid atmosphere to prevent the leaves from turning brown.

WATERING From spring to autumn, keep the compost moist but not wet (fronds can rot in soggy compost); allow the top of the compost to dry out between waterings in winter. Mist regularly or place on a tray of damp pebbles.

FEEDING Apply a half-strength balanced liquid fertilizer once a month from spring to early autumn.

PLANTING AND CARE Grow in a 12.5–15cm (5–6in) pot in a 50:50 mix of multipurpose and soil-based composts, and place out of direct sunlight in filtered light or part shade. A bathroom with good ventilation is an ideal home. Repot into a container one size larger every 2–3 years if the plant becomes root-bound.

BUTTON FERN
Pellaea rotundifolia AGM

TEMPERATURE 5–24°C (41–75°F)
LIGHT Filtered sun/Light shade
HUMIDITY Moderate
CARE Easy
HEIGHT & SPREAD 30 x 30cm
(12 x 12in)

The arching fronds of this graceful fern are composed of tiny button-shaped leaves that add a light, airy note to a display of foliage plants. It also makes an elegant subject for a small hanging basket, and can be used as edging for a large pot of taller shade-loving plants. Despite its delicate appearance, the button fern is easier to care for than many of its cousins, tolerating drier compost and lower humidity levels.

WATERING From spring to autumn, water when the top of the compost feels almost dry; reduce watering slightly in winter. Set on a tray of damp pebbles or mist the foliage every few days.

FEEDING Apply a half-strength balanced liquid feed once a month year-round.

PLANTING AND CARE Grow in a 15cm (6in) pot, or one that fits the root ball, and plant in ericaceous compost with a handful of horticultural grit for added drainage. Place your fern in filtered light or a slightly shaded area, out of direct sun – it will not suffer in draughts and is tolerant of low winter temperatures (not freezing). Repot in fresh compost every year or two, or when it becomes root-bound.

STAGHORN FERN
Platycerium bifurcatum AGM

TEMPERATURE 10–24°C (50–75°F)
LIGHT Filtered sun
HUMIDITY High
CARE Challenging
HEIGHT & SPREAD 30 x 90cm
(12 x 36in)

Impossible to overlook, the spectacular antler-shaped fronds of the staghorn fern make this demanding plant a popular choice. It actually produces two types of fronds: those at the base are round, flat, and green, and turn brown with age, so do not worry if this happens, the large, antler-shaped fronds grow from these smaller leaves.

WATERING Keep the compost moist from spring to early autumn – set the pot in a tray of water for about 15 minutes if the round leaves have covered the compost, as soaking these can cause them to rot. Allow the top of the compost to dry out between waterings in winter. Mist the leaves every day in the morning, and set on a tray of damp pebbles, or install a room humidifier.

FEEDING From spring to early autumn, apply a balanced liquid fertilizer monthly.

PLANTING AND CARE Plant young ferns in a medium-sized 12.5–15cm (5–6in) pot or basket of orchid compost, and keep the plant out of direct sunlight in a humid atmosphere, such as a bathroom. Repot every 2–3 years in spring.

CRETAN BRAKE FERN
Pteris cretica AGM

TEMPERATURE 13–75°C (55–75°F)
LIGHT Filtered sun/Light shade
HUMIDITY Moderate
CARE Fairly easy
HEIGHT & SPREAD 60 x 60cm
(2 x 2ft)

This much-loved, dainty fern is best displayed on its own, where the wiry stems topped with slim, finger-like fronds, have space to expand. Choose between the plain green fronds of the species and variegated forms that features a white stripe through the centre of each leaflet.

WATERING Ensure the compost is moist, but not wet, from spring to autumn; in winter, allow the top of the compost to dry out between waterings. Mist the foliage every day or two.

FEEDING Apply a half strength balanced liquid fertilizer once a month from spring to early autumn.

PLANTING AND CARE Plant this fern in a 12.5–15cm (5–6in) pot in a 2:1:1 mix of soil-based compost, multipurpose compost, and charcoal. Set out of direct sunlight in a shady spot and a humid atmosphere, such as a bathroom. Cut back brown or tatty fronds at the base and repot every 2 years in spring.

PALMS

Transform your home into a tropical paradise with an elegant palm or palm-like plant, or include a few in a conservatory or bright room to evoke a parlour of the *Belle Époque* era when palms were first popular. Many of these tall, leafy plants are easy to grow, but check before buying if you are a beginner, as some are quite demanding. They are long-lived, and will provide many years of beauty, if given the right care.

PONY TAIL PALM
Beaucarnea recurvata AGM

TEMPERATURE 5–26°C (41–79°F)
LIGHT Sun/Filtered sun
HUMIDITY Low
CARE Easy
HEIGHT & SPREAD up to 2 x 1m (6 x 3ft)

Native to Mexico, the ponytail palm's fountain of hair-like leaves and textured, distinctive trunk, with its large swollen base, make it a star attraction in any house plant display. Although not officially a palm (it is a relative of the yucca), its similar features mean that it is often grouped with them.

WATERING In summer, water once a week, allowing the top of the compost to dry out between waterings; its bulbous stem stores water and will keep it alive if you forget occasionally. In winter the compost should be almost dry.

FEEDING Apply a half-strength balanced liquid fertilizer once a month in spring and summer.

PLANTING AND CARE Grow your plant in a large 25–30cm (10–12in) pot in a 3:1 mix of soil-based compost and sharp sand. Set in bright light. Replenish the top layer of compost every spring, and repot this slow-growing plant every 2–3 years in a container just one size larger.

PARLOUR PALM
Chamaedorea elegans AGM

TEMPERATURE 10–27°C (50–80°F)
LIGHT Light shade
HUMIDITY Low to moderate
CARE Easy
HEIGHT & SPREAD 1.2 x 0.6m (4 x 2ft)

This popular palm produces an elegant fountain of lush, feathery foliage. Happy in shade and tolerant of low levels of humidity, it is a very easy plant to grow and also helps to purify the air. Clusters of tiny yellow flowers sometimes appear on mature plants.

WATERING Allow the top of the compost to dry out between waterings in summer; reduce in winter so that the compost is almost dry. Mist the leaves regularly.

FEEDING Apply a balanced liquid feed once a month from spring to autumn.

PLANTING AND CARE Grow your palm in a large 20–30cm (8–12in) pot in an equal mix of soil-based and multipurpose composts. Set in light shade; it will not be happy in deep shade. Cut out any brown fronds at the base; it is normal for fronds to die off from time to time. Repot every 2–3 years when root-bound.

FISHTAIL PALM
Caryota mitis

TEMPERATURE 13–24°C (55–75°F)
LIGHT Filtered sun
HUMIDITY Moderate to high
CARE Fairly easy
HEIGHT & SPREAD Up to 2.5 x 1.5m (8 x 5ft)
WARNING! All parts are toxic

The unusual triangular foliage of this palm make it an intriguing house plant. The fishtail-shaped, serrated leaves look like they have been torn or nibbled, while the stems fan out elegantly.

WATERING From spring to autumn, water when the top of the compost feels just dry; reduce watering a little in winter. Stand on a tray of damp pebbles and mist the foliage every day or two.

FEEDING Apply a balanced liquid fertilizer monthly from spring to autumn.

PLANTING AND CARE Grow in soil-based compost in a pot that just fits the root ball (it likes to be constricted). Set in filtered light, out of direct summer sun. Repot young plants every 2–3 years; replace the top layer of compost each spring when mature.

SAGO PALM
Cycas revoluta AGM

TEMPERATURE 13–24°C (55–75°F)
LIGHT Filtered sun
HUMIDITY Moderate
CARE Easy
HEIGHT & SPREAD 60 x 60cm
(24 x 24in)
WARNING! All parts are toxic

Although not a true palm, this chunky plant's textured trunk, topped with arching fronds, certainly looks like one. While it is, in fact, a cycad (an ancient group of slow-growing plants), it would not look out of place on a tropical beach. Beware the sharp, needle-like leaves when positioning it.

WATERING From spring to autumn, allow the top of the compost to dry out a little before watering. In winter, the compost should be almost dry. Overwatering, or watering the crown (where the leaves emerge), can cause rot. Mist the leaves in summer.

FEEDING Feed with a half-strength balanced liquid fertilizer once a month from spring to autumn.

PLANTING AND CARE Grow in a 20–30cm (8–12in) pot in an equal mix of soil-based and multipurpose composts. Set it in good light, out of direct summer sun, and away from radiators in winter. It is a slow-growing plant, and will need repotting every 3 years or when root-bound.

ARECA PALM
Dypsis lutescens AGM

TEMPERATURE 13–24°C (55–75°F)
LIGHT Filtered sun
HUMIDITY Moderate
CARE Fairly easy
HEIGHT & SPREAD 2 x 1m (6 x 3ft)

Also known as the butterfly palm, this popular house plant has arching, wide, glossy green fronds. Sprays of small yellow flowers may appear in summer. It is easy to grow, and one of the best house plants for removing air pollutants.

WATERING From spring to early autumn, allow the top of the compost to dry out between waterings; reduce watering in winter so the compost is almost dry. Mist every day or two, or stand on a tray of damp pebbles.

FEEDING Apply a balanced liquid fertilizer 2–3 times during the growing season from spring to autumn.

PLANTING AND CARE Grow in a 20–30cm (8–12in) pot in soil-based compost. Set in filtered light, and away from heaters in winter. Remove dead fronds at the base, and repot every 3 years in spring if root-bound.

KENTIA PALM
Howea forsteriana AGM

TEMPERATURE 13–24°C (55–75°F)
LIGHT Light shade
HUMIDITY Moderate
CARE Fairly easy
HEIGHT & SPREAD Up to 3 x 2m
(8 x 5ft)

Perfect for a shady room, the kentia palm has tall stems of dark green, glossy leaves that fan out elegantly to create a striking feature plant. Relatively easy to grow, it is a good choice for beginners.

WATERING Water from spring to autumn when the top of the compost feels slightly dry; in winter reduce so that the compost is just moist. Stand on a tray of damp pebbles or mist every few days.

FEEDING Apply a balanced liquid fertilizer every 2 weeks from spring to early autumn.

PLANTING AND CARE Plant this palm in a 20–30cm (8–12in) pot in 3:1 mix of soil-based compost and sharp sand. Stand in light shade and away from draughts. Replace the top of the compost annually in spring, but repot only when the plant is tightly root-bound.

MINIATURE DATE PALM
Phoenix roebelenii AGM

TEMPERATURE 10–24°C (50–75°F)
LIGHT Filtered sun/Light shade
HUMIDITY Moderate
CARE Fairly easy
HEIGHT & SPREAD 1.8 x 1.5m (6 x 5ft)

Like one of the classic palms along the Côte d'Azur, this plant's textured stem and fine, feathery fronds have a stylish elegance. Almost as wide as it is tall, it needs plenty of space to show off its sculptural silhouette. Mature plants bear cream summer flowers and edible fruits.

WATERING Keep the compost moist from spring to autumn; in winter, allow the top to dry out between waterings. Stand on a tray of damp pebbles, and mist the leaves regularly in warm weather.

FEEDING Apply a balanced liquid fertilizer monthly from spring to autumn.

PLANTING AND CARE Grow in a pot that just fits the root ball, in soil-based compost. Stand in filtered light or a little shade, away from draughts. If possible, move to a cooler room in winter. Replace the top of the compost each spring; repot every 2–3 years when root-bound.

BAMBOO PALM
Rhapis excelsa AGM

TEMPERATURE 10–25°C (50–77°F)
LIGHT Light shade/Shade
HUMIDITY Low to moderate
CARE Easy
HEIGHT & SPREAD Up to 2 x 2m (6 x 6ft)

If you are looking for a palm with a difference, try this unusual plant. Its bamboo-like stems and large fronds, composed of blunt-ended, ribbed leaves, catch the eye when displayed in a large room or hallway. Slow-growing and tolerant of low light conditions, it is one of the easiest palms to grow, making it ideal for a beginner. The smaller *Rhapis humilis* is another good choice.

WATERING Keep the compost moist from spring to autumn, but avoid waterlogging. Reduce in winter so that the top of the compost feels dry between waterings. Mist the leaves every few days in summer.

FEEDING Apply a balanced liquid fertilizer 2–3 times during the growing season from spring to autumn, or use a slow-release fertilizer once in early spring.

PLANTING AND CARE Grow in a pot that just fits the root ball in a 3:1 mix of multipurpose compost and horticultural grit. Stand in light shade; it will tolerate deeper shade in summer but may need moving closer to the window in winter. Trim off old, brown fronds close to the trunk when they appear. Repot every 2–3 years, but only when root-bound.

TRAILING AND CLIMBING PLANTS

Cover your walls with flowers and foliage and inject colour into the space above your head with these climbing and trailing plants. Some climbers can be grown up a mossy pole to keep them compact, or you can attach their twining stems to wires and trellises fixed to your walls. Easy to grow in hanging baskets or cascading from shelves, trailers are the perfect option when floor space is tight.

LIPSTICK PLANT
Aeschynanthus pulcher AGM

TEMPERATURE 18–27°C (65–80°F)
LIGHT Filtered sun
HUMIDITY Moderate
CARE Fairly easy
HEIGHT & SPREAD 20 x 70cm (8 x 28in)

Cascading stems of fleshy green leaves create a lush foliage effect all year round, but the show really starts in summer when this trailer's spectacular red tubular flowers open, emerging from darker cases (sepals) like bright lipsticks.

WATERING From spring to autumn, apply tepid rainwater or distilled water when the top of the compost feels dry. Keep it a little drier in winter. Mist every day or two.

FEEDING Use a half-strength balanced liquid fertilizer once a month in spring and summer.

PLANTING AND CARE Grow in a pot that just fits the root ball, in a 4:1:1 mix of soil-based compost, sand, and horticultural grit. Hang in bright filtered light, out of direct sun, and keep warm year-round. Repot plants in spring when tightly root-bound.

PAPER FLOWER
Bougainvillea × buttiana

TEMPERATURE 10-26°C (50-79°F)
LIGHT Sun
HUMIDITY Low
CARE Fairly easy
HEIGHT & SPREAD Up to 1.5 x 1.5m
(5 x 5ft)
WARNING! All parts are toxic to pets

This climber will cover a wall in a sunny room with twining stems of small green leaves and bright flowers, or you can train it up canes or a hoop to keep it compact. The papery blooms comprise red, pink, or white bracts (petal-like modified leaves) and tiny cream flowers.

WATERING From spring to early autumn, keep the compost moist; reduce watering in winter so the compost is just moist.

FEEDING Apply a balanced liquid fertilizer every 2 weeks from spring to late summer, replacing it with a high-potash feed at every third application.

PLANTING AND CARE Grow in a pot that fits the root ball in soil-based compost. Stand in full sun, and tie the stems to canes, a hoop, or wires fixed to a wall. Prune sideshoots in autumn. Repot young plants every 2 years; refresh the top layer of compost each spring when mature.

SPIDER PLANT
Chlorophytum comosum

TEMPERATURE 7-25°C (45-76°F)
LIGHT Filtered sun/Light shade
HUMIDITY Low
CARE Easy
HEIGHT & SPREAD 12 x 60cm (1x 2ft)

Do not dismiss the spider plant just because it is widely available and easy to grow. It makes an eye-catching feature in a pot on a stand or in a hanging basket, its arching green and yellow leaves flowing gracefully over the sides, while baby plantlets dangle from long stems like spiders on silken threads.

WATERING Keep the compost moist from spring to autumn, and allow the top to dry out between waterings in winter.

FEEDING From mid-spring to early autumn, apply a balanced liquid feed every 2-3 weeks.

PLANTING AND REPOTTING Plant in a 50:50 mix of multipurpose and soil-based composts in a pot that will accommodate the root ball. Set in filtered light or a little shade, out of direct sun. It will tolerate gloomier areas but may not produce plantlets. Repot every 2-3 years in spring when the plant is root-bound.

GRAPE IVY
Cissus rhombifolia AGM

TEMPERATURE 12–24°C (59–75°F)
LIGHT Filtered sun/Light shade
HUMIDITY Low
CARE Easy
HEIGHT & SPREAD up to 2 x 2m (6 x 6ft)

The glossy lobed foliage of this easy-care plant will trail from a basket or scramble up a trellis to cover wall. The leaves are have a silvery sheen when young, and then mature to dark green, giving a two-toned effect.

WATERING Keep the compost moist from spring to autumn, and reduce in winter so it is just moist.

FEEDING Apply a balanced liquid fertilizer monthly from spring to autumn.

PLANTING AND CARE Plant in soil-based compost in a 15–20cm (6–8in) pot. If you grow it as a climber, tie the shoots in regularly to their supports. Trim back long growth in spring, and repot every 2–3 years or when root-bound, or replace the top layer of compost of mature plants each spring.

DEVIL'S IVY
Epipremnum aureum AGM

TEMPERATURE 15–24°C (59–75°F)
LIGHT Filtered sun/Light shade/Shade
HUMIDITY Low
CARE Easy
HEIGHT & SPREAD up to 2 x 2m (6 x 6ft)
WARNING! All parts are toxic

One of the best house plants for beginners, the almost indestructible devil's ivy produces trailing or climbing stems of large heart-shaped leaves that create a lush tropical effect. Display it in a hanging basket or set the pot on a tall plant stand anywhere in your home, apart from areas in full sun.

WATERING Allow the top of the compost to dry out between waterings from spring to autumn; in winter keep just moist.

FEEDING Apply a balanced liquid fertilizer monthly from spring to autumn.

PLANTING AND CARE Plant in soil-based compost in a pot that fits the root ball. Set in bright or low light, out of direct sun. If grown as a climber, tie stems to a moss pole, trellis, or wires. Prune in spring. Repot every 2 years; replace the top layer of compost of mature plants each spring.

CREEPING FIG
Ficus pumila 'Snowflake'

TEMPERATURE 13-24°C (55-75°F)
LIGHT Filtered sun/Light shade
HUMIDITY Low
CARE Fairly easy
HEIGHT & SPREAD Up to 90 x 90cm (3 x3ft)
WARNING! All parts are toxic to pets

Use this dainty little trailing plant to dress up a hanging basket or flow over the sides of a pot of flowering or larger foliage plants. It can also be persuaded to climb a trellis, creating a textured screen of small, round, cream-edged leaves. While fairly easy to grow, if the plant is not watered regularly and left to drain, the foliage can soon dry out.

WATERING Keep the compost moist at all times, but a little drier in winter. Mist every day or two in hot summer weather.

FEEDING Apply a balanced liquid fertilizer monthly in spring and summer.

PLANTING AND CARE Plant in a 10-20cm (4-8in) pot in soil-based compost. Set in filtered sun or light shade. Pinch out the stem tips to produce bushy growth. If plants start to look leggy, cut them back hard to promote new leafy growth. Repot every 2 years in spring.

JASMINE
Jasminum polyanthum AGM

TEMPERATURE 10-24°C (50-75°F)
LIGHT Filtered sun
HUMIDITY Low
CARE Fairly easy
HEIGHT & SPREAD Up to 3 x 3m (10 x 10ft)

When it flowers in midwinter, this climber's sweet scent will fill a cool room, such as a hallway, with fragrance. The blooms are pink in bud, and appear over many weeks between the dark green leaves. This is a large plant, and while you can train it up canes when young, it soon becomes a tangle of stems if not given space to expand on wires or a trellis.

WATERING Keep the compost moist from spring to late summer; reduce watering a little in winter, but ensure the compost is moist when in bud and flower.

FEEDING Apply a balanced liquid fertilizer every 2 weeks from spring to autumn.

PLANTING AND CARE Plant in a pot that just fits the root ball in soil-based compost, mixed with a few handfuls of horticultural grit. Keep cool, as jasmine will suffer in warm, centrally heated rooms. Prune after flowering – you can be quite brutal to keep it compact. Only repot young plants; for mature plants, just replace the top layer of compost each spring.

MANDEVILLA
Mandevilla × amoena 'Alice du Pont' AGM

TEMPERATURE 15–24°C (59–75°F)
LIGHT Filtered sun
HUMIDITY Moderate
CARE Challenging
HEIGHT & SPREAD Up to 7 x 7m
(23 x 23ft)

It is easy to be tempted by the large, pink, tropical flowers of this twining climber, but remember that it needs a large space to thrive, and may sulk in the average living room. However, it makes an outstanding feature on a wall in a conservatory or room with a skylight.

WATERING Keep the compost moist from spring to autumn; reduce in winter so the compost is just moist. Mist the foliage every day in summer.

FEEDING Apply a balanced liquid fertilizer once a month in spring and switch to a high-potash feed in summer.

PLANTING AND CARE Grow in a large 25–30cm (10–12in) pot in a 3:1 mix of soil-based compost and grit. Stand in bright light, out of direct summer sun. Prune in spring to create a framework of 3–5 strong shoots; if there is only one shoot, reduce it by a third to prompt more to form. Replace the top layer of compost annually in spring, rather than repotting.

SWISS CHEESE PLANT
Monstera deliciosa AGM

TEMPERATURE 18-27°C (65-80°F)
LIGHT Filtered sun/Light shade
HUMIDITY Moderate
CARE Easy
HEIGHT & SPREAD Up to 8 x 2.5m
(26 x 8ft)

WARNING! All parts are toxic

This classic climbing plant first became popular in the 1970s. Admired for its glossy, heart-shaped, lobed and perforated leaves, which give rise to its name, this easy-care plant is often sold with the stems tied to a mossy pole.

WATERING Water when the top of the compost feels dry; reduce watering slightly in winter. Mist every few days or set on a tray of damp pebbles.

FEEDING Apply a half-strength balanced liquid fertilizer every month from spring to autumn.

PLANTING AND CARE Grow in a 20–30cm (8-12in) pot in 3:1 mix of soil-based compost and sand. Set in filtered sun or light shade; shaded foliage will not produce holes. Prune in spring, and wipe the leaves regularly to remove dust. Repot every 2–3 years, or replace the top layer of compost annually in spring.

RED PASSION FLOWER
Passiflora racemosa AGM

TEMPERATURE 12-24°C (54-75°F)
LIGHT Filtered sun
HUMIDITY Moderate
CARE Challenging
HEIGHT & SPREAD Up to 3 x 1m (10 x 3ft)

The most widely available passion flower is the blue form (*Passiflora caerulea*), which is hardy and easier to grow outside in mild regions, while this more unusual red type is tender. Its showy, bowl-shaped, summer flowers lend a tropical note to a conservatory or bright room with a skylight. It also produces pale green edible fruits.

WATERING Keep the compost moist from spring to autumn. In winter, water only when the top of the compost feels dry. Mist plants every day in summer or set on tray of damp pebbles.

FEEDING Apply a balanced liquid fertilizer every 2 weeks from mid-spring to late summer.

PLANTING AND CARE Grow in a 20–30cm (8-12in) pot in soil-based compost. Stand in bright filtered sun, and prune in early spring. Repot young plants in spring; when mature, just replace the top layer of compost annually.

HEART-LEAF
Philodendron scandens AGM

TEMPERATURE 16-24°C (60-75°F)
LIGHT Filtered sun/Light shade
HUMIDITY Low to moderate
CARE Easy
HEIGHT & SPREAD Up to 1.5 x 1.5m (5 x 5ft)
WARNING! All parts are toxic

This impressive climber will cover a wall with its large, heart-shaped leaves, which can grow up to 20cm (10in) in length, transforming a living room into a lush jungle in no time. It is easy to care for, grows well in low light, and can be trained up a mossy pole to keep it compact in a small space.

WATERING Keep the compost moist from spring to autumn; reduce in winter, watering only when the top of the compost feels dry. Mist the leaves every few days in spring and summer.

FEEDING Apply a balanced liquid fertilizer once a month from spring to early autumn.

PLANTING AND CARE Plant in a large 20-30cm (8-12in) pot in a 2:1 mix of soil-based compost and sand or horticultural grit. Young plants can be grown in a hanging basket, with the stems trailing down. As they grow larger, attach the stems to a mossy pole, trellis, or horizontal wires fixed to a wall. Stand in filtered sun or light shade; it tolerates darker shade but may not grow as vigorously. Wipe leaves regularly to remove dust. Prune in late winter and repot in spring, or replace the top layer of compost annually.

CAPE IVY
Senecio macroglossus 'Variegatus' AGM

TEMPERATURE 10-25°C (50-77°F)
LIGHT Sun/Filtered sun in summer
HUMIDITY Low
CARE Easy
HEIGHT & SPREAD Up to 1.5 x 1.5m (5 x 5ft)
WARNING! All parts are toxic

Masquerading as a regular ivy, this beautiful house plant has a little more class, with its glossy, fleshy, green and yellow leaves and dark twining stems. Use it to trail from a basket or grow it on a hoop or up a tripod or trellis.

WATERING Allow the top of the compost to dry out between waterings from spring to late summer; reduce watering in autumn and winter so it is just moist.

FEEDING Apply a half-strength balanced liquid fertilizer from spring to autumn.

PLANTING AND CARE Plant Cape ivy in a 15cm (6in) pot in cactus compost or a 3:1 mix of soil-based compost and sharp sand. Stand in direct sun, moving to bright filtered light in midsummer. Trim the shoot tips in spring if they get too long, and tie the stems to their support regularly. Repot every 2-3 years or when the plant becomes root-bound.

MIND-YOUR-OWN-BUSINESS
Soleirolia soleirolii

TEMPERATURE -5-24°C (23-75°F)
LIGHT Filtered sun/Light shade
HUMIDITY Moderate
CARE Easy
HEIGHT & SPREAD 5 x 90cm (2 x 36in)

Also known as baby's tears, this pretty plant forms a mound of tiny leaves on wiry stems, which look like a mop of curly hair trailing daintily from its pot. It suits contemporary displays, flowing from the top of three identical tall pots. Take care when planting it up with partners; it is fast-growing and can take over if not trimmed regularly. Tiny pink-white flowers appear in summer.

WATERING Keep the compost moist from spring to autumn, and slightly drier in winter. If left to dry out, the leaves will shrivel and die. Mist every few days.

FEEDING Apply a half-strength balanced liquid fertilizer every month from spring to autumn.

PLANTING AND CARE Plant this trailer in a 10-20cm (4-8in) pot in a 3:1 mix of soil-based compost and grit. Display in filtered sun or light shade, out of direct sun. Trim the stem tips to maintain bushy growth. Repot every 1-2 years.

STEPHANOTIS
Stephanotis floribunda AGM

TEMPERATURE 10–23°C (50–73°F)
LIGHT Filtered sun
HUMIDITY Moderate
CARE Fairly easy
HEIGHT & SPREAD Up to 3 x 3m
(10 x 10ft)

This climber's long, twining stems of glossy green leaves and fragrant, long-lasting waxy white flowers combine to create a spectacular visual and sensory effect in summer. Given a large pot and good care, it can be grown along wires to cover a wall, or train it over a large hoop or on a trellis and prune the stems regularly to keep it more compact.

WATERING Keep the compost moist from spring to autumn; allow the top to dry out between waterings in winter. Stand on a tray of damp pebbles and mist the leaves every day or two in summer.

FEEDING Apply a high-potash liquid fertilizer every 2 weeks from spring to autumn.

PLANTING AND CARE Grow in a pot that fits the root ball in soil-based compost. Set in bright filtered light, out of direct sun. Keep plants cool in summer – around 21–23°C (70–73°F) is ideal – and a little cooler still (but not cold) in winter. Trim back lightly in spring, and replace large, overgrown plants. Repot every 2–3 years or renew the top layer of compost each spring.

SILVER-INCH PLANT
Tradescantia zebrina AGM

TEMPERATURE 12–24°C (54–75°F)
LIGHT Filtered sun
HUMIDITY Low to moderate
CARE Easy
HEIGHT & SPREAD Up to 15 x 60cm
(6 x 24in)

The gently trailing stems of the silver-inch plant make a striking feature in a hanging basket or pot on a shelf in a bright room. The fleshy silver and green striped leaves are purple when young, and the undersides remain purple as they mature, creating a colourful three-toned effect. Small pinkish-purple flowers appear throughout the year.

WATERING From spring to autumn, water when the top of the compost is almost dry; in winter, reduce so that the compost is just moist. Mist the leaves every few days in spring and summer.

FEEDING Apply a balanced liquid fertilizer once a month from spring to early autumn.

PLANTING AND CARE Grow in a 3:1 mix of soil-based compost and sharp sand or horticultural grit and a 15–20cm (6–8in) pot. In summer, stand in bright filtered light, out of direct sun. Trim the stem tips in spring to maintain bushy growth. Repot every 2–3 years or when root-bound.

CARNIVOROUS PLANTS

These fascinating plants make intriguing house plants. They have developed a range of colourful pitchers or sticky leaves and stems to trap and consume insects and other small creatures, which provide them with essential nutrients. Most need boggy soil to thrive, and some require more specialist care, so check that you can provide the conditions they need.

CALIFORNIA PITCHER PLANT
Darlingtonia californica AGM

TEMPERATURE -5–26°C (23–78°F)
LIGHT Sun
HUMIDITY Moderate
CARE Challenging
HEIGHT & SPREAD 40 x 20cm (14 x 8in)

Also known as the cobra lily, the pitchers of this unusual plant are hooded and feature fang-like structures that resemble a snake's head. Purple-veined flowers appear in spring, followed by red-veined pitchers that emit a honey scent to attract their prey. This plant is quite demanding, so ensure you can offer the exacting conditions it needs.

WATERING Water your plant daily with rainwater or distilled water, or set in a shallow water-filled tray.

FEEDING Do not feed this pitcher plant.

PLANTING AND CARE Plant in an equal mix of sustainably sourced moss, perlite, and horticultural sand (potting compost will kill this plant). Set in sun during the summer. When dormant in winter, place the plant outside in a sheltered area or in a cold, bright, unheated room. You may see tiny insects if you look into the pitchers. These little creatures live inside the plant and eat other prey that fall in; the pitcher then digests their faeces.

VENUS FLY TRAP
Dionaea muscipula

TEMPERATURE 9–27°C (48–80°F)
LIGHT Sun
HUMIDITY Moderate
CARE Fairly easy
HEIGHT & SPREAD Up to 10 x 20cm
(4 x 8in)

This plant's snapping jaw-like leaves trap flying insects that come within reach, but it will soon die if coaxed to perform this trick too often. It has two types of leaf: the spring foliage is broader and produces traps close to the centre of the plant, while the summer leaves are longer and develop red-tinged traps further away. White tubular flowers appear in spring.

WATERING Place the pot in a deep tray of rainwater or distilled water from spring to late summer; from autumn to late winter, when dormant, remove it from the tray but keep the growing medium moist.

FEEDING Do not feed Venus fly traps.

PLANTING AND CARE Plant in a 10–15cm (4–6in) pot, in a 50:50 mix of sustainably sourced moss and perlite; potting compost will kill the plant. Place in a sunny spot and open windows regularly to allow insects in. Remove the flowers, which can weaken the plant. In winter, when dormant, move it away from radiators and heaters. Repot every year in late winter or early spring.

CAPE SUNDEW
Drosera capensis

TEMPERATURE 7–29°C (45–85°F)
LIGHT Sun/Filtered sun
HUMIDITY Moderate
CARE Easy
HEIGHT & SPREAD 15 x 20cm (6 x 8in)

The easiest sundew to grow, this plant's long slim leaves are covered with colourful tentacles that produce a sticky mucilage that looks like drops of water (hence the name). The leaves ensnare insects and then curl around their trapped prey, which is then slowly absorbed by the plant. In late spring or early summer, pink flowers appear that last just one day, opening in the morning then closing in the afternoon.

WATERING Set the pot in a deep tray of rainwater or distilled water. In its natural habitat, the plant is dormant in winter and requires less water, but in a warm home, leave it in its water tray to continue growing throughout the year.

FEEDING Do not feed Cape sundews.

PLANTING AND CARE Plant in a tall 10–15cm (4–6in) pot in an equal mix of sustainably sourced moss and perlite; potting compost will kill the plant. Set in a bright spot and open windows regularly to allow insects in. These will be attracted to the plant, which needs just 2–3 per month to survive. Remove dead leaves and repot annually in fresh growing medium. Remove flowers to prevent self-seeding.

MONKEY CUPS
Nepenthes hybrids

TEMPERATURE 13–25°C (55–77°F)
LIGHT Filtered sun
HUMIDITY Moderate to high
CARE Fairly easy
HEIGHT & SPREAD Up to 30 x 45cm
(12 x 18in)

The dark red pitchers that dangle from slender stems of this unusual tropical plant look otherworldly, emerging from the tips of spear-shaped green leaves. The pitchers' colour and nectar attracts insects, which drown when they fall in.

WATERING Never stand in a tray of water but keep the compost moist. Water from above with rainwater or distilled water. Mist daily or set on a tray of damp pebbles.

FEEDING Apply a pre-mixed foliar feed spray and mist the leaves every 2 weeks. You can give it an occasional fresh fly or insect, although this is rarely needed.

PLANTING AND CARE Plant in a pot or hanging basket with nepenthes compost (chopped pine bark, sustainably sourced moss, and perlite) from a specialist supplier; potting compost will kill the plant. Set in a bright spot out of direct sun with good ventilation. Repot every 2–3 years when root-bound.

BUTTERWORT
Pinguicula - Mexican hybrids

TEMPERATURE 18–29°C (65–85°F)
LIGHT Filtered sun
HUMIDITY Moderate
CARE Easy
HEIGHT & SPREAD 15 x 10cm (6 x 4in)

The delicate small red, pink, or blue flowers that appear on this plant in summer belie its grisly secret. They are held on slim stems above a rosette of lime green or bronze foliage, which is covered with a sticky mucilage that traps insects, such as fungus gnats. An enzyme in the leaves then digests the prey.

WATERING Keep moist by watering from above with rainwater or distilled water. When the plant is dormant, usually in winter, reduce watering, allowing the top of the compost to dry out between waterings.

FEEDING No fertilizer is required, as most homes harbour a few insects; butterworts need just 2–3 insects per month to thrive.

PLANTING AND CARE Grow in a small 10–15cm (4–6in) pot in specialist carnivorous plant compost or a 3:1:1 mix of silica sand, sustainably sourced moss, and perlite (never use potting compost). Set in bright filtered light, out of direct summer sun. Plants can become dormant at any time of the year when they grow small fleshy leaves. Repot when dormant.

NORTH AMERICAN PITCHER PLANTS
Sarracenia species and hybrids

TEMPERATURE -5–25°C (23–77°F)
LIGHT Sun
HUMIDITY Moderate
CARE Fairly easy
HEIGHT & SPREAD: Up to 30 x 15cm (12 x 6in)

These colourful carnivorous plants come in a range of sizes, and produce pitchers in shades of burgundy, red, pink, and green, often with decorative vein patterns. The nectar around the pitcher mouth lures insects, which then fall in. While some *Sarracenia* will grow happily outside in boggy soil, those from warmer climes make fascinating house plants for a cool, bright room or an unheated conservatory (they need cool winters). Pendulous red or green flowers appear in summer.

WATERING In summer, stand the plant pot in a tray of rainwater or distilled water about 1–2cm (¼–½in) deep. In winter, remove the plant from the tray and keep the compost just moist.

FEEDING Do not use a fertilizer on this plant; stand it outside or on a windowsill in summer, which will provide it with plenty of insect prey.

PLANTING AND CARE Plant in a small to medium-sized 10–15cm (4–6in) plastic pot in a specialist compost mix from a carnivorous plant supplier (or a 2:1:1 mix of fine fir bark, coarse lime-free grit, and perlite). Do not use potting compost, which will kill the plant. In late autumn, it will become dormant and should be moved to a cool, bright room at 10°C (50°F) or colder until early spring. Repot every 2–3 years when dormant in autumn, but do not plant in a large container, as it needs to be quite root-bound to thrive.

Sarracenia mitchelliana 'Bella' AGM

One of the many beautiful hybrids, 'Bella' has bright pink, red, and white vein patterns on the pitchers and lids, and bears bright red flowers in spring.

Sarracenia psittacina

Known as the parrot pitcher plant, this type will catch crawling insects with its rosette of decoratively veined red, white, or green horizontal traps. The dark spring flowers can vary in colour.

Sarracenia purpurea

The purple pitcher plant has short, fat pitchers in a deep burgundy colour, with dark red or pink flowers in spring. It is quite hardy and can also be grown outside in the garden or on a patio.

Sarracenia flava

The elegant yellow pitcher plant has tall, slender yellow-green pitchers with upright lids, and nodding yellow flowers in spring.

Sarracenia 'Judith Hindle' AGM

The profusion of slim pitchers with frilly lids set this pretty hybrid apart. Young pitchers emerge green and mature to dark red, with marbled veining. Dark red flowers appear in spring.

FOLIAGE PLANTS

These leafy plants can be used as focal points or grouped together to create a calming green oasis. Choose a selection of plain-leaved types to create a simple backdrop for more intricately patterned foliage plants or add bright blooms to create a colourful display. Many foliage plants are easy to care for, with a few exceptions, and most are happy in rooms that receive little direct sunlight.

CHINESE EVERGREEN
Aglaonema commutatum

TEMPERATURE 16–25°C (60–77°F)
LIGHT Light shade/Shade
HUMIDITY Moderate
CARE Easy
HEIGHT & SPREAD up to 45cm x 45cm (18in x 18in)
WARNING! All parts are poisonous

This elegant plant has spear-shaped leaves, with silver, cream, or pink patterning. All varieties are easy to care for, given warmth and sufficient moisture. Remove the small flowers to divert the plant's energy into growing leaves.

WATERING Keep the compost moist, but do not leave the pot in standing water, which may cause it to rot. In winter, allow the top of the compost to dry out between waterings. Mist twice a week.

FEEDING Apply a balanced liquid fertilizer every 2 weeks from spring to autumn.

PLANTING AND CARE Grow in a 15–20cm (6–8in) pot in soil-based compost mixed with a handful or two of horticultural grit. Set in light shade, or slightly darker shade, and keep out of draughts. Repot every 3 years in spring.

AMAZONIAN ELEPHANT'S EAR
Alocasia × amazonica AGM

TEMPERATURE 18–25°C (65–77°F)
LIGHT Filtered sun/Light shade
HUMIDITY High
CARE Challenging
HEIGHT & SPREAD Up to 1.2 x 1m (4 x 3ft)
WARNING! All parts are poisonous

This showstopper has large, dramatic foliage that sets it apart from the crowd. The arrow-shaped dark green leaves are purple beneath and feature distinctive silver vein patterns and wavy edges. Remove the small flowers to allow the plant to focus its energy on the foliage.

WATERING Use rainwater or distilled water to keep the compost moist from spring to autumn; in winter, allow the top to dry out between waterings. Mist the leaves every day and set on a tray of damp pebbles, or install a room humidifier.

FEEDING Feed every 2–3 weeks from spring to early autumn with a balanced liquid fertilizer.

PLANTING AND CARE Grow in an equal mix of composted bark, soil-based compost and sand in a 25–30cm (8–10in) pot. Set in a bright area, out of direct sun and draughts. Repot every 2–3 years.

ZEBRA PLANT
Aphelandra squarrosa

TEMPERATURE 13–25°C (55–77°F)
LIGHT Filtered sun
HUMIDITY Moderate to high
CARE Challenging
HEIGHT & SPREAD 60 x 60cm (24 x 24in)

With dazzling striped green and cream foliage, this plant is ideal for a bathroom with high humidity. The colourful autumn flowers are composed of yellow bracts (modified petal-like leaves) around small orange blooms.

WATERING Using rainwater or distilled water, keep the compost moist; dryness may cause leaf drop. In winter, water when the top of the compost is almost dry. Mist daily and set on a tray of damp pebbles, or install a humidifier.

FEEDING Apply a balanced liquid fertilizer once every 2 weeks during spring and summer.

PLANTING AND CARE Plant in a 15–20cm (6–8in) pot in soil-based compost. Set in a bright spot, out of direct sun. Remove faded flower stems, and then prune to leave two sets of leaves at the bottom of the stems to keep plants compact. Repot annually in spring.

CAST IRON PLANT
Aspidistra elatior AGM

TEMPERATURE 5–20°C (41–68°F)
LIGHT Light shade/Shade
HUMIDITY Low
CARE Easy
HEIGHT & SPREAD 60 x 60cm (24 x 24in)

Ideal for beginners, the cast iron plant is almost foolproof, and can be tucked into shady areas where few others will thrive. While the plain green type is not very exciting, plants with cream splashes, stripes or spots, inject more drama into a display.

WATERING Water when the top of the compost is dry; reduce watering in winter. Never allow the compost to become waterlogged or soggy.

FEEDING From spring to late summer, apply a half-strength balanced liquid fertilizer once a month.

PLANTING AND CARE Plant in a 50:50 mix of soil-based and multipurpose composts and a 12.5–20cm (5–8in) pot. Set in a lightly shaded area, well away from direct sun. Repot every 2–3 years in a container just one size larger than the original.

PAINTED LEAF BEGONIAS
Begonia species

TEMPERATURE 15–22°C (58–72°F)
LIGHT Filtered sun/Light shade
HUMIDITY Moderate
CARE Fairly easy
HEIGHT & SPREAD Up to 90 x 45cm (36 x 18in)
WARNING! The roots are toxic

Forget the flowery bedding plants you see in summer; these demure beauties offer a completely different look. Celebrated for their decorative patterned foliage and small elegant flowers, there are hundreds of colours and forms to choose from. Most are derived from the *Begonia rex* species, which are also known as angel wing begonias because of the shape of their leaves. Taller cane types, such as the polka dot begonia, add structure to an indoor display, and have slightly large flowers. Plants grow from tubers but most are for sale as young plants.

WATERING Keep the compost moist, but not wet, from spring to autumn; allow the top of the compost to dry out between waterings in winter. Stand on a tray of damp pebbles, but do not mist the leaves.

FEEDING Feed every 2 weeks from late spring to early autumn with a high nitrogen fertilizer. For begonias with larger flowers, switch to a high potash feed when the buds appear, and use this until the blooms fade.

PLANTING AND CARE Choose a pot that accommodates the plant's root ball easily. Plant in a 50:50 mix of soil-based and multipurpose composts. Set in filtered sun or light shade and keep away from radiators and heaters in winter. Repot when root-bound in spring.

Begonia 'Rumba'

One of the many red-leaved *Rex* begonias, this elegant beauty has rich, pink-red foliage with near-black markings, and red undersides. Stand it in filtered sun for the best colours.

Begonia 'Escargot'

One of the *Rex* begonias, this popular variety has green and silver leaves that form a swirling pattern, like a snail's shell. The textured foliage is also covered with delicate pink hairs.

Begonia maculata

Known as the polka dot begonia, this large cane type is a real show-off, with its large green and white spotty leaves and cascading trusses of small cream flowers, which appear in summer. Its long stems will need staking.

Begonia soli-mutata

Few plants can beat this unusual begonia for leaf texture. While the dark burgundy and bright green markings on the heart-shaped foliage catch the eye, a closer inspection reveals the rough, sandpaper-like surface.

CROTON
Codiaeum variegatum

TEMPERATURE 15-25°C (60-76°F)
LIGHT Filtered sun
HUMIDITY High
CARE Challenging
HEIGHT & SPREAD Up to 1.5 x 0.75m
(5ft x 2ft 6in)
WARNING! All parts are toxic

The bright red, yellow, and green
spear-shaped or lobed leaves of
this potentially large shrub look best
when set centre stage against a neutral
backdrop. Not the easiest plant to grow,
it demands high humidity and constant
warmth – a bathroom would make an
ideal home.

WATERING Keep the compost moist
with tepid water from spring to autumn;
allow the top to dry out betwee waterings
in winter. Set it on a tray of damp pebbles,
but do not mist the leaves.

FEEDING Apply a balanced liquid
fertilizer every 2 weeks from spring
to autumn.

PLANTING AND CARE Plant in soil-based
compost in a pot that will accommodate
the root ball. Repot every 2-3 years. Set in
bright filtered light, away from draughts
and heaters, and in constant warmth –
never below 15°C (60°F). Wearing gloves,
trim to keep it to size.

NEVER-NEVER PLANT
Ctenanthe burle-marxii

TEMPERATURE 10-25°C (50-76°F)
LIGHT Filtered sun
HUMIDITY Moderate
CARE Easy
HEIGHT & SPREAD 60 x 45cm
(24 x 18in)

The never-never plant's profusion of
striped dark and pale green leaves are
given an extra lift with a splash of red
on the undersides, lending a three-tone
effect. This undemanding, compact
plant adds a glamorous note to a
bright room.

WATERING Keep the compost moist
from spring to autumn, but allow the
top of the compost to dry out between
waterings in winter. If the leaves roll up,
add more water. Mist occasionally or
stand on a tray of damp pebbles.

FEEDING Apply a balanced liquid
fertilizer monthly from spring to autumn.

PLANTING AND CARE Plant in a
12.5-15cm (5-6in) pot in an equal mix
of soil-based and multipurpose composts.
Repot every 2-3 years when the plant
becomes root-bound.

DIEFFENBACHIA
Dieffenbachia seguine

TEMPERATURE 16–23°C (61–73°F)
LIGHT Filtered sun/Light shade
HUMIDITY Moderate
CARE Fairly easy
HEIGHT & SPREAD Up to
1.5 x 1m (5 x 3ft)
WARNING! All parts are toxic

The huge, patterned leaves of the dieffenbachia create an impressive feature in a large room or hallway in need of an eye-catching statement plant. The green, oval-shaped foliage features a splash or spots of cream in the centre.

WATERING Keep the compost moist from spring to autumn, and just moist in winter. Stand on a tray of damp pebbles or mist occasionally.

FEEDING Apply a balanced liquid fertilizer every month from spring to autumn.

PLANTING AND CARE Plant in soil-based compost in a pot that fits the root ball. Stand in filtered sun or light shade; it will survive in gloomier spots but may not grow much. Wear gloves when pruning as the sap is toxic. Repot when root-bound every 2–3 years.

DRAGON PLANT
Dracaena fragrans

TEMPERATURE 15–24°C (60–75°F)
LIGHT Filtered sun/Light shade
HUMIDITY Low to moderate
CARE Easy
HEIGHT & SPREAD Up to 1.2 x 0.9m
(4 x 3ft)
WARNING! All parts are toxic for pets

A great choice for beginners looking for a stalwart with foliage interest, the dragon plant produces fountains of strappy, variegated leaves, which form a rosette atop tall, cane-like stems on mature plants. Choose from green leaves with a yellow central stripe, or foliage with green and yellow striped edges and a dark green centre.

WATERING Keep the compost moist from spring to autumn, and just moist in the winter. Mist occasionally or set on a tray of damp pebbles.

FEEDING Apply a half-strength balanced liquid fertilizer every 2 weeks from spring to autumn.

PLANTING AND CARE Plant in soil-based compost in a pot large enough to hold the root ball. Plants thrive best in filtered sun or light shade, but also grow well in lower light conditions. Cut the top of the canes when they reach a desirable height. Repot every 2–3 years.

MADAGASCAR DRAGON TREE
Dracaena marginata

TEMPERATURE 15–24°C (60–75°F)
LIGHT Filtered sun/Light shade
HUMIDITY Low to moderate
CARE Easy
HEIGHT & SPREAD Up to 1.5 x 0.9m
(5 x 3ft)
WARNING! All parts are toxic for pets

The sprays of spiky leaves held on woody stems lend this popular plant an attractive, palm-like appearance. Tall and stately, with green, pink, and cream striped foliage, it is one of the best plants for removing toxins from the air. It is also very easy to grow.

WATERING Keep the compost moist from spring to autumn, and just moist in the winter.

FEEDING Apply a half-strength balanced liquid fertilizer every 2 weeks from spring to autumn.

PLANTING AND CARE Plant in soil-based compost in a pot that will fit the root ball. Prune the stems to limit the plant's size. Repot every 3 years or when root-bound.

JAPANESE ARALIA
Fatsia japonica

TEMPERATURE 10–25°C (60–76°F)
LIGHT Filtered sun/Light shade
HUMIDITY Low to moderate
CARE Easy
HEIGHT & SPREAD Up to 2 x 2m
(6 x 6ft)

The Japanese aralia is perfect for a room in light shade, since its large, glossy, hand-shaped leaves thrive in low-light conditions. Choose from dark green or variegated leaves – the latter will need a little more light to retain their colours. Spherical cream flowers may appear in autumn. This relatively undemanding plant is a great choice for beginners.

WATERING Keep the compost moist from spring to autumn, and just moist in the winter.

FEEDING Apply a half-strength balanced liquid fertilizer every 2 weeks from spring to late summer.

PLANTING AND CARE Plant in a pot large enough to accommodate the root ball with an equal mix of soil-based and ericaceous composts. Set in filtered sun or light shade; move the plant to a cool room in winter. Trim back to keep the plant in check. Repot every 2–3 years.

WEEPING FIG
Ficus benjamina

TEMPERATURE 16–24°C (65–75°F)
LIGHT Filtered sun/Light shade
HUMIDITY Moderate
CARE Challenging
HEIGHT & SPREAD Up to 3.5 x 1.2m
(10 x 4ft)
WARNING! All parts are poisonous

Tall and elegant, this plant should be given space to show off its arching stems of small green or variegated, cream leaves. Not the easiest of plants, it has a tendency to drop its leaves, but makes a striking focal point if you can provide the exact conditions it demands.

WATERING Use tepid rainwater or distilled water and allow the top of the compost to dry out between each watering. Keep just moist in winter. Mist the leaves in summer.

FEEDING Apply a half-strength balanced liquid fertilizer once a month from spring to autumn.

PLANTING AND CARE Plant in soil-based compost in a pot that fits the root ball. Do not move or repot plants, as this can lead to leaf drop. In spring, replace the top layer of compost.

INDIA RUBBER PLANT
Ficus elastica

TEMPERATURE 15–24°C (60–75°F)
LIGHT Filtered sun/Light shade
HUMIDITY Low to moderate
CARE Easy
HEIGHT & SPREAD 1.8 x 1.2m (6 x 4ft)
WARNING! The sap is an irritant

Popular for its broad, glossy, dark green leaves and easy-going nature, the India rubber plant brings a tree-like shape to a group of smaller plants and tolerates low-light conditions. Rubber plants with variegated leaves will need more light, but all types are drought-tolerant.

WATERING Allow the top of the compost to dry out between waterings, and keep it just moist in winter. Mist the leaves every few days in summer.

FEEDING Apply a half-strength balanced liquid fertilizer every 2 weeks from spring to autumn.

PLANTING AND CARE Plant in soil-based compost with some horticultural grit for added drainage in a pot large enough to accommodate the root ball. Set in filtered sun or light shade, away from draughts. Prune to keep the plant size in check. Repot every 2–3 years when root-bound.

FIDDLE-LEAF FIG
Ficus lyrata AGM

TEMPERATURE 15–24°C (60–75°F)
LIGHT Filtered sun
HUMIDITY Low to moderate
CARE Fairly easy
HEIGHT & SPREAD 1.8 x 1.2m (6 x 4ft)
WARNING! The sap is an irritant

The large, slightly lobed leaves of this tall, stately plant are shaped like a violin or fiddle, hence the name. They also have distinctive pale veins and the stems sprout from a sturdy, tree-like trunk. The plant is also available in the more compact 'Bambino' form.

WATERING Allow the top of the compost to dry out between waterings from spring to autumn, and keep just moist in winter. Ensure you do not overwater the plant, as the roots will rot in soggy conditions.

FEEDING Apply a half-strength balanced liquid fertilizer once a month from spring to autumn.

PLANTING AND CARE Plant in a 3:1 mix of soil-based compost and horticultural grit in a pot that fits the root ball. Place in indirect light, away from direct sun and draughts. In winter, move it away from heaters. Repot every 2–3 years when root-bound.

MOSAIC PLANT
Fittonia albivenis Verschaffeltii Group AGM

TEMPERATURE 17-26°C (62-79°F)
LIGHT Filtered sun
HUMIDITY High
CARE Fairly easy
HEIGHT & SPREAD 15 x 20cm (6 x 8in)

The beautiful patterns on the foliage of the mosaic plant make a striking feature. It is small enough for any room, but demands high humidity so it is best kept in a bathroom, kitchen, or terrarium. The dark or pale green leaves have bright pink veins and make a good match for the aluminium plant (*Pilea cadierei*), which is also small and requires similar conditions.

WATERING Keep the compost moist year-round but avoid waterlogging – yellow leaves can indicate overwatering. Mist the plant daily and place on a tray of damp pebbles, or install a humidifier.

FEEDING Apply a half-strength balanced liquid fertilizer once a month from spring to autumn.

PLANTING AND CARE Plant in soil-based compost in a small 7.5-10cm (3-4in) pot. The mosaic plant thrives in bright filtered light, away from direct sun. Remove the summer flowers to allow the plant to focus on its leaves. It needs warmth and moisture year-round, and high levels of humidity to keep its leaves healthy. Repot every 2-3 years when root-bound.

ETERNAL FLAME
Goeppertia crocata AGM
(syn. *Calathea crocata*)

TEMPERATURE 16-24°C (61-75°F)
LIGHT Filtered sun
HUMIDITY Moderate to high
CARE Fairly easy
HEIGHT & SPREAD 60 x 60cm (24 x 24in)

The torch-like orange summer flowers give this plant its name, but it can also be grown for its colourful foliage, which makes a feature in its own right. The broad, oval-shaped, slightly wrinkled leaves are green with a metallic sheen on the upper sides and dark burgundy beneath.

WATERING Keep the compost moist all year round, but guard against waterlogging. Mist daily with tepid water, and place on a tray of damp pebbles.

FEEDING From spring to early autumn, apply a balanced liquid fertilizer monthly.

PLANTING AND CARE Plant in soil-based compost in a medium-sized 12.5-15cm (5-6in) pot. Stand in a bright area out of direct sunlight, and in a room with high humidity, such as a bathroom. Make sure that winter temperatures do not dip below 16°C (61°F). Repot every 2-3 years or when root-bound.

RATTLESNAKE PLANT
Goeppertia lancifolia
(syn. *Calathea lancifolia*)

TEMPERATURE 15-24°C (60-75°F)
LIGHT Filtered sun/Light shade
HUMIDITY Moderate
CARE Fairly easy
HEIGHT & SPREAD 75 x 45cm (30 x 18in)

This plant's star attraction is its dazzling, wavy-edge foliage, with its lime and dark green snake-like markings on the upper surfaces, and burgundy shading beneath. A native of Brazil, it loves warm, humid conditions, so a bathroom or kitchen would make an ideal home.

WATERING Keep the compost moist with rainwater or distilled water from spring to autumn; allow the top of the compost to dry out between waterings in winter. Mist daily with tepid water and set on a tray of damp pebbles, or install a humidifier.

FEEDING Apply a half-strength balanced liquid fertilizer every 2 weeks from spring to autumn.

PLANTING AND CARE Use a 2:1 mix of soil-based compost and horticultural grit and plant in a 12.5-15cm (5-6in) pot. Stand in filtered light or a little shade, out of direct sun and draughts. Keep warm all year round. Repot every 2-3 years when root-bound.

PEACOCK PLANT
Goeppertia makoyana
(syn. *Calathea makoyana*) AGM

TEMPERATURE 16–24°C (61–75°F)
LIGHT Filtered sun/Light shade
HUMIDITY High
CARE Challenging
HEIGHT & SPREAD 60 x 60cm
(24 x 24in)

The silver leaves of this crowd-pleaser are impossible to overlook, with dark green brushstrokes on the upper surface and burgundy markings beneath. While not the easiest to care for, the plant's striking appearance makes it well worth the effort.

WATERING Use rainwater or distilled water to keep the compost moist from spring to autumn, and just moist in the winter. Mist daily with tepid water and place on a tray of damp pebbles, or install a humidifier.

FEEDING Apply a half-strength balanced liquid fertilizer every 2 weeks from spring to autumn.

PLANTING AND CARE Plant in a 2:1 mix of soil-based compost and horticultural grit in a 12.5–15cm (5–6in) pot. Set in filtered light or some shade, out of direct sun and draughts. Keep warm all year round. Repot every 2–3 years when root-bound.

VELVET PLANT
Gynura aurantiaca

TEMPERATURE 15–24°C (60–75°F)
LIGHT Filtered sun
HUMIDITY Moderate
CARE Fairly easy
HEIGHT & SPREAD 20 x 20cm (8 x 8in)

The soft, velvety leaves of this compact plant are simply irresistible and call out to be touched. Fine purple hairs cover the lobed, metallic-green foliage, giving it a downy, two-tone appearance, while the leafy stems will trail elegantly over the sides of a pot.

WATERING Keep the compost moist from spring to autumn, and only just moist in winter. Avoid watering the foliage, which should be kept dry. Set on a tray of damp pebbles but do not mist, as this causes spots on the leaves.

FEEDING Apply a half-strength balanced liquid fertilizer every 2 weeks from spring to autumn.

PLANTING AND CARE Plant in an equal mix of multipurpose and soil-based composts in a wide 15–20cm (6–8in) pot. Set in filtered light, out of direct sun. Pinch out the stem tips to create a bushier plant, and the yellow flowers, which have a rather unpleasant smell. Repot every 2–3 years or when root-bound.

POLKA DOT PLANT
Hypoestes phyllostachya AGM

TEMPERATURE 18–27°C (65–80°F)
LIGHT Filtered sun
HUMIDITY Moderate
CARE Fairly easy
HEIGHT & SPREAD 25 x 25cm
(10 x 10in)

Compact and colourful, this plant's green, heart-shaped leaves are speckled with pink, red, or cream spots, although on many varieties they look more like splashes than the round polka dots suggested by the name. Try a few varieties in different colours in a terrarium or bottle garden. Small magenta flowers appear in summer.

WATERING Allow the top of the compost to dry out between waterings from spring to autumn, and keep just moist in winter. Stand on a tray of damp pebbles, or mist the leaves every few days.

FEEDING Apply a half-strength balanced liquid fertilizer every 2 weeks from spring to autumn.

PLANTING AND CARE Plant in soil-based compost in a 12.5–15cm (5–6in) pot. Stand in bright, filtered light, ideally in an area with high humidity, such as a bathroom or kitchen. Pinch out the stem tips to create a bushier plant. Repot every 2–3 years or when the plant becomes root-bound.

PRAYER PLANT
Maranta leuconeura var. *kerchoveana* AGM

TEMPERATURE 15–24°C (60–75°F)
LIGHT Filtered sun
HUMIDITY Moderate
CARE Fairly easy
HEIGHT & SPREAD 60 x 60cm
(24 x 24in)

It is difficult to believe that the intricately decorated foliage of this spectacular plant has not been painted by human hands. The oval-shaped leaves feature pale and dark green feathered patterns and red veins on the surface, while the undersides are dark red. To add to its charms, the foliage folds up as if in prayer at night, and unfolds at dawn.

WATERING Keep the compost moist from spring to autumn, and slightly drier in winter. Stand on a tray of damp pebbles and mist the foliage regularly.

FEEDING Apply a half-strength balanced liquid fertilizer every 2 weeks from spring to autumn.

PLANTING AND CARE Plant in soil-based compost in a shallow 12.5–15cm (5–6in) pot. Set in filtered light, out of direct sun and draughts. Repot every 2–3 years.

MONEY TREE
Pachira aquatica

TEMPERATURE 12–24°C (54–75°F)
LIGHT Filtered sun
HUMIDITY Moderate
CARE Fairly easy
HEIGHT & SPREAD 1.8 x 1.2m
(6 x 4ft)

Folklore says that growing this palm-like plant will bring good fortune, and it certainly delivers on looks, if not money. The slim stems are often plaited, and the large glossy foliage is divided into leaflets that splay out from a central point like giant green flower petals.

WATERING Water from spring to autumn when the top of the compost is dry; keep just moist in winter. Mist every few days or set on a tray of damp pebbles.

FEEDING Apply a balanced liquid fertilizer every 2 weeks from spring to autumn.

PLANTING AND CARE Plant in soil-based compost with some horticultural grit in a 20–25cm (8–10in) pot. Stand in filtered light, out of direct sun. To keep the plant compact, pinch out the stem tips. Replace the top layer of compost annually rather than repotting.

WATERMELON PEPPER
Peperomia argyreia

TEMPERATURE 15–24°C (60–75°F)
LIGHT Light shade
HUMIDITY Moderate
CARE Fairly easy
HEIGHT & SPREAD 20 x 20cm
(8 x 8in)

Held on slim red stalks, the striped silver and dark green foliage of this elegant plant looks like the skin of a watermelon, and it makes a beautiful focal point in the centre of a table. Despite its glamorous looks, it is quite easy to care for and remains compact.

WATERING Allow the top of the compost to dry out between waterings from spring to autumn, and keep it almost dry over winter. Set on a tray of damp pebbles, or mist the leaves every few days.

FEEDING Apply a half-strength balanced liquid fertilizer once a month from spring to autumn.

PLANTING AND CARE Plant in soil-based potting compost in a 10–12.5cm (4–5in) pot. Set in light shade in summer, and a bright area in winter when light levels are lower, but out of direct sun. Replenish the top of the compost annually. Repot every 3 years, as it prefers to be root-bound.

RADIATOR PLANT
Peperomia caperata

TEMPERATURE 15–24°C (60–75°F)
LIGHT Light shade
HUMIDITY Moderate to high
CARE Fairly easy
HEIGHT & SPREAD 25 x 25cm
(10 x 10in)

Also known as the emerald ripple plant, this peperomia's heart-shaped red or green foliage has an intricately corrugated texture that produces a beautiful two-tone effect when it catches the light. The long, thin, cream summer flowers look like candlewicks shooting out from the foliage.

WATERING Allow the top of the compost to dry out between waterings from spring to autumn. Keep the compost almost dry over winter. Set on a tray of damp pebbles, but do not mist the foliage.

FEEDING Apply a half-strength balanced liquid fertilizer once a month from spring to autumn.

PLANTING AND CARE Grow in soil-based compost mixed with a handful of horticultural grit in a small 10cm (4in) pot. Set in a lightly shaded area with high humidity, such as a bathroom or kitchen. Repot every 2–3 years when root bound.

XANADU PHILODENDRON
Philodendron xanadu

TEMPERATURE 15–24°C (60–75°F)
LIGHT Light shade/Shade
HUMIDITY Moderate
CARE Easy
HEIGHT & SPREAD Up to 1 x 1.2m
(3 x 4ft)
 WARNING! All parts are poisonous

The bold, lobed foliage of this leafy philodendron will add a touch of class to a shady corner or hallway where a bulky plant is needed. Its fountain of glossy, dark green leaves, which can grow up to 45cm (18in) in length, forms a compact dome.

WATERING Keep the compost moist from spring to autumn; allow the top to dry out between waterings in winter. Mist the leaves every few days or set on a tray of damp pebbles.

FEEDING Apply a balanced liquid fertilizer monthly from spring to autumn.

PLANTING AND CARE Plant in soil-based compost in a large pot that will fit the root ball. Keep away from direct sun. Wipe the surface of the leaves with a damp cloth every few weeks to remove dust and keep the plant looking its best. Repot every 2–3 years or when root-bound.

ALUMINIUM PLANT
Pilea cadierei AGM

TEMPERATURE 15-24°C (60-75°F)
LIGHT Light shade
HUMIDITY Moderate
CARE Fairly easy
HEIGHT & SPREAD 30 x 25cm
(12 x 10in)
WARNING! All parts are toxic

The lacy, aluminium-silver markings
on the foliage of this pretty little plant
give it its name, while an easy-going
nature make it a good choice for
beginners. Use it to add sparkle to a
leafy collection in a lightly shaded room.

WATERING Keep the compost moist
from spring to autumn; allow the top
of the compost to dry out between
waterings in winter. Mist regularly.

FEEDING Apply a balanced liquid
fertilizer every 2 weeks from spring
to autumn.

PLANTING AND CARE Use a 2:1 mix
of soil-based compost and horticultural
grit and plant in a 12.5-15cm (5-6in) pot.
Stand in little shade, out of direct sunlight
and keep the plant warm year-round.
Pinch out the flower buds on the stem
tips to keep the plant bushy. Repot every
year or two when root-bound.

MISSIONARY PLANT
Pilea peperomioides AGM

TEMPERATURE 15-24°C (60-75°F)
LIGHT Filtered sun/Light shade
HUMIDITY Moderate
CARE Fairly easy
HEIGHT & SPREAD 30 x 30cm
(12 x 12in)
WARNING! All parts are toxic

Balanced on the stems like spinning
plates, the round leaves of this unusual
plant create an intriguing display,
elevating it to the top of many plant
collectors' wish lists. The loose dome
of leaves looks great on a windowsill or
table in a lightly shaded spot.

WATERING Allow the top of the compost
to dry out between waterings from spring
to autumn; keep it just moist in winter.
Mist the foliage regularly.

FEEDING Apply a half-strength balanced
liquid fertilizer every 2 weeks from spring
to autumn.

PLANTING AND CARE Plant in a 2:1 mix
of soil-based compost and horticultural
grit in a 12.5-15cm (5-6in) pot. Stand in
light shade, out of direct sun and away
from draughts. Keep the plant warm all
year round, and repot every 1-2 years in
spring when it is root-bound.

BRAZILIAN COLEUS
Plectranthus oertendahlii AGM

TEMPERATURE 15–24°C (60–75°F)
LIGHT Light shade/Shade
HUMIDITY Low
CARE Easy
HEIGHT & SPREAD 20 x 60cm
(8 x 24in)

Grown for its handsome, rough, silver-veined foliage and spires of small white spring flowers, the lax stems of this easy-care plant make it a good choice for a tall pot. It thrives in light shade, but will also grow happily in gloomier positions, adding colour and texture to rooms without any direct sun.

WATERING Allow the top of the compost to dry out between waterings from spring to autumn. In winter, keep the compost just moist.

FEEDING Apply a half-strength balanced liquid fertilizer every 2 weeks from spring to autumn.

PLANTING AND CARE Use a 2:1 mix of soil-based compost and horticultural grit and plant in a 12.5–15cm (5–6in) pot. Set in light shade, out of direct sun. Repot every 2–3 years when root-bound.

CHINA DOLL PLANT
Radermachera sinica AGM

TEMPERATURE 12–24°C (54–75°F)
LIGHT Filtered sun
HUMIDITY Low to moderate
CARE Fairly easy
HEIGHT & SPREAD Up to 1.8 x 1.2m
(4 x 6ft)

This handsome plant will fill an empty corner in a bright room with its elegant leafy stems. The glossy foliage is rich green in colour and divided up into small leaflets, which lend this tree-like plant a light, airy look.

WATERING From spring to early autumn, water when the top of the compost feels dry. Reduce watering in winter so the compost is just moist. Mist occasionally.

FEEDING Apply a half-strength balanced liquid fertilizer every 2 weeks from spring to autumn.

PLANTING AND CARE Plant in soil-based compost in a pot that will accommodate the root ball. Stand in bright filtered light, out of direct sun. Prune in spring to keep it to size, and pinch out stem tips. Repot this fast-growing plant every 2 years.

DWARF UMBRELLA TREE
Schefflera arboricola AGM

TEMPERATURE 15–24°C (60–75°F)
LIGHT Filtered sun/Light shade
HUMIDITY Low to moderate
CARE Easy
HEIGHT & SPREAD 2.4 x 1.2m
(8 x 4ft)
WARNING! All parts are toxic

This impressive plant is loved for its hand-shaped green or variegated leaves and its ability to grow in centrally heated homes in sun or shade. Plants are often sold with their stems tied to a mossy pole. bathroom. Repot every 2–3 years.

WATERING Allow the top of the compos to dry out between waterings from spring to autumn; water once a month in winter.

FEEDING Apply a half-strength balanced liquid fertilizer every month from spring to autumn.

PLANTING AND CARE Plant in a heavy pot that will fit the root ball, in 2:1 mix of soil-based compost and sand. Keep out of direct sun in a warm room. Prune in spring, and repot every 2 years.

COLEUS
Solenostemon scutellarioides hybrids

TEMPERATURE 15-24°C (60-75°F)
LIGHT Filtered sun
HUMIDITY Moderate
CARE Fairly easy
HEIGHT & SPREAD 60 x 30cm
(24 x 12in)
 WARNING! All parts toxic to pets

With a huge choice of leaf shapes and colours - from lime green and lipstick pink to brooding burgundy, burnt orange, and everything in between - there is a coleus to suit any design scheme. The fancy foliage makes a great partner for plain-leaved plants, or use some of the muted colours as foils for flowers.

WATERING Keep the compost moist from spring to autumn; allow the top of the compost to dry out between waterings in winter.

FEEDING Apply a balanced liquid fertilizer every 2 weeks from spring to autumn.

PLANTING AND CARE Grow in an equal mix of multipurpose and soil-based composts in a 15cm (6in) pot. Pinch out the stem tips to keep it bushy. Set in a bright position, out of direct sunlight. Prune the stems back by two-thirds in late winter or early spring, or grow from seed every spring (see pp344-45).

STROMANTHE
Stromanthe sanguinea 'Triostar'

TEMPERATURE 15-24°C (60-75°F)
LIGHT Filtered sun
HUMIDITY High
CARE Fairly easy
HEIGHT & SPREAD 45 x 60cm
(18 x 24in)

A jewel among foliage plants, few can compete with the stromanthe's striking leaves, splashed with shades of pink, red, green, and cream. It needs space to show off its spreading, spear-shaped foliage, and is best displayed in a plain container that complements, but does not compete with, its dazzling hues.

WATERING Keep the compost moist from spring to summer, and water less frequently in winter. Mist daily, and set on a tray of damp pebbles, or install a room humidifier.

FEEDING Apply a half-strength balanced liquid fertilizer every 2 weeks from spring to late autumn.

PLANTING AND CARE Plant in an equal mix of multipurpose and soil-based composts in a 12.5-15cm (5-6in) pot - shallow containers are ideal. Stand the plant in a bright spot, out of direct sun and draughts, ideally in a kitchen or bathroom. Repot every 2-3 years.

GOOSEFOOT PLANT
Syngonium podophyllum AGM

TEMPERATURE 15–29 °C (60–85°F)
LIGHT Filtered sun/Light shade
HUMIDITY Moderate
CARE Fairly easy
HEIGHT & SPREAD Up to 90 x 60cm
(3 x 2ft)
WARNING! All parts are toxic

The arrow-shaped, cream, and green variegated foliage of the goosefoot plant will add a jungly note to a foliage display in a bright or lightly shaded room. It is usually sold as a compact foliage plant, but, if left to its own devices, it will grow tall and may need tying onto a support if it starts to climb.

WATERING Allow the top of the compost to dry out between waterings from spring to late autumn; reduce watering slightly in winter. Mist leaves regularly or set on a tray of damp pebbles.

FEEDING Apply a half-strength balanced liquid fertilizer every 2 weeks from spring to autumn.

PLANTING AND CARE Plant in soil-based compost in a 15–20cm (6–8in) pot. It will thrive in a bright spot out of direct sun, ideally in a humid area, such as a kitchen or bathroom. Prune every year in spring to keep it compact and bushy, and when it reaches an ideal size, do not repot, but replace the top layer of the compost annually in spring.

BOAT LILY
Tradescantia spathacea

TEMPERATURE 15–27°C (60–80°F)
LIGHT Filtered sun
HUMIDITY Moderate
CARE Easy
HEIGHT & SPREAD 60 x 60cm
(24 x 24in)

The boat lily's green and purple sword-shaped leaves make an eye-catching bouquet. Small, white flowers appear throughout the year, nestled between the leaves, but the star attraction is the foliage. This compact plant will thrive in the humidity in a small bathroom or kitchen.

WATERING Allow the top of the compost to dry out between waterings from spring to autumn; keep it just moist in winter. Mist every day or two, or set on a tray of damp pebbles.

FEEDING Apply a balanced liquid fertilizer once a month from spring to autumn.

PLANTING AND CARE Plant in a 2:1 mix of soil-based compost and sand or horticultural grit in a 15–20cm (6–8in) pot. Set in a bright spot, out of direct sun it tolerates some shade, but may lose its purple tones. Repot every 2–3 years.

FERN ARUM
Zamioculcas zamiifolia

TEMPERATURE 15–24°C (60–75°F)
LIGHT Filtered sun/Light shade
HUMIDITY Low
CARE Easy
HEIGHT & SPREAD 75 x 60cm
(30 x 24in)
WARNING! All parts are toxic

The long, leafy stems of the fern arum form a large, vase-shaped plant that will grow almost anywhere, as it tolerates both sun and shade, and low levels of humidity. Perfect for beginners, the glossy foliage makes a good foil for more glamorous leaves and flowers.

WATERING Allow the top of the compost to dry out between waterings from spring to autumn; water once a month in winter.

FEEDING Apply a half-strength balanced liquid fertilizer once a month from spring to autumn.

PLANTING AND CARE Grow in a 2:1 mix of soil-based compost and sand in a pot that fits the root ball. Light shade or filtered sun is ideal, but it will also grow in gloomier spots. Trim in spring to create a good shape. Repot every 2–3 years.

SPINELESS YUCCA
Yucca elephantipes AGM

TEMPERATURE 10–27°C (50–80°F)
LIGHT Sun/Filtered sun
HUMIDITY Low
CARE Easy
HEIGHT & SPREAD 1.5 x 0.75m
(5 x 2ft 6in)
WARNING! All parts toxic to pets

One of the few plants that will bask happily in full summer sun, this yucca's spiky, sword-like foliage grows from a palm-like trunk, forming a dramatic sculptural shape that makes a bold statement in a sunny room.

WATERING Allow the top of the compost to dry out between waterings from spring to autumn; water once a month in winter.

FEEDING Apply a half-strength balanced liquid fertilizer once a month from spring to autumn.

PLANTING AND CARE
Plant in a 2:1 mix of soil-based and sand in a pot that fits the root ball. If it grows too big, cut the trunk to size in spring; new foliage will soon appear. Repot every 2–3 years.

CACTI

The feature that distinguishes cacti from other succulents (see pp244–99) is the round, cushion-like areas on their stems, known as "areoles", from which spines can grow. They also almost exclusively hail from the Americas. Cacti can range from tiny spiky globe-shaped plants to elegant smooth-stemmed trailers, and can generally be grouped into two types: desert-dwelling specimens, which prefer low humidity and bright light conditions; and tropical types such as the Christmas cactus (see p238), which hail from rainforests and thrive in shadier spots with higher levels of humidity.

ACANTHOCEREUS

The distinctive upright or arching ribbed stems of *Acanthocereus* are covered with rows of vicious thorny spines. In summer, mature plants produce white or yellow flowers that open at night – in some species the blooms are also scented. The flowers are then followed by inedible red fruits. Only cultivars of *Acanthocereus tetragonus* are widely available as house plants, but since they can grow up to 1.8m (6ft) in height indoors, allow sufficient space to display their spiky, statuesque stems.

TEMPERATURE 10–30°C (50–86°F)

LIGHT Position in full sun, but provide some shade in summer.

WATERING During the spring and summer, water when the top 2cm (¾in) of compost is dry. In autumn, reduce watering. Keep plants dry in winter.

FEEDING Apply an all-purpose granular fertilizer in spring at half the dose recommended on the label.

COMPOST Plant in cactus compost, or a 50:50 mix of loam-based (John Innes No. 2 Peat-Free) compost and 4mm grit.

FLOWERING Flowers appear only on mature plants and rarely form on house plants.

PROPAGATION Sow seed or take offsets.

COMMON PROBLEMS These plants are prone to rotting in wet compost. Check regularly for mealybugs, scale insect, and spider mites.

ACANTHOCEREUS TETRAGONUS 'FAIRY CASTLES'
syn. *Cereus tetragonus* 'Fairy Castles'
Fairy-castle cactus

One of the most popular cultivars of *Acanthocereus tetragonus*, the fairy-castle cactus produces bright green ribbed stems that soon form small clusters. The ribs are edged with woolly clusters of short, creamy-white bristles, which produce a decorative striped pattern down the stems. The nocturnal white or yellow flowers are rarely produced on plants grown indoors, as this cactus needs to be large and mature to bloom.

HEIGHT AND SPREAD Up to 1m x 30cm (36 x 12in).

CARE NOTES See opposite.

 WARNING! Wear cactus gloves when handling this plant.

ARIOCARPUS

An unusual cactus, many plants in the *Ariocarpus* group look like little green starfish and make a great contrast to a collection of round or column-shaped species. While most other cacti have "tubercules" in the form of raised bumps, on *Ariocarpus* they resemble triangular leaf-like sections. Only the seedlings have soft spines, which fall off as the plant matures, making this a good choice for homes with children or pets. The funnel-shaped flowers appear only when the plants are mature, so you may have to be patient. When they do arrive, the blooms develop from a woolly section at the top of the plant in autumn. They come in a range of colours, including white, yellow, pink, purple, and magenta.

TEMPERATURE -10–30°C (14–86°F); this plant will survive -10°C (14°F) if the soil is dry.

LIGHT Position in full sun, but provide some shade in summer.

WATERING During the spring and summer, water when the top 1cm (½in) of compost is dry. In autumn, reduce watering to once a month. Keep plants dry in winter.

FEEDING Apply a half-strength high-potash fertilizer fortnightly during late spring and summer.

COMPOST Plant in cactus compost, or a 50:50 mix of loam-based (John Innes No. 2 Peat-Free) compost and 4mm grit.

FLOWERING Flowers only appear on mature plants; buy one in bloom to guarantee flowers the following year.

PROPAGATION Sow seed.

COMMON PROBLEMS These plants are prone to rotting in wet compost. Check regularly for mealybugs and spider mites.

ARIOCARPUS RETUSUS

syn. *Mammillaria areolosa;*
Mammillaria prismatica
Star rock; Cobbler's thumb

One of the most widely available *Ariocarpus*, the star rock produces a rosette of fat, triangular, blue-green or grey tubercules (leaf-like sections). These are arranged in a star shape, hence the name. The flowers appear in autumn and are white or pink. This *Ariocarpus* is very slow-growing and suitable only for those with the patience to watch it develop over many years.

HEIGHT AND SPREAD Up to 8 x 20cm (3 x 8in).

CARE NOTES See left.

ASTROPHYTUM

Admired for their round or columnar shape, patterned stems, and colourful flowers, these cacti are popular with keen collectors. The green or blue-green ribbed stems are, in some species, covered with tiny hairy scales that give them a silvery sheen. While many plants are spineless, others are armed with long or twisted spines. The daisy-like flowers, which can be white, yellow, pink, or red, appear in summer at the top of the plant and resemble pompoms on a cap.

TEMPERATURE -7–30°C (19–86°F); plants will tolerate short periods below freezing if the soil is dry.

LIGHT Position in full sun, but provide a little shade in summer.

WATERING During the spring and summer, water when the top 1cm (½in) of compost is dry. In autumn, reduce watering to once a month. Keep plants dry in winter. Provide good air circulation to reduce risk of rot.

FEEDING Apply a half-strength cactus fertilizer once a month during late spring and summer.

COMPOST Plant in cactus compost, or a 50:50 mix of loam-based (John Innes No. 2 Peat-Free) compost and 4mm grit.

FLOWERING Flowers appear on mature plants; water regularly and provide a little fertilizer to guarantee blooms.

PROPAGATION Sow seed.

COMMON PROBLEMS These plants will rot in wet compost. Look out for mealybugs, scale insects, thrips, and spider mites.

ASTROPHYTUM CAPRICORNE AGM

syn. *Echinocactus capricornis*
Goat's horn cactus

The distinctive long curly spines of the goat's horn cactus are guaranteed to turn heads. While the ribbed stems of young plants are round, they soon form columns that can reach over 1m (3ft) in height, although restricting them to a pot usually keeps them smaller. The white woolly flecks on the stem also produce a decorative pattern, and the yellow and red flowers have a sweet fragrance.

HEIGHT AND SPREAD Up to 1m x 15cm (36 x 6in).

CARE NOTES See opposite.

ASTROPHYTUM MYRIOSTIGMA AGM

syn. *Cereus callicoche;*
Echinocactus myriostigma
Bishop's cap

The bishop's cap has broad ribs that look like the ceremonial head-dress of a bishop, after which this cactus is named. Young plants are round but soon grow into short columns, and their shimmering silver colour is produced by a coat of harmless hairy scales. Fragrant pale yellow flowers, sometimes reddish in the centre, appear intermittently from early spring to autumn.

HEIGHT AND SPREAD Up to 60 x 10cm (24 x 4in).

CARE NOTES See opposite.

ASTROPHYTUM ORNATUM AGM

syn. *Echinocactus ornatus*
Monk's hood cactus

One of the largest and easiest to grow of the *Astrophytum* species, the monk's hood cactus is globe-shaped when young but grows into a column as it matures. The stems are decorated with an unusual pattern of white scales, while the ribs are armed with clusters of brown or yellow spines. Yellow flowers appear in summer.

HEIGHT AND SPREAD Up to 30 x 15cm (12 x 6in).

CARE NOTES See opposite.

CAUTION Wear cactus gloves when handling this plant.

CEPHALOCEREUS

In their native Mexican habitat, these woolly-coated cacti can grow to a towering 12m (40ft). Restricted to a pot, however, this popular species maintains more manageable proportions. The stems form tall ribbed columns and some – including the popular *Cephalocereus senilis* – are covered with fine hairs that give them a distinctive cuddly appearance. Do not be fooled, though, as the long spines that protrude from the coat are sharp and dangerous. The flowers appear only on mature cacti and may never develop on those grown as house plants.

TEMPERATURE 5–30°C (41–86°F).

LIGHT Position in full sun.

WATERING During the spring and summer, water when the top 2cm (¾in) of compost is dry. In autumn, reduce watering. Keep plants dry in winter.

FEEDING Apply a slow-release general-purpose granular fertilizer in spring at half the dose recommended on the label.

COMPOST Plant in cactus compost, or a 50:50 mix of loam-based (John Innes No. 2 Peat-Free) compost and 4mm grit.

FLOWERING Flowers will appear only on mature plants (around 10–20 years old).

PROPAGATION Sow seed or take stem cuttings.

COMMON PROBLEMS These plants will rot in wet compost. Look out for mealybugs, scale, and spider mites.

CEPHALOCEREUS SENILIS

syn. *Cephalophorus senilis; Cereus senilis; Pilocereus senilis*
Old man cactus

The tall spiny stems of the old man cactus are wrapped in a yellowish-white hairy coat that resembles a scruffy beard – hence the name. This woolly covering may turn brown and become less dense on older plants. As it can grow quite big, display the plant's sculptural form on a wide sill next to a tall window or under a bright skylight. The trumpet-shaped blooms are whitish-yellow and open at night, but they are rarely seen on indoor plants and tend to develop only on mature cacti in the wild that are 6m (20ft) or more in height.

HEIGHT AND SPREAD Up to 1m x 8cm (3ft x 3in).

CARE NOTES See left.

WARNING! Wear cactus gloves when handling this plant.

CEREUS

These South American desert cacti are tall and tree-like in the wild, but smaller species and cultivars are grown indoors as house plants. However, even these may be too large for some homes, so check their heights and spreads before buying to ensure you can accommodate their tall, ribbed, spiny stems. This group of cacti are sometimes known as "night-blooming cereus" because their large, generally white, fragrant flowers open after dark. Plants may have pink, purple, or yellow blooms, and they usually appear in summer.

TEMPERATURE 5–30°C (41–86°F).

LIGHT Position in full sun, but provide some shade in summer.

WATERING During the spring and summer, water when the top 2cm (¾in) of compost is dry. In autumn, reduce watering to once a month. Keep plants dry in winter.

FEEDING Apply a half-strength high-potash fertilizer once a month during late spring and summer.

COMPOST Plant in cactus compost, or a 50:50 mix of loam-based (John Innes No. 2 Peat-Free) compost and 4mm grit.

FLOWERING Flowers only appear on mature plants; buy one in bloom to guarantee flowers.

PROPAGATION Sow seed or take stem cuttings.

COMMON PROBLEMS These plants are prone to rotting in wet compost. Check regularly for mealybugs, scale insect, and spider mites.

CEREUS URUGUAYANUS 'MONSTROUS'

syn. *Cereus hildmannianus*
subsp. *uruguayanus*
Spiny hedge cactus;
Peruvian apple

If you have the space, the spiny hedge cactus will create a large sculptural feature in a bright sunny room. The blue-green cylindrical stems feature distinctive ribs covered with long golden or brown spines. Clusters of white summer flowers develop along the stems, and plants will flower and fruit when they are just 4 years old. In its native Uruguay, this cactus is grown for its edible fruits, which grow to the size of a goose egg.

HEIGHT AND SPREAD Up to 2m x 15cm (6ft 6in x 6in).

CARE NOTES See opposite.

WARNING! Wear cactus gloves when handling this plant.

CEREUS VALIDUS

syn. *Cereus forbesii;*
Cereus hankeanus

This tall, sculptural *Cereus* is a cactus for the more experienced grower. Even in a pot, the blue-green cylindrical stems, armed with long spines, will eventually grow into a tree-like, branched plant. In spring to early summer, it produces large funnel-shaped white or pinkish-white flowers, followed by inedible red fruits.

HEIGHT AND SPREAD Each stem can grow up to 1.5m x 10cm (5ft x 4in).

CARE NOTES See opposite.

WARNING! Wear cactus gloves when handling this plant.

CEREUS VALIDUS 'SPIRALIS'

syn. *Cereus forbesii* 'Spiralis'
Spiralled cereus; Twisted cereus

Look no further than the spiralled cereus if you need a star performer for your cactus collection. The tall blue-green branched stems, which feature spiralling ribs edged with short spines, look like giant green corkscrews. This incredible cactus also produces a profusion of white and pink blooms in summer.

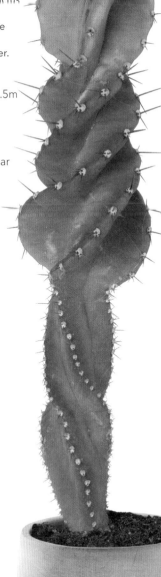

HEIGHT AND SPREAD Up to 1.5m x 60cm (5 x 2ft).

CARE NOTES See opposite.

WARNING! Wear cactus gloves when handling this plant.

CLEISTOCACTUS

Prickly desert-dwelling South American natives, *Cleistocactus* form either tall, slim, columnar structures or fountains of trailing stems, ideal for large hanging baskets. The cylindrical ribbed stems are covered with spines, which are soft in some species. Their long slim flowers, which look a little like tubes of lipstick, shoot out from the sides. The blooms can appear throughout the year on mature plants but are most prevalent in spring and summer. Some do not flower until they are 10–15 years old, so buy mature plants if this is a feature you want to enjoy.

TEMPERATURE 10–30°C (50–86°F)

LIGHT Position in full sun for most of the year, but provide some shade in summer.

WATERING During the spring and summer, water when the top 2cm (¾in) of compost is dry. In autumn, reduce watering to once a month. Keep the compost dry in winter.

FEEDING Apply a half-strength high-potash fertilizer fortnightly during late spring and summer.

COMPOST Plant in cactus compost, or a 50:50 mix of loam-based (John Innes No. 2 Peat-Free) compost and 4mm grit.

FLOWERING Flowers appear on mature plants. Water regularly in spring and summer to encourage blooms to form.

PROPAGATION Sow seed or take stem cuttings.

COMMON PROBLEMS These plants will rot in wet compost. Pests to look out for include mealybugs and spider mites.

CLEISTOCACTUS COLADEMONONIS AGM

syn. *Cleistocactus winteri* subsp. *colademononis*; *Hildewintera colademononis*; *Winterocereus colademononis* Rat's tail; Monkey's tail

Resembling white furry octopus tentacles, the stems of this striking plant are a guaranteed talking point. The hairs are actually long soft spines growing on stems that can reach up to 2m (6ft 6in) in length. Bright red tubular flowers, up to 7.5cm (3in) long, appear along the stems in spring and sometimes at other times of the year. Display this stunning cactus in a large hanging basket where it will form an eye-catching feature in a sunny room.

HEIGHT & SPREAD Each stem grows up to 5cm x 2m (2in x 6ft 6in).

CARE NOTES See left.

WARNING! Plant is toxic if eaten.

CLEISTOCACTUS PARVIFLORUS

syn. *Cereus parviflorus*

One of the columnar species, *Cleistocactus parviflorus* produces towering, slim, ribbed stems up to 3cm (1½in) in diameter, covered with fine brown to greenish-yellow spines. The small tubular flowers are usually yellow, although some plants may produce red blooms.

HEIGHT & SPREAD Each stem grows up to 3m x 7cm (10ft x 3in).

CARE NOTES See left.

WARNING! Plant is toxic if eaten.

CLEISTOCACTUS STRAUSII AGM

syn. *Borzicactus strausii;*
Cephalocereus strausii;
Cereus strausii
Silver torch

One of the most widely available *Cleistocactus*, the silver torch produces tall, grey-green, ribbed stems covered with a coat of fine white hair-like spines. Mature plants that are over 45cm (18in) tall produce burgundy red flowers in late summer. The long, cylindrical blooms make a colourful display, emerging from sides of the stems like shooting stars.

HEIGHT & SPREAD Up to 3m x 6cm (10ft x 2½in).

CARE NOTES See opposite.

WARNING! Plant is toxic if eaten.

CLEISTOCACTUS WINTERI AGM

syn. *Hildewintera aureispina;*
Winteria aureispinar;
Winterocereus aureispinus
Golden rat's tail

If you like the weird and wonderful, the golden rat's tail cactus is the plant for you. Its jumble of spreading, trailing stems look more like long, spiny sausages or snakes than its common name would suggest. Orange to salmon-pink tubular flowers emerge in spring and summer. Grow it in a large pot or hanging basket where the long, furry stems can sprawl freely.

HEIGHT & SPREAD Clumps grow up to 1 x 0.6m (36in x 24in).

CARE NOTES See opposite.

WARNING! Plant is toxic if eaten.

COPIAPOA

These pretty little cacti, originally from the dry coastal deserts of northern Chile, are perfect for a small windowsill collection. The olive-brown or blue–green stems, which can be spherical or slightly columnar, typically feature well-defined ribs and black or brown spines, though a few species are spineless. As the plants mature, the stems multiply to form decorative clusters. *Copiapoa* produce tubular yellow flowers from woolly crowns at the top of the plant in summer.

TEMPERATURE 10–30°C (50–86°F)

LIGHT Position in full sun, with some shade in summer.

WATERING Water from early spring to autumn with rainwater, leaving the top 1cm (½in) of the compost to dry out between waterings. Keep the compost dry in winter.

FEEDING Apply a half-strength high-potash fertilizer once a month in spring and summer.

COMPOST Plant in cactus compost, or a 50:50 mix of loam-based (John Innes No. 2 Peat-Free) compost and 4mm grit.

FLOWERING Plants, even young ones, will flower readily if they receive adequate water and a little fertilizer in the growing season.

PROPAGATION Sow seed or take offsets.

COMMON PROBLEMS These cacti will quickly rot in wet soil. Watch out for mealybugs and spider mite infestations.

COPIAPOA HYPOGAEA AGM

syn. *Chileorebutia hypogaea;*
Neochilenia hypogaea;
Pilocopiapoa hypogaea
Underground copiapoa

The underground copiapoa is so called because in its native Chile its round low-growing dimpled stems grow partly beneath the soil surface to protect themselves from the harsh sun. Young plants feature sparse spines that protrude from small white felted areas, giving the plant a spotty appearance. Golden-yellow scented flowers appear in summer.

HEIGHT & SPREAD Each stem grows up to 7 x 12cm (3 x 5in).

CARE NOTES See left.

WARNING! Wear cactus gloves when handling this plant.

CORYPHANTHA

Round or short and cylindrical, these cacti have attractive dimpled stems. While some produce just a few spines, the long, curved spines on others are the main attraction. The blooms appear in spring or summer at the top of the plant and come in shades of yellow or pink, or occasionally creamy-white. Plants remain small and compact, even when mature, making them ideal candidates where space is limited.

TEMPERATURE 5–30°C (41°F–86°F); some are frost hardy down to -10°C (14°F) if the soil is dry.

LIGHT Position in full sun, but provide some shade in midsummer.

WATERING From mid-spring to early autumn, water when the top 2cm (¾in) of compost is dry. Keep plants drier in winter, watering lightly once a month.

FEEDING Apply a half-strength high potash fertilizer fortnightly from late spring to late summer.

COMPOST Plant in cactus compost, or a 50:50 mix of loam-based (John Innes No. 2 Peat-Free) compost and 4mm grit.

FLOWERING Mature plants will flower in summer when given sufficient fertilizer and water.

PROPAGATION Sow seed or take offsets.

COMMON PROBLEMS Prone to rotting in damp compost. Check plants regularly for mealybugs and spider mites.

COPIAPOA TENUISSIMA

syn. *Copiapoa humilis* subsp. *tenuissima;* *Copiapoa hypogaea* subsp. *tenuissima*

The olive-green dimpled stems of this compact cactus are covered with fine hair-like spines that look like starbursts. The stems are slow to form clumps, but it flowers reliably in spring or summer when small scented yellow blooms develop at the top of the plant.

HEIGHT & SPREAD Up to 7 x 12cm (3 x 5in).

CARE NOTES See opposite.

 WARNING! Wear cactus gloves when handling this plant.

CORYPHANTHA MACROMERIS

syn. *Echinocactus macromeris;* *Lepidocoryphantha macromeris;* *Mammillaria macromeris*

Pincushion cactus; Big needle cactus

Hailing from the deserts of Mexico and the southern United States, the pincushion cactus is easy to grow and a great choice for a beginner. The short, cylindrical stems are dimpled and spiky, and they quickly multiply to create small clusters. Long brown needle-like spines form at the top of the plant, while shorter white spines cover the rest of the stem. The daisy-like, bright rose-pink or magenta flowers appear in the summer.

HEIGHT & SPREAD Up to 15 x 10cm (6 x 4in).

CARE NOTES See left.

 WARNING! Wear cactus gloves when handling this plant.

DISOCACTUS

Dramatically different from their desert-dwelling cousins, *Disocactus* are from the tropical regions of Central America, the Caribbean, and South America, where they cling to trees and rocks. Their long trailing stems, which can be cylindrical or flat and ribbon-like, make impressive displays in hanging baskets. The large red or pink starry flowers, which appear in spring or summer, make a striking visual impression.

TEMPERATURE 6–24°C (43°F–75°F); keep at 11–14°C (52–57°F) in winter.

LIGHT Position in bright light but not direct sun, with shade from midday sun in summer.

WATERING From mid-spring to early autumn, soak the compost when watering, but reapply only when the top 1cm (½in) of compost is dry. Keep the compost just moist in winter. Mist stems occasionally to increase humidity levels.

FEEDING Use a half-strength liquid fertilizer sprayed onto the stems of the plant once every 2 weeks from early spring to autumn.

COMPOST Plant in cactus compost with added horticultural grit, or a 3:2:1 mix of loam-based compost (John Innes No. 2 Peat-Free), 4mm grit, and peat-free multipurpose compost.

FLOWERING Move the plants to a cooler area (11–14°C/52–57°F) in winter, and keep the compost just moist, to promote flower buds to form.

PROPAGATION Sow seeds or take stem cuttings in spring.

COMMON PROBLEMS Check plants regularly for mealybugs and spider mites.

DISOCACTUS FLAGELLIFORMIS AGM

syn. *Aporocactus flagelliformis*
Rat tail cactus

One of the most widely available and easy-to-grow, the trailing stems of the rat tail cactus grow quickly, soon forming a prickly fountain up to 1m (3ft) or more in length. The ribbed, cylindrical stems are covered with tiny reddish-yellow spines that look like fine hairs – but beware, they are sharp and painful if touched. The spectacular crimson and pink flowers are a bonus when they appear for a few days in late spring. Display this plant in a large basket and suspend it high enough to allow the stems to develop to their full potential.

HEIGHT & SPREAD Clumps grow up to 1.5 x 0.6m (5 x 2ft).

CARE NOTES See left.

WARNING! Wear cactus gloves when handling this plant.

ECHINOCACTUS

The classic round barrel shape and neat spiny ribs makes *Echinocactus* a favourite among collectors and beginners alike. Adding colour and texture to a desert cactus display, the long yellowish, cream, or occasionally red sharp spines form along the edges of the ribs, creating distinctive prickly stripes in many species. Small flowers, which can be yellow or pink, appear like little rosettes at the top of the stems in summer.

TEMPERATURE 10–30°C (50–86°F).

LIGHT Position in full sun; provide a little shade in summer.

WATERING From mid-spring to early autumn, water only when the top 2cm (¾in) of compost is dry. Keep plants dry in winter.

FEEDING Apply a half-strength cactus fertilizer once a month during late spring and summer.

COMPOST Plant in cactus compost, or a 50:50 mix of loam-based (John Innes No. 2 Peat-Free) compost and 4mm grit.

FLOWERING Mature plants will flower in summer, given a little fertilizer and water (see above).

PROPAGATION Sow seed.

COMMON PROBLEMS This plant is prone to root rot when grown in damp compost. Check plants regularly for aphids, mealybugs, and scale insects.

ECHINOCACTUS GRUSONII AGM
Golden barrel cactus

With its colourful prickly stems, the golden barrel cactus makes an exciting, textured feature. The pale green, heavily ribbed globes feature rows of short, densely packed yellow spines and a creamy wool top. While its classic cactus silhouette is highly appealing, the small yellow flowers are less than inspiring, often going unnoticed as they merge with the creamy-coloured "wool" at the top of the stem. This cactus generally grows a solitary stem, although older plants may form small clusters.

HEIGHT & SPREAD Up to 60 x 60cm (24 x 24in).

CARE NOTES See opposite.

WARNING! Wear cactus gloves when handling this plant.

ECHINOCEREUS

Ideal for beginners, these natives of the southern United States and Mexico are among the easiest cacti to grow. Their cylindrical stems feature spine-covered ribs; in some species, the spines are colourful or long and curved, creating an intricate lacy pattern over the entire plant. As well as the decorative stems, these pretty cacti are grown for their large, dramatic flowers, which range in colour from pinks and reds to yellows, browns, and greens, many are bicoloured too. The blooms appear in spring or summer at the top of the plant and are followed by edible fruits. Mature plants develop to form large clusters of prickly stems.

TEMPERATURE 5–30°C (41–86°F).

LIGHT Position in full sun with a little shade in midsummer.

WATERING During the spring and summer, water when the top 2cm (¾in) of compost is dry. In autumn, reduce watering to once a month, and keep plants dry in winter.

FEEDING Apply a half-strength cactus fertilizer once a month from spring to early autumn.

COMPOST Plant in cactus compost, or a 50:50 mix of loam-based (John Innes No. 2 Peat-Free) compost and 4mm grit.

FLOWERING Keep plants on a sunny windowsill, except in the summer (see above), to encourage flowers to form.

PROPAGATION Sow seed or take offsets.

COMMON PROBLEMS Susceptible to rot if overwatered. Check regularly for mealybugs and scale insects.

ECHINOCEREUS PENTALOPHUS AGM
syn. *Cereus pentalophus*;
Cereus pentalophus var. *radicans*;
Cereus pentalophus var. *simplex*
Lady finger cactus;
Dog tail

A must for any cactus collection, the lady finger cactus produces a mass of slim green stems that look like sprawling spiny fingers. The stems have long, sharp white or yellowish spines along the ribs, and in late spring, bright pink flowers with yellow or cream centres appear at the ends of the "fingers". The blooms are followed by edible green fruits. Grow it in a hanging basket or tall pot, where the stems and blooms can trail over the sides.

HEIGHT & SPREAD Clumps grow up to 20 x 20cm (8 x 8in).

CARE NOTES See left.

WARNING! Wear cactus gloves when handling this plant.

ECHINOCEREUS PULCHELLUS

syn. *Cereus pulchellus;*
Echinocactus pulchellus;
Echinonyctanthus pulchellus;
Echinopsis pulchella

The dainty, blue-green, globe-shaped stems of this diminutive cactus feature tiny white clusters of spines that emerge from woolly areas along the ribs, giving the plant a spotty appearance. Pink or pinkish-white daisy-like flowers appear at the top of each domed stem in summer.

HEIGHT & SPREAD Up to 6 x 7cm (2 x 2½in).

CARE NOTES See p205.

WARNING! Wear cactus gloves when handling this plant.

ECHINOCEREUS REICHENBACHII AGM

syn. *Cereus reichenbachianus;*
Echinocactus reichenbachianus;
Echinocactus reichenbachii
Black lace cactus;
Lace hedgehog cactus

Small and cylindrical, the dark green stems of the black lace cactus are often almost obscured by its multicoloured brown, black, pink, or white curved spines. These spines appear to form a lacy design, hence the plant's common name. The spines grow from ribs, which on some plants form a slightly spiralling pattern, adding to this little plant's charms. In spring or summer, large purple or pink flowers with a sweet fragrance appear at the top of each stem.

HEIGHT & SPREAD Up to 25 x 10cm (10 x 4in).

CARE NOTES See p205.

WARNING! Wear cactus gloves when handling this plant.

ECHINOCEREUS RIGIDISSIMUS subsp. RUBISPINUS

syn. *Echinocereus pectinatus*
var. *rubispinus; Echinocereus*
rigidissimus var. *rubispinus*
Rainbow cactus

The popular rainbow cactus is prized for the dark red and violet spines that cover its cylindrical stems. As if the colourful spines were not enough to catch the eye, in summer, large white-throated magenta or red flowers appear around the sides of stems. The plant also forms small clumps as it matures.

HEIGHT & SPREAD Up to 25 x 60cm (10 x 24in).

CARE NOTES See p205.

WARNING! Wear cactus gloves when handling this plant.

ECHINOCEREUS VIERECKII

syn. *Echinocereus viereckii subsp. viereckii*
Hedgehog cactus

The bright apple-green ribbed stems of the hedgehog cactus form dense clusters, while its yellow spines make a colourful contrast. If you have children, try the more widely available *Echinocereus viereckii* subsp. *morricalii* (pictured), which is almost spineless and safer to handle. Large, funnel-shaped magenta-purple flowers appear in summer on both species.

HEIGHT & SPREAD Each stem can reach up to 30 x 7.5cm (12 x 3in).

CARE NOTES See p205.

WARNING! Wear cactus gloves when handling this plant.

ECHINOPSIS

This group of cacti comes in a wide range of shapes and sizes, from tiny and squat to large and tree-like, but the majority are spiny, ribbed, and globe-like or cylindrical. The plants' beautiful, tubular blooms are available in many colours, including white, red, pink, violet, orange, and yellow. Although each flower only lasts a day, they appear in succession over a long period in spring and summer.

The group is collectively known as hedgehog cacti, which can sometimes lead to *Echinopsis* being confused with *Echinocereus* (see pp205–206), which share the same common name.

TEMPERATURE 5–30°C (41–86°F); keep cool and dry in winter; will tolerate spells below freezing to -5°C (23°F) if the soil is dry.

LIGHT Position in full sun; provide a little shade in midsummer.

WATERING From late spring to early autumn, water when the top 2cm (¾in) of compost is dry. In autumn, reduce watering to once a month. Keep plants dry in winter.

FEEDING Apply a half-strength high-potash fertilizer every 2 weeks in summer.

COMPOST Plant in cactus compost, or a 50:50 mix of loam–based (John Innes No. 2 Peat-Free) compost and 4mm grit.

FLOWERING Encourage plants to flower by keeping them at over 21°C (70°F) and in bright sunlight during the spring and early summer.

PROPAGATION Sow seed or take offsets.

COMMON PROBLEMS Stems will rot in damp compost. Check regularly for mealybugs and scale insects.

ECHINOPSIS CHAMAECEREUS AGM

syn. *Cereus silvestrii; Chamaecereus silvestrii; Lobivia silvestrii*
Peanut cactus

The peanut cactus forms clusters of short, finger-like, ribbed stems that are said to resemble the nuts after which it is named. The stems have soft spines when young but plants become spineless as they mature. Initially growing upright, they then trail slightly to make a beautiful feature in a small hanging basket. Flushes of large, dark-eyed, bright red flowers shoot out from the stems throughout spring and summer.

HEIGHT & SPREAD Up to 15 x 30cm (6 x 12in).

CARE NOTES See left.

WARNING! Wear cactus gloves when handling this plant

ECHINOPSIS FORMOSA

syn. *Lobivia formosa;*
Soehrensia formosa

The ribbed columns of this prickly cactus are covered with long spines, which can be white, brown, or beige. The stems tend to be solitary and rarely form clusters, while the early summer flowers are normally yellow, although on some plants they may be orange or reddish-orange.

HEIGHT & SPREAD Up to 60 x 30cm (24 x 12in).

CARE NOTES See p207.

WARNING! Wear cactus gloves when handling this plant.

ECHINOPSIS SUBDENUDATA 'TUFTY'

syn. *Echinopsis ancistrophora;*
Echinopsis subdenudatus
Easter lily cactus

The small, globe-shaped stems of this dainty cactus are grey–green and generally compact, although older plants are taller and more cylindrical. Safe for children to handle, this cactus is almost spineless, or has very short spines, while the marked woolly areas create its distinctive spots. The spectacular white flowers are also hard to beat, providing an almost continuous show from late spring to late summer. Sweetly fragrant, each bloom lasts just one day, but more follow in succession.

HEIGHT & SPREAD Up to 30 x 7.5cm (12 x 3in).

CARE NOTES See p207.

EPIPHYLLUM

Grown for their long, often wavy-edged, smooth-faced stems and large, orchid-like flowers, these tropical cacti have similar needs to *Disocactus* (see p204). The trailing stems form a lush, leafy display in a hanging basket, while the fragrant flowers, which appear in summer or autumn, come in a range of colours, including white, orange, red, or yellow; some are bicoloured. In Mexico this plant is prized for its edible fruits.

TEMPERATURE 6–24°C (43°F–75°F); keep at 11–14°C (52–57°F) in winter.

LIGHT Position in bright light but not direct sun. In summer, keep shaded from the midday sun.

WATERING For most of the year, soak the compost thoroughly when watering, but reapply only when the top 1cm (½in) of compost is dry. Do not water for a month during winter, to give the plant a rest period. These cacti require moderately high humidity.

FEEDING Apply cactus fertilizer every 2 weeks during spring and summer.

COMPOST Plant in cactus compost with added grit, or a 3:2:1 mix of loam-based compost (John Innes No. 2 Peat-Free), 4mm grit, and peat-free multipurpose compost.

FLOWERING Move the plants to a cooler area (11–14°C/52–57°F) in winter, and keep the compost just moist to promote flower buds to form. Move to a warmer spot in spring.

PROPAGATION Sow seeds or take stem cuttings.

COMMON PROBLEMS Check plants regularly for mealybugs and spider mites.

EPIPHYLLUM ANGULIGER

Fishbone cactus

This deservedly popular plant produces a waterfall of unusual wavy-edged leaves that resemble fishbones, hence its common name. The white scented flowers open in the evenings in autumn – each flower lasts for just one or two days – and are followed by edible greenish fruits that taste a little like gooseberries then follow the blooms. The plant makes an attractive feature in a bright room in a hanging basket or pot on a plant stand.

HEIGHT & SPREAD Clumps grow up to 20 x 30cm (8 x 12in).

CARE NOTES See opposite.

ERIOSYCE

The spiny armour of a few *Eriosyce* species have made them very popular among collectors looking for something a little out of the ordinary. While the round globe-like or cylindrical stems are unremarkable, the plants' long, curved cream, black, or brown spines, which in some species almost cover the entire stem, draw the eye. In summer, bright pink, yellow, or cream flowers appear at the top of the plant.

TEMPERATURE 5–30°C (41–86°F); tolerates short spells below freezing to -4°C (25°F) if the soil is dry.

LIGHT Position in full sun, but provide a little light shade in midsummer.

WATERING From late spring to autumn, water when the top 2cm (¾in) of compost is dry. In autumn, reduce watering to once a month. Keep plants dry in winter.

FEEDING Apply a half-strength high-potash fertilizer every 2 weeks in summer.

COMPOST Plant in cactus compost, or a 50:50 mix of loam-based (John Innes No. 2 Peat-Free) compost and 4mm grit.

FLOWERING Plants will flower reliably if the care advice above is followed.

PROPAGATION Sow seed.

COMMON PROBLEMS Prone to rotting if overwatered. Check regularly for mealybugs and scale insects.

ERIOSYCE SENILIS AGM

syn. *Echinocactus senilis;*
Euporteria senilis;
Neoporteria nidus f. *senilis*

Despite its diminutive size, *Eriosyce senilis* will stand out from the crowd in any cactus collection. The star attraction is the tangle of curved, bristly white spines that cover the purplish spherical or short columnar stems like candyfloss. Magenta flowers, which are not especially large, add to the plant's allure when they appear in summer.

HEIGHT & SPREAD Each stem can reach up to 18 x 8cm (7 x 3in).

CARE NOTES See left.

WARNING! Wear cactus gloves when handling this plant.

ESPOSTOA

Tall, slim, and covered with a woolly coat that protects them against the harsh climate of their native Andes, these fluffy-looking pillar-shaped plants add height and texture to a mixed cactus display. Mature plants may also produce large bell-shaped flowers in summer, followed by sweet edible fruits, although the blooms are rarely seen on *Espostoa* grown as house plants.

TEMPERATURE 12–30°C (54–86°F)

LIGHT Position in full sun, but provide light shade in midsummer.

WATERING From late spring to autumn, water when the top 1cm (½in) of compost is dry. Reduce watering in autumn. Keep compost dry in winter.

FEEDING Apply a half-strength cactus fertilizer once a month from spring to autumn.

COMPOST Plant in cactus compost, or a 50:50 mix of loam-based (John Innes No. 2 Peat-Free) compost and 4mm grit.

FLOWERING Flowers will only appear on mature plants when exposed to sufficient sunlight.

PROPAGATION Sow seed.

COMMON PROBLEMS Prone to rotting if overwatered. Check plants regularly for mealybugs and scale insects.

ESPOSTOA LANATA AGM

syn. *Cleistocactus lanatus; Oreocereus lanatus*
Peruvian old man cactus

The Peruvian old man cactus makes a striking silhouette, with its tall ribbed columns covered in a dense thicket of hair-like spines. Despite its cuddly appearance, this furry coat disguises sharp spines: do not be tempted to stroke it. The stems soon multiply to form clusters and mature plants will also branch out. This plant is shy to bloom, especially when grown indoors; when they do appear, the nocturnal white to purple flowers appear from late spring to early summer.

HEIGHT & SPREAD Each stem can reach up to 3m x 20cm (10ft x 8in).

CARE NOTES See left.

WARNING! Wear cactus gloves when handling this plant.

ESPOSTOA MELANOSTELE AGM

syn. *Cephalocereus melanostele; Cereus melanostele*
Peruvian old lady cactus

Like its close cousin (see left), the Peruvian old lady cactus grows into a tall, columnar plant, with greyish-green stems covered with sharp yellow spines buried amongst fine, white, hair-like spines that look like wool. Plant in a large pot as the stems will soon multiply to fill it. The white flowers rarely appear on cacti grown as house plants.

HEIGHT & SPREAD Clusters grow up to 1 x 0.6m (3 x 2ft).

CARE NOTES See left.

WARNING! Wear cactus gloves when handling this plant.

FEROCACTUS

Natives of the southern United States and Mexico, this group of cacti are popular for their chubby barrel shape, and fierce, spiny armour. The ribbed stems are adorned with thick, sharp spines that may be hooked or straight, and in a few species, bright pink or red. The small, funnel-shaped flowers come in yellow, purple, or red, with buds emerging through the dense spiny thickets in summer. Keep this group of cacti out of reach of children and pets.

TEMPERATURE 10–30°C (64–86°F); keep plants cool at 10–12°C (54–50°F) from late autumn to late winter.

LIGHT Position in full sun, with a little shade in midsummer.

WATERING From spring to early autumn, allow the top 2cm (¾in) of the compost to dry out before watering, then water well and leave to drain. From late autumn to late winter, keep compost almost dry.

FEEDING Apply a diluted cactus fertilizer every 3–4 weeks from spring to early autumn.

COMPOST Plant in a cactus compost or mixture of a 3:1:1 mix of soil-based compost, sand, and horticultural grit.

FLOWERING Plants will flower given sufficient light and a little fertilizer.

PROPAGATION Sow seed.

COMMON PROBLEMS Susceptible to rotting in wet compost or a humid atmosphere. Mealybugs and scale insects may be a problem.

FEROCACTUS EMORYI subsp. RECTISPINUS

syn. *Ferocactus rectispinus;*
Echinocactus emoryi var. *rectispinus;*
Echinocactus rectispinus
Long-spined barrel cactus

With its armour of terrifying red spines measuring up to 25cm (10in) in length, the long-spined barrel cactus is aptly named. While the spines are a guaranteed talking point, the plant also produces beautiful large pale yellow flowers in summer. Take care to avoid injury when displaying this cactus – a shelf wider than the spines out of reach of children and pets would be best.

HEIGHT & SPREAD Up to 60 x 30cm (24 x 12in).

CARE NOTES See left.

WARNING! Wear cactus gloves when handling this plant.

FEROCACTUS FORDII subsp. BOREALIS AGM

syn. *Echinocactus fordii*
Ford barrel cactus

Impossible to overlook when in bloom, the colourful Ford barrel cactus creates a focal point in a collection, or you could display it as a feature plant on its own. Its long, dramatic, red-tinged curved spines, surrounded by thinner white spines, grow in starry clusters along grey-green ribs, while large purplish-pink flowers appear at the top of the plant in summer. For a similar cactus with even longer, sword-like spines, look out for the true species, *Ferocactus fordii.*

HEIGHT & SPREAD Up to 45 x 30cm (18 x 12in).

CARE NOTE See left.

WARNING! Wear cactus gloves when handling this plant.

FEROCACTUS GLAUCESCENS AGM

syn. *Ferocactus pfeifferi*;
Echinocactus glaucescens;
Echinocactus pfeifferi
Glaucous barrel cactus

The bluish colour and rounded shape of young plants give the glaucous barrel cactus its common name, although it may develop a more cylindrical silhouette as it matures. Easy to grow, this cactus has long yellow spines that sprout from the edges of well-defined ribs in starry clusters, while long-lasting funnel-shaped yellow flowers appear in summer. The stems of this decorative cactus soon multiply to form clusters.

HEIGHT & SPREAD Up to 60 x 50cm (24 x 20in).

CARE NOTES See p211.

WARNING! Wear cactus gloves when handling this plant.

FEROCACTUS GRACILIS AGM

syn. *Ferocactus peninsulae* var. *gracilis*
Fire barrel cactus

With its dramatic bright pink spines, the colourful fire barrel cactus is one to look out for. Like its cousins, young plants are spherical, becoming more columnar as they mature, but the stems are very slow to produce clusters. Pinky-red flowers appear in early summer at the top of the plant.

HEIGHT & SPREAD Up to 60 x 30cm (24 x 12in).

CARE NOTES See p211. Bring plants into more light in summer if the spines start to lose their colouration.

WARNING! Wear cactus gloves when handling this plant.

FEROCACTUS LATISPINUS AGM

syn. *Ferocactus latispinus* var. *latispinus;*
Echinocactus cornigerus var. *latispinus;*
Echinocactus latispinus
Devil's tongue cactus

It's easy to see how the devil's tongue cactus came by its common name: one of its curved red spines is larger and longer than the others, like a tongue sticking out. When combined with smaller red and creamy-white spines, this produces a stunning effect. The blue-green ribbed stem of this barrel cactus also maintains a more rounded shape than many other mature ferocactus. Purplish-pink flowers develop in summer on established plants.

HEIGHT & SPREAD Up to 25 x 25cm (10 x 10in).

CARE NOTES See p211.

WARNING! Wear cactus gloves when handling this plant.

FEROCACTUS MACRODISCUS

syn. *Echinocactus macrodiscus*
Candy cactus

As the candy cactus matures, it produces a low, wide, domed stem that sets it apart from the more rounded plants in this group. The grey-green ribs also sport curved, cream-coloured spines. While these are not as spectacular as the spines of some barrel cacti, the large white and pink striped flowers help to compensate when they appear in spring, even on young plants.

HEIGHT & SPREAD Up to 10 x 25cm (4 x 10in).

CARE NOTES See p211.

WARNING! Wear cactus gloves when handling this plant.

FEROCACTUS VIRIDESCENS AGM

syn. *Echinocactus viridescens*
Coast barrel cactus

The coast barrel cactus has a pleasing rounded shape and bright green ribbed stems. Its curved yellow spines are pink when young, giving the plant a two-tone look, and in early summer, green or red-tinged flowers appear. Use this unassuming cactus as a foil for more brightly coloured types.

HEIGHT & SPREAD Up to 25 x 30cm (10 x 12in).

CARE NOTES See p211.

WARNING! Wear cactus gloves when handling this plant.

GYMNOCALYCIUM

Perfect for a narrow windowsill, these easy-care South American cacti are round and compact, with white, brown or black spines that radiate from woolly areas on the ribs. The stems are grey-green or blue-green, and in some species the ribs are unusually wide, dividing the plant into triangular segments that look like little chins, hence the common name, "chin cactus". Most *Gymnocalycium* plants produce white, cream, or pale pink flowers in spring or summer, although some of the most popular species have dark red or yellow blooms.

TEMPERATURE 10–30°C (50–86°F); some species tolerate temperatures down to -15°C (5°F).

LIGHT Position in full sun, and in light shade in summer.

WATERING From late spring to early autumn, allow the top 1cm (½in) of the compost to dry out before watering, then water well and leave to drain. Do not water from late autumn to late winter.

FEEDING Apply a half-strength high-potash fertilizer once a month from spring to late summer.

COMPOST Plant in a cactus compost or mixture of a 3:1:1 mix of soil-based compost, sand, and horticultural grit.

FLOWERING Plants will flower readily but need high heat and good light to open; increase exposure to sunlight if flowers fail to form.

PROPAGATION Sow seed.

COMMON PROBLEMS Prone to rotting in damp compost. Check plants regularly for mealybugs.

GYMNOCALYCIUM BALDIANUM AGM

syn. *Echinocactus baldianus;*
Gymnocalycium platense var. *baldianum;*
Gymnocalycium venturianum
Dwarf chin cactus; Spider cactus

Free-flowering and easy to grow, the dwarf chin cactus is ideal for beginners. Unlike those of many of its cousins, the ribs of this *Gymnocalycium* have a more dimpled surface, from which sprout pale brown spines that look like tiny spiders, giving rise to its other common name. The large purple-red or pinkish-purple early summer flowers are produced when plants are quite young.

HEIGHT & SPREAD Up to 10 x 13cm (4 x 5in).

CARE NOTES See left.

WARNING! Wear cactus gloves when handling this plant.

GYMNOCALYCIUM BALDIANUM var. ALBIFLORUM

syn. *Gymnocalycium kieslingii*
White-flowered dwarf chin cactus

Almost identical to *Gymnocalycium baldianum* (see right), and equally easy to grow, this variety produces elegant white flowers in summer that create a striking contrast to the dark blue-green stems.

HEIGHT & SPREAD Up to 10 x 13cm (4 x 5in).

CARE NOTES See left.

WARNING! Wear cactus gloves when handling this plant.

GYMNOCALYCIUM BRUCHII AGM

syn. *Astrophytum bruchii;*
Frailea bruchi
Chin cactus

This miniature cactus has round flat-topped blue-green stems, and the ribs are covered with long, curved white spines. The flowers, which appear in clusters in spring at the top of the plant like a bouquet of tiny water lilies, are an unusual shade of lavender-white. Inedible green fruits follow the blooms. This cactus is hardier than most, tolerating -15°C (5°F) if the soil is dry.

HEIGHT & SPREAD Up to 4 x 6cm (1½ x 2½in).

CARE NOTES See opposite.

 WARNING! Wear cactus gloves when handling this plant.

GYMNOCALYCIUM CALOCHLORUM

syn. *Echinocactus calochlorus;*
Gymnocalycium proliferum var.
calochlorum; Gymnocalycium
quehlianum var. *calochlorum*
Clustering chin cactus

Highly prized for its small, round, dimpled stems, the clustering chin cactus is covered in white curved spines that produce a pretty lacy pattern over the surface. The large, elegant pale pink to white flowers, which appear on spineless tubes in late spring or summer, are followed by inedible green fruits. It forms small clusters of stems after a few years.

HEIGHT & SPREAD Up to 4 x 6cm (1½ x 2½in).

CARE NOTES See opposite.

 WARNING! Wear cactus gloves when handling this plant.

GYMNOCALYCIUM HORSTII var. BUENEKERI

syn. *Gymnocalycium buenekeri*
Chin cactus

This chin cactus has the classic wide-ribbed rounded shape that gives *Gymnocalycium* their common name. Sparse long yellow curved spines contrast with the blue-green stems, which multiply quickly to produce small clumps. Large pale pink flowers appear in summer. This cactus is frost-resistant down to -4°C (25°F) if the soil is dry.

HEIGHT & SPREAD Up to 10 x 10cm (4 x 4in).

CARE NOTES See opposite.

 WARNING! Wear cactus gloves when handling this plant.

LEUCHTENBERGIA

This cactus group includes just one species, *Leuchtenbergia principis*, which is native to the Chihuahaun desert in Mexico. An excellent choice for those searching for an unusual addition to their collection, the three-sided stems resemble the leaves of an agave, giving rise to its common name of "agave cactus". Pale yellow flowers appear on mature plants in the summer months.

TEMPERATURE -8–30°C (18–86°F).

LIGHT Position in full sun.

WATERING From autumn to late spring, apply plenty of water when the top 1cm (½in) of compost is dry. Do not water in winter.

FEEDING Apply a half-strength cactus fertilizer once a month during spring and summer.

COMPOST Plant in cactus compost.

FLOWERING Plants are more likely to flower if grown outside in summer, where they can benefit from stronger direct sunlight.

PROPAGATION Sow seed.

COMMON PROBLEMS Damp compost will cause stems to rot. Check regularly for scale insects, mealybugs, and spider mites.

LEUCHTENBERGIA PRINCIPIS
Agave cactus

Not everyone's idea of a beautiful plant, the agave cactus is notable for its strange appearance. Soft, papery spines grow in tufts from the ends of the stem sections, while large fragrant pale yellow flowers appear in summer. Each bloom lasts only two or three days, but they appear in succession over many weeks.

HEIGHT & SPREAD Up to 60 x 30cm (24 x 12in).

CARE NOTES See opposite.

LOPHOPHORA

Small and elegant, these low-growing, globe-shaped cacti look like tiny apples. There are just two species in this group: *Lophophora diffusa,* which has smooth yellow–green stems, and *Lophophora williamsii,* with dimpled blue-green ribbed stems. Both are spineless but feature soft creamy-coloured wool that in some plants looks like tufts of hair sprouting in patches over the stems. Slow to flower, mature lophophora plants produce small pale pink blooms in summer from a woolly area at the top of the plant.

TEMPERATURE 5–40°C (41–104°F); will tolerate freezing temperatures of -7°C (20°F) if the soil is dry.

LIGHT Position in full sun and provide light shade in summer.

WATERING Water well during the summer months, but allow the top 1cm (½in) of compost to dry out between waterings; water sparingly in spring and autumn and do not water at all in winter.

FEEDING Apply a half-strength cactus fertilizer twice in summer.

COMPOST Plant in cactus compost with added grit, or a 3:2:1 mix of loam-based compost (John Innes No. 2 Peat-Free), 4mm grit, and peat-free multipurpose compost.

FLOWERING Flowers appear on plants that are at least 5 years old. Keep in a warm room in direct sunlight, and leave unwatered for several weeks in early spring, then water well.

PROPAGATION Sow seed.

COMMON PROBLEMS Prone to rotting if overwatered. Check plants regularly for mealybugs.

LOPHOPHORA WILLIAMSII

syn. *Echinocactus lewinii; Echinocactus williamsii; Echinocactus williamsii* var. *anhaloninicus; Echinocactus williamsii* var. *pellotinicus*
Dumpling cactus; Peyote

The hair-like wool that dots the surface of the dumpling cactus can be long and tufty in some plants, while in others, it is barely noticeable. The stems slowly multiply to make attractive clusters, and when mature, plants produce pale pink flowers in summer. Plant in a deep pot to accommodate the large root.

HEIGHT & SPREAD Up to 6 x 12cm (2½ x 4½in).

CARE NOTES See left.

WARNING! Plant is toxic if eaten.

MAMMILLARIA

One of the most popular and widely available groups of cacti, *Mammillaria* includes over 200 species and varieties. Most are globe- or ball-shaped, although a few form short cylindrical columns, and they either grow as solitary stems or in domed clusters. The spines may be stiff and stout, or hair-like, and some plants also feature wool or bristles. The flowers tend to be small and appear in rings around the stems, producing a beautiful haloed effect. They also come in a wide range of colours.

TEMPERATURE 5–30°C (41–86°F).

LIGHT Position in full sun, but provide some shade in summer.

WATERING From spring to autumn, water thoroughly but allow the top 1–2cm (½–¾in) of compost to dry out between waterings. Do not water in winter, but mist plants occasionally.

FEEDING Apply a half-strength cactus fertilizer once a month from spring to early autumn.

COMPOST Plant in cactus compost with added grit, or a 3:2:1 mix of loam-based compost (John Innes No. 2 Peat-Free), 4mm grit, and peat-free multipurpose compost.

FLOWERING To encourage flowering, keep plants in a cool place in winter and do not water. Then, in spring, resume watering and increase the temperature.

PROPAGATION Sow seed or take offsets.

COMMON PROBLEMS Plants are susceptible to rotting if overwatered. Check plants regularly for mealybugs.

MAMMILLARIA BAUMII AGM

syn. *Dolichothele baumii;*
Ebnerella baumii
Pincushion cactus

Starry clusters of soft white spines cover this little rounded cactus like spun sugar, almost obscuring the grey-green stems. It soon forms small clumps, which are decorated with relatively large, scented golden-yellow flowers in late spring.

HEIGHT & SPREAD Each stem grows up to 7 x 15cm (3½ x 6in).

CARE NOTES See left.

WARNING! Wear cactus gloves when handling this plant.

MAMMILLARIA BOMBYCINA AGM

syn. *Chilita bombycina; Ebnerella bombycine; Escobariopsis bombycine; Neomammillaria bombycina*
Silken pincushion cactus

The short cylindrical stems of the silken pincushion cactus quickly multiply to form large dome-shaped clusters. Each stem is covered in a mass of short white spines and longer brown curved spines that protrude from a downy base to create a fascinating spotty, two-tone effect. Circular clusters of magenta-pink flowers appear on the upper surfaces of the stems in spring and summer.

HEIGHT & SPREAD Clumps grow up to 20 x 30cm (8 x 12in).

CARE NOTES See left.

WARNING! Wear cactus gloves when handling this plant.

MAMMILLARIA ELONGATA AGM

syn. *Leptocladia elongate;*
Leptocladodia elongata;
Neomammillaria elongata
Ladyfinger cactus;
Golden star cactus

MAMMILLARIA CARMENAE AGM

syn. *Escobariopsis carmenae*
Isla Carmen pincushion cactus

The Isla Carmen pincushion cactus produces small dimpled globes covered with dense clusters of soft fine white or pale yellow spines that look like sparkling starbursts. In spring and summer, small yellow-centred white or pink-tinged flowers appear in a halo around the top of the plant.

HEIGHT & SPREAD Each stem grows up to 10 x 10cm (4 x 4in).

CARE NOTES See opposite.

WARNING! Wear cactus gloves when handling this plant.

The popular ladyfinger cactus produces clusters of prickly finger-like stems adorned with a network of creamy-yellow to brown curved spines. The upright or slightly trailing stems make this little cactus a good candidate for a hanging basket. Small pale yellow or pink-tinged blooms appear in spring.

HEIGHT & SPREAD Clusters grow up to 15 x 20cm (6 x 8in).

CARE NOTES See opposite.

WARNING! Wear cactus gloves when handling this plant.

MAMMILLARIA HAHNIANA AGM

syn. *Neomammillaria hahniana*
Old lady of Mexico

The long, soft, silvery spines that cloak the old lady of Mexico look like wispy hair. Globe-shaped or short and cylindrical, this cactus flowers prolifically, even when young, producing an abundance of rose-red blooms in spring, followed by inedible red fruits. Easy to grow, this is an ideal choice for beginners.

HEIGHT & SPREAD Clusters grow up to 10 x 20cm (4 x 8in).

CARE NOTES See opposite.

WARNING! Wear cactus gloves when handling this plant.

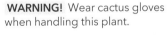

MAMMILLARIA LONGIFLORA

syn. *Neomammillaria longiflora;*
Phellosperma longiflora
Pincushion cactus

Squat, round, and dimpled when young, the stems of this cactus become slightly taller and more domed-shaped with age. Short white spines, with a longer reddish-brown hooked spine in the centre of each cluster, give it a colourful spidery look. The pink funnel- or bell-shaped flowers are often as big as the stem.

HEIGHT & SPREAD Up to 6 x 9cm (2½ x 3½in).

CARE NOTES See p218.

WARNING! Wear cactus gloves when handling this plant.

MAMMILLARIA MAGNIMAMMA AGM

syn. *Mammillaria centricirrha*
var. *magnimamma;*
Neomammillaria magnimamma
Mexican pincushion

The curved spines of the Mexican pincushion can vary from plant to plant, with some as long as 5cm (2in), while others are much shorter. The spines cover globe-shaped, grey–green stems, which soon multiply to form mounded clusters. White or cream flowers, which have delicate red or purplish-pink veining, develop in rings at the top of the stems in spring.

HEIGHT & SPREAD Clusters grow up to 30 x 45cm (12 x 18in).

CARE NOTES See p218.

WARNING! Wear cactus gloves when handling this plant.

MAMMILLARIA PLUMOSA AGM

syn. *Escobariopsis plumosa;*
Neomammillaria plumosa
Feather cactus

At first glance, the feather cactus does not really look like a plant at all, as it is covered with dense clusters of fine, downy-looking spines that completely disguise the small round stems. In fact, this feathery cloak evolved to protect the plant from the blistering sun of its native Mexico. Small creamy-white or pale pink flowers, which are sweetly scented, appear at the top of the stems in late summer.

HEIGHT & SPREAD Clusters grow up to 10 x 40cm (4 x 16in).

CARE NOTES See p218.

WARNING! Wear cactus gloves when handling this plant.

MAMMILLARIA SPINOSISSIMA AGM

syn. *Mammillaria spinosissima* f. *rubrispina*;
Neomammillaria spinosissima
Spiny pincushion cactus

Rusty red bristly spines are produced at the top of the spiny pincushion cactus, while shorter and finer white spines cover the rest of the plant. The stems are round or form short columns, and they quickly multiply to create decorative clusters. Haloes of small purplish or pink flowers appear at the top of the stems in spring.

HEIGHT & SPREAD Clusters grow up to 10 x 30cm (4 x 12in).

CARE NOTES See p218.

WARNING! Wear gloves when handling this plant.

MAMMILLARIA ZEILMANNIANA AGM

syn. *Mammillaria crinita* f. *zeilmanniana*;
Neomammillaria zeilmanniana
Rose pincushion

The rose pincushion cactus quickly forms eye-catching clusters of prickly pink-hued globes. The effect is produced by long reddish spines, surrounded by fine white spines, which cover the round to short cylindrical green stems. Each stem is topped with a ring of rosy-purple flowers in summer, although the blooms can appear at other times of the year too.

HEIGHT & SPREAD Up to 12 x 20cm (5 x 8in).

CARE NOTES See p218.

WARNING! Wear cactus gloves when handling this plant.

MATUCANA

A good choice for beginners, *Matucana* are globe-shaped or short cylindrical plants with bright green or blue–green stems. Some species are spineless when mature; others produce clusters of long, sharp spines, that can be yellow, white, black, or brown. Plants flower at an early age, the funnel-shaped blooms (some larger than the stems) appearing at the top of the plant in late spring or summer. The flowers come in a range of colours, but are most commonly red, yellow, or pink.

TEMPERATURE 10–30°C (50–86°F).

LIGHT Position in full sun; provide a light shade in midsummer.

WATERING During the spring and summer, water when the top 2cm (¾in) of compost is dry. In autumn, reduce watering to once a month. Keep plants dry in winter.

FEEDING Apply a half-strength cactus fertilizer once in spring.

COMPOST Plant in cactus compost, or a 50:50 mix of loam-based (John Innes No. 2 Peat-Free) compost and 4mm grit. Plant in a relatively deep pot to accommodate the roots.

FLOWERING Stand plants in full sun and provide good air circulation to encourage them to bloom.

PROPAGATION Sow seed or take offsets.

COMMON PROBLEMS These plants will rot in wet compost. Check plants regularly for mealybugs and spider mites.

MATUCANA AURANTIACA AGM

syn. *Arequipa aurantiaca;*
Borzicactus aurantiacus;
Echinocactus aurantiacus;
Submatucana aurantiaca
Orange matucana

The orange matucana forms a cluster of small, globe-shaped, light green stems with long, reddish-brown spines radiating out from woolly areas along the ribs. The large orange-red flowers can reach up to 10cm (4in) in length, dwarfing the little stems and producing a dazzling display when they appear in summer.

HEIGHT & SPREAD Each stem grows up to 15 x 15cm (6 x 6in).

CARE NOTES See left.

WARNING! Wear cactus gloves when handling this plant.

MATUCANA AUREIFLORA

syn. *Borzicactus aureiflorus;*
Submatucana aureiflora

The unusual spines and bright flowers make this prickly flat-topped globe popular with cactus enthusiasts. Clusters of long, curved spines decorate the ribs and are amber coloured at the base and almost translucent at the tips. Several flushes of large, golden–yellow flowers appear in spring and summer, and unusually for cacti, they remain open day and night.

HEIGHT & SPREAD Each stem grows up to 10 x 12cm (4 x 5in).

CARE NOTES See left.

WARNING! Wear cactus gloves when handling this plant.

MATUCANA INTERTEXTA AGM

syn. *Borzicactus intertextus;*
Submatucana intertexta

Resembling a round green coral covered with baby sea urchins, this pretty little cactus is shaped like a spiky ball. Clusters of curved, brown-tipped, white spines create the sea-urchin effect, while tubular orange flowers appear in late spring or early summer.

HEIGHT & SPREAD Each stem grows up to 20 x 18cm (8 x 7in).

CARE NOTES See opposite.

WARNING! Wear cactus gloves when handling this plant.

MATUCANA KRAHNII

syn. *Borzicactus krahnii*

The grey–green, globe-shaped stems of this diminutive cactus soon form small clusters, but the plant will remain compact and suitable for a narrow windowsill even when mature. The knobbly ribs feature black- and brown-tipped spines, and bouquets of small, bright red flowers appear in flushes over a few weeks in spring and summer.

HEIGHT & SPREAD Each stem grows up to 8 x 8cm (3 x 3in).

CARE NOTES See opposite.

WARNING! Wear cactus gloves when handling this plant.

MATUCANA POLZII

syn. *Matucana aurantiaca* subsp. *polziiare*

Quick to form offsets, the baby plants of this small cactus nestle around the mother stem, giving it a quirky look. The dark red to orange funnel-shaped blooms it produces are quite showy, but only appear on mature stems.

HEIGHT & SPREAD Clusters grow up to 5 x 15 cm (2 x 6in).

CARE NOTES See opposite.

224

MELOCACTUS

Despite its resemblance to desert cacti, *Melocactus* are tropical plants, hailing from the Caribbean and Central and South America. Not the easiest to grow, those willing to nurture them will be rewarded with beautiful spiny stems topped with unusual red or white bristly areas (known as "cephalium") that are said to resemble little fez hats. When the cephalium appears, the stem stops growing but the caps continue to develop. Small flowers grow from the cephalium, followed by large edible red or pink tubular fruits that look like candles.

TEMPERATURE 12–30°C (54–86°F).

LIGHT Position in full sun, with some shade in summer.

WATERING Keep the compost moist from late spring to late summer, reapplying water when the top of the compost feels dry. Keep plants slightly moist in autumn and winter; do not allow the compost to dry out completely.

FEEDING Apply a half-strength balanced liquid fertilizer every 2 weeks from spring to autumn.

COMPOST Plant in cactus compost with added horticultural grit.

FLOWERING Flowers appear on mature plants grown in good light in a well-ventilated area in moist, but not wet compost.

PROPAGATION Sow seed.

COMMON PROBLEMS These plants will rot in wet compost. Pests to look out for include mealybugs and spider mites.

MELOCACTUS MATANZANUS
Turk's cap cactus

One of the smallest and most popular *Melocactus,* the Turk's cap cactus flowers when quite young form red cephalium (see left) at the top of the plant. Starry clusters of brown or white spines form in vertical lines on ribbed globe-shaped stems. A ring of small rose-pink flowers, followed by lilac-pink fruits emerge on 4- to 5-year-old plants. Buy one in flower if you want to be sure of blooms.

HEIGHT & SPREAD Each stem grows up to 18 x 9cm (7 x 3½in).

CARE NOTES See left.

WARNING! Wear cactus gloves when handling this plant.

OPUNTIA

One of the most recognizable of all cactus groups, *Opuntia* range from compact, low-growing, spreading plants to tree-sized species that reach 5m (16ft) or more in the wild. The stems are made up of distinctive flat, paddle-shaped segments, known as "cladodes", which are protected by clusters of fine, hair-like prickles (glochids) that irritate the skin when touched. Some species also produce longer spines. Known as prickly pears due to their red edible fruits, these cacti also produce beautiful yellow, pink, or orange flowers in spring or summer.

TEMPERATURE 5–30°C (41–86°F); some species are frost-hardy down to -10°C (14°F) if the soil is dry.

LIGHT Position in full sun all year.

WATERING During the spring and summer, water when the top 2cm (¾in) of compost is dry. Reduce watering in autumn. Keep plants dry in winter.

FEEDING Apply a half-strength cactus fertilizer once a month from spring to autumn.

COMPOST Plant in cactus compost, or a 50:50 mix of loam-based (John Innes No. 2 Peat-Free) compost and 4mm grit.

FLOWERING Flowers can appear on mature plants, but need high light levels and lower winter temperatures to develop.

PROPAGATION Sow seed or take cuttings.

COMMON PROBLEMS These plants will rot in wet compost. Pests to look out for include mealybugs and spider mites.

OPUNTIA CANTABRIGIENSIS

syn. *Opuntia engelmannii* var. *cuija*
Engelman prickly pear

If you buy two Engelman prickly pear plants, you may find that they look slightly different, as there is some variation in this species, but all form spreading shrub-like plants comprised of oval or round stem segments. This is a large cactus and needs space to show off its elegant shape and long, sharp spines. Large yellow flowers appear in spring and are followed by reddish-purple, pear-shaped fruits.

HEIGHT & SPREAD Up to 0.9 x 1.2m (3 x 4ft).

CARE NOTES See opposite; keep at or just above 10–18°C (50–65°F) in winter.

WARNING! Wear cactus gloves when handling this plant.

OPUNTIA MICRODASYS AGM

Bunny ears cactus;
Polka dot cactus

Its relatively small size and cartoon-like silhouette makes the bunny ears cactus a favourite among collectors and beginners alike. Evenly spaced spots of glochids form a polka-dot pattern – hence its other common name – while the oval stem segments always appear in pairs like rabbit's ears. Do not be tempted to touch the plant. It may look soft and cute but, as with all *Opuntia*, the prickles irritate the skin. Yellow flowers form along the edges of the pads in summer and are followed by purple to red fruits.

HEIGHT & SPREAD Up to 45 x 60cm (18 x 24in).

CARE NOTES See opposite.

WARNING! Wear cactus gloves when handling this plant.

OPUNTIA MICRODASYS 'ALBATA' AGM

syn. *Opuntia microdasys* var. *albispina*
White bunny ear's cactus

A beautiful cultivar of the species *Opuntia microdasys* (see left), 'Albata' has white polka-dot glochids, which look like snow sprinkled over the stems. Lemon-yellow flowers appear in summer, followed by red fruits. They may appear beautiful and inviting but do not touch them, as the glochids are painful and difficult to remove from the skin.

HEIGHT & SPREAD Up to 45 x 60cm (18 x 24in).

CARE NOTES See opposite.

WARNING! Wear cactus gloves when handling this plant.

OPUNTIA MONACANTHA
syn. *Cactus monacanthos*
Drooping prickly pear

In the wild, the drooping prickly pear is a tree-like cactus. Growing it in a pot will restrict its size, but make sure you can display it where the large spiky branched stems will not cause injury. The plant forms a short trunk and slim, oval- to oblong-shaped green stem segments, covered with long, sharp brown spines that detach easily when touched. The yellow or orange flowers appear in late spring and are followed by pear-shaped, reddish-purple fruits.

HEIGHT & SPREAD Up to 90 x 80cm (3 x 2½ft).

CARE NOTES See p224.

WARNING! Wear cactus gloves when handling this plant.

OREOCEREUS

The name *Oreocereus* means "mountain cereus", and refers to its natural home high up in Andes Mountains in South America. To protect it from this harsh environment, the short columnar stems are covered with a white woolly coat that looks like fine hair, with long, sharp spines hidden among the soft wrapping. In spring, this cactus produces dazzling red or orange flowers.

TEMPERATURE 5–30°C (41–86°F); plants will tolerate -10°C (14°F) if the soil is dry.

LIGHT Position in full sun, but provide some shade in summer.

WATERING During the spring and summer, water when the top 2cm (¾in) of compost is dry. In autumn, reduce watering. Keep plants dry in winter.

FEEDING Apply a half-strength cactus fertilizer once a month from spring to late summer.

COMPOST Plant in cactus compost, or a 50:50 mix of loam-based (John Innes No. 2 Peat-Free) compost and 4mm grit.

FLOWERING Flowers only appear on mature plants; buy one in flower to guarantee blooms.

PROPAGATION Sow seed.

COMMON PROBLEMS These plants will rot in wet compost. Check them regularly, particularly for mealybugs and spider mites.

OREOCEREUS CELSIANUS

syn. *Borzicactus celsianus;*
Cereus celsianus;
Cleistocactus celsianus;
Pilocereus celsianus
Old man of the Andes

The ribbed columnar stems of the old man of the Andes are covered with silky white hairs that are more profuse towards the top of the plant. Yellowish-brown spines protrude from the fuzzy coat like sharp needles. In spring, funnel-shaped blooms, which are pale purplish-pink to dark red, appear along the stem.

HEIGHT & SPREAD Up to 60 x 8cm (24 x 3in).

CARE NOTES See opposite.

WARNING! Wear cactus gloves when handling this plant.

OROYA

Hailing from the Andes, these cacti are named after the Peruvian town of la Oroya where they were first discovered. The beautiful spiky globes or short, fat columns, which can grow up to 30cm (12in) in diameter, make dramatic displays on a wide windowsill or under a skylight. The ribs are covered with long curved spines, while a ring of small yellow or pink flowers, held on long pink or red stems, appears at the top of the plant in spring or summer.

TEMPERATURE 5–30°C (41–86°F); some species will tolerate -7°C (19°F) if the soil is dry.

LIGHT Position in full sun for most of the year, but provide some shade in summer.

WATERING During the spring and summer, water when the top 2cm (¾in) of compost is dry. In autumn, reduce watering to once a month. Keep plants dry in winter.

FEEDING Apply a half-strength cactus fertilizer once a month from spring to early autumn.

COMPOST Plant in cactus compost, or a 50:50 mix of loam-based (John Innes No. 2 Peat-Free) compost and 4mm grit.

FLOWERING Give plants sufficient light and a little fertilizer.

PROPAGATION Sow seed.

COMMON PROBLEMS These plants will rot in wet compost. Pests to look out for include mealybugs and spider mites.

OROYA PERUVIANA

syn. *Echinocactus peruvianus*

One of the most popular *Oroya* and among the easiest to grow, this spiny cactus looks a little like a bird's nest. The bright green or blue-green stems, which are globe-shaped when young but eventually grow to form short columns, are covered with a tangle of long, curved, straw-coloured and reddish-brown spines. Clusters of pink or orange-red flowers are produced, even on young plants, from spring to summer.

HEIGHT & SPREAD Up to 25 x 15cm (10 x 6in).

CARE NOTES See left.

WARNING! Wear cactus gloves when handling this plant.

PARODIA

Easy to grow and generally quite small in size, *Parodia* are perfect plants for beginners. This group includes about 50 species, ranging in shape from little globes to tall cylindrical columns. The ribbed and spiny stems are topped with single flowers in spring, which may be yellow, orange, or red, although some hybrids offer other colours. The stems of some species multiply to form clusters, while others are solitary.

TEMPERATURE 10–30°C (50–86°F).

LIGHT Position in full sun; provide light shade in midsummer.

WATERING From mid-spring to late summer, water when the top 1cm (½in) of compost is dry. Reduce watering at other times, and keep plants almost dry in winter, misting them occasionally on warm days in late winter.

FEEDING Apply a half-strength cactus fertilizer once a month from mid-spring to late summer.

COMPOST Plant in cactus compost, or a 50:50 mix of loam-based (John Innes No. 2 Peat-Free) compost and 4mm grit.

FLOWERING Flowers appear on mature plants when light levels are high enough.

PROPAGATION Sow seed or take offsets or cuttings.

COMMON PROBLEMS These plants will rot in wet compost. Check regularly for mealybugs and spider mites.

PARODIA CHRYSACANTHION AGM

syn. *Echinocactus chrysacanthion*

Golden powder puff

You can see at first glance how this little cactus gets its common name. Covered in long, fine, hair-like spines, the small round stems look exactly like golden powder puffs, although the plant is more prickly than it looks, so take care and wear gloves when handling it. In spring, a cluster of golden flowers emerges from the woolly area at the top of the plant.

HEIGHT & SPREAD Each stem grows up to 12 x 10cm (5 x 4in).

CARE NOTES See left.

WARNING! Wear cactus gloves when handling this plant.

PARODIA LENINGHAUSII AGM

syn. *Echinocactus leninghausii; Eriocactus leninghausii; Notocactus leninghausii*

Yellow tower cactus

The tall, candle-like stems of the yellow tower cactus are covered with soft, harmless golden spines, making it ideal for homes with children or pets. The ribbed, furry-looking stems branch and multiply from the base to form small clusters. Groups of sunny yellow flowers develop at the top of mature plants, usually when the stems reach 20cm (8in) or more in height, creating a bouquet of bright colourful blooms.

HEIGHT & SPREAD Each stem grows up to 60 x 12cm (24 x 5in).

CARE NOTES See left.

WARNING! Wear cactus gloves when handling this plant.

PARODIA SCOPA
subsp. SCOPA AGM

syn. *Cereus scopa;*
Echinocactus scopa;
Echinopsis scopa;
Notocactus scopa;
Parodia scopa
Silver ball

The striking globes of young silver balls are covered with white woolly areas and dense, fine white or pale brown spines that shimmer in the sunlight. The spiny ribs form beautiful striped or spiralling patterns on the stems, which become more column-shaped as they age. Bright yellow flowers are produced in a ring from a woolly area on the top of the plant, producing an eye-catching combination of stem and blooms.

HEIGHT & SPREAD Each stem grows up to 50 x 15cm (20 x 6in).

CARE NOTES See opposite.

WARNING! Wear cactus gloves when handling this plant.

PARODIA
MAGNIFICA AGM

syn. *Eriocactus magnificus;*
Notocactus magnificus
Green ball cactus;
Balloon cactus

The dramatic stems of the green ball cactus feature deep ribs edged with rows of fine yellow spines that form a graphic pattern of vertical stripes around the plant. Initially globe-shaped, the stems of older plants form short columns, and they soon multiply to create small clusters. Vibrant yellow flowers appear at the top of each stem, and mature plants may produce a few flushes throughout summer.

HEIGHT & SPREAD Each stem grows up to 30 x 15cm (12 x 6in).

CARE NOTES See opposite.

WARNING! Wear cactus gloves when handling this plant.

PARODIA
SUBTERRANEA

syn. *Notocactus occultus;*
Parodia maassii var. *subterranean*
Underground parodia

Seek out the underground parodia for its unusual flat-topped, globe- or column-shaped stems, which in the wild grow mostly beneath the soil surface to protect them from harsh sun and wind. The ribs often spiral around the plant and feature short, claw-like brown spines surrounded by finer white bristles. Flowers appear in summer from a woolly area at the top of the stem and are usually red, although on some plants they may be bright orange or purple.

HEIGHT & SPREAD Each stem grows up to 45 x 10cm (18 x 4in).

CARE NOTES See opposite.

WARNING! Wear cactus gloves when handling this plant.

PILOSOCEREUS

Often sporting decorative blue spiny branched stems, *Pilosocereus* are shrubby or tree-like cacti that can grow up to 10m (33ft) in their native Brazil. They produce long spines along their ribbed stems, and tubular flowers in summer. Although this group of cacti includes a few species, only *Pilosocereus pachycladus* (see right) is commonly available as a house plant.

TEMPERATURE 12–30°C (54–86°F).

LIGHT Position in full sun.

WATERING During the spring and summer, water when the top 2cm (¾in) of compost is dry. In autumn, reduce watering to once a month. Keep plants dry in winter.

FEEDING Apply a half-strength cactus fertilizer once a month from spring to late summer.

COMPOST Plant in cactus compost, or a 50:50 mix of loam-based (John Innes No. 2 Peat-Free) compost and 4mm grit.

FLOWERING Flowers appear only on mature plants that are 1m (3ft) or more in height.

PROPAGATION Sow seed or take offsets.

COMMON PROBLEMS These plants will rot in wet compost. Pests to look out for include mealybugs and spider mites.

PILOSOCEREUS PACHYCLADUS

syn. *Pilosocerus azureus;*
Pseudopilocereus pachycladus;
Pseudopilocereus pernambucoensis
Blue torch cactus

If you are looking for a desert cactus that conjures up images of old cowboy films, the blue torch cactus is the one for you. The cylindrical stems are a vivid sky blue and topped with soft tufts of orange-white hair. Short yellow spines fringe the edges of the ribs and the plant will eventually become tall and branched, creating a classic cactus silhouette. Even without the large, night-opening white or red flowers, which appear from the hairy tops on mature plants in summer, this stunning cactus is a real show-stopper. It is a large species, so ensure you have space to accommodate it before buying.

HEIGHT & SPREAD Each stem grows up to 1m x 15cm (3ft x 6in).

CARE NOTES See left.

WARNING! Wear cactus gloves when handling this plant.

PYGMAEOCEREUS

These tiny cacti produce clumps of short cylindrical stems. The ribs in some species may spiral around the stem, and they are covered with soft spines. Cactus-lovers grow *Pygmeaocereus* for their night-opening, scented, usually white flowers, which look like fireworks shooting out from the sides of the stems on long tubes.

TEMPERATURE 5–30°C (41–86°F).

LIGHT Position in full sun and light shade in midsummer.

WATERING During the spring and summer, water when the top 2cm (¾in) of compost is dry. In autumn, reduce watering, and keep plants dry in winter when dormant. Provide good ventilation in summer.

FEEDING Apply a half-strength cactus fertilizer once in late spring.

COMPOST Plant in cactus compost, or a 50:50 mix of loam-based (John Innes No. 2 Peat-Free) compost and 4mm grit.

FLOWERING Flowers will develop if light levels are high enough.

PROPAGATION Sow seed or take offsets.

COMMON PROBLEMS These plants will rot in wet compost. Pests to look out for include mealybugs, spider mites, scale, thrips, and aphids.

PYGMAEOCEREUS BYLESIANUS
syn. *Arthrocereus bylesianus*

The dark green stems of this little column-shaped cactus have wavy ribs and rust-coloured or grey spines. The plant's main attraction is the series of white summer flowers, each of which opens for just one night and emits an unusual scent. This cactus is more suitable for experienced growers than beginners because it requires strong sunlight and good ventilation, and mature plants are very prone to rotting if overwatered.

HEIGHT & SPREAD Each stem grows up to 8 x 2cm (3 x 1in).

CARE NOTES See opposite.

REBUTIA

With their colourful flowers and little globe-shaped, dimpled stems, these easy-to-grow cacti are perfect for beginners. Clusters of short spines, which sprout from woolly areas on the stems, give plants a spotty appearance. The flowers come in a range of colours, including white, pink, red, and yellow, and appear around the base of the stems in spring or summer, even on relatively young plants. *Rebutia* also produce large numbers of seeds that germinate freely around the parent plant.

TEMPERATURE 5-30°C (41-86°F); keep cool in winter at about 5-10°C (41-50°F).

LIGHT Position in full sun for most of the year, but provide light shade in summer.

WATERING During the spring and summer, water when the top 1cm (½in) of compost is dry. In autumn, reduce watering. Keep plants dry in winter.

FEEDING Apply a half-strength cactus fertilizer once a month from spring to late summer.

COMPOST Plant in cactus compost, or a 50:50 mix of loam-based (John Innes No. 2 Peat-Free) compost and 4mm grit.

FLOWERING Flowers appear freely, but are more likely to develop when plants are kept cool in winter.

PROPAGATION Sow seed or take offsets.

COMMON PROBLEMS These plants will rot in wet compost. Pests to look out for include mealybugs and spider mites.

REBUTIA ARENACEA AGM
syn. *Sulcorebutia arenacea*
Arenaceous crown cactus

A beautiful little species, the arenaceous crown cactus forms green, globe-shaped, flat-topped stems decorated with a symmetrical swirling pattern of pale yellow and orange spines. As plants mature, they develop into attractive clumps, and in spring, clusters of yellowish-orange flowers appear around the base of the stems.

HEIGHT & SPREAD Each stem grows up to 4 x 6cm (1½ x 2½in).

CARE NOTES See left.

WARNING! Wear cactus gloves when handling this plant.

REBUTIA 'CARNIVAL'

syn. *Aylostera* 'Carnival';
Sulcorebutia 'Carnival'
Carnival crown cactus

Popular for their brightly coloured flowers, the carnival crown cactus is a group of hybrids that produce red, pink, white, and orange flowers – some may be bicoloured. The small globe-shaped stems become more cylindrical with age, and feature a dense covering of short white or sandy-coloured spines. The blooms appear in spring.

HEIGHT & SPREAD Each stem grows up to 4 x 6cm (1½ x 2½in).

CARE NOTES See p231.

WARNING! Wear cactus gloves when handling this plant.

REBUTIA FLAVISTYLA

syn. *Aylostera flavistyla*
Flame crown cactus

For a week in spring, an explosion of bright orange, daisy-like flowers almost cover the tiny body of the flame crown cactus. Deservedly popular, the dimpled, globe-shaped stems feature short, glassy-white spines that are soft to the touch and look like hair.

HEIGHT & SPREAD Up to 5 x 5cm (2 x 2in).

CARE NOTES See p231.

WARNING! Wear cactus gloves when handling this plant.

REBUTIA HELIOSA

syn. *Aylostera heliosa*
Heliosa crown cactus

The large daisy-like orange flowers of the heliosa crown cactus make a dramatic focal point when they appear in spring, smothering the tiny spherical or short cylindrical stems so that the plant looks like a tiny florist's bouquet. This cactus is covered with short brown and white fine, hair-like spines and the stems quickly make small clumps.

HEIGHT & SPREAD Clumps grow up to 4 x 10cm (1½ x 4in).

CARE NOTES See p231.

REBUTIA HELIOSA
x ALBIFLORA
syn. *Aylostera heliosa*
White heliosa crown cactus

A good choice for those who find the orange flowers of the heliosa crown cactus a little too bright and brash, this plant has similar stems, but more subtle cream-coloured flowers with pale pink streaks. You may find this plant labelled *Rebutia heliosa* 'Sunrise'.

HEIGHT & SPREAD Clumps grow up to 4 x 10cm (1½ x 4in).

CARE NOTES See p231.

WARNING! Wear cactus gloves when handling this plant.

REBUTIA
MINISCULA
'KRAINZIANA' AGM
syn. *Rebutia krainziana*
Krainziana crown cactus

Loved for its dark green dimpled stems and a neat spotty pattern of white spines that are soft to the touch, the Krainziana crown cactus also produces a striking display of daisy-like flowers in early spring. Because it has some natural variation, you may see this little cactus with bright red, orange, yellow, or white blooms.

HEIGHT & SPREAD Each stem grows up to 7 x 10cm (2¾ x 4in).

CARE NOTES See p231.

WARNING! Wear cactus gloves when handling this plant.

REBUTIA
SENILIS AGM
syn. *Rebutia senilis* var. *senilis*
Fire crown cactus

Clusters of tiny flat-topped, globe-shaped stems covered with long, glassy-white bristly spines form a backdrop to the fire crown cactus' large flowers, which are its star attraction when they appear in spring. The blooms are usually orange or crimson, but can be white, red, or yellow.

HEIGHT & SPREAD Each stem grows up to 7 x 7cm (2¾ x 2¾in).

CARE NOTES See p231.

WARNING! Wear cactus gloves when handling this plant.

REBUTIA
VIOLACIFLORA
syn. *Rebutia minuscula* subsp. *violaciflora;*
Rebutia minuscula f. *violaciflora*
Violet crown cactus

Bristly yellow or tan spines, which are longer than those found growing on many *Rebutia* species, create a pattern of starry clusters over the violet crown cactus' tiny globe-shaped stems. The plant gets its name from the colour of the funnel-shaped spring flowers, which are a delicate pale violet.

HEIGHT & SPREAD Up to 2 x 4cm (¾ x 1½in).

CARE NOTES See p231.

RHIPSALIS

Not immediately recognizable as cacti, *Rhipsalis* are from the tropical rainforests of South America, the Caribbean, and Central America. They are epiphytic, which means they grow on trees, and most species have long, trailing, or sprawling spineless stems that are best displayed in a large hanging basket. They also prefer shade, unlike their desert-dwelling cousins. Some plants have cylindrical stems that hang down like green hair, while others are flattened ribbons, and a few feature bristles or spines. The small flowers are usually white, although some have yellow or red blooms. These develop along the length of the stems in winter or early spring, and are followed by inedible white berries.

TEMPERATURE 10–30°C (50–86°F).

LIGHT Position in light shade out of direct sun.

WATERING During the spring and summer, water well when the top of compost is just dry. In autumn and winter, reduce watering but do not let plants dry out completely. Mist stems regularly to raise humidity levels.

FEEDING Apply a balanced fertilizer once a month from spring to early autumn.

COMPOST Plant in orchid compost.

FLOWERING These plants bloom profusely if grown in an even, high temperature and shade. They will drop their buds if plants are moved.

PROPAGATION Take stem cuttings.

COMMON PROBLEMS Plants are generally problem-free.

RHIPSALIS BACCIFERA
syn. *Cassytha baccifera;*
Rhipsalis baccifera subsp. *baccifera;*
Rhipsalis cassytha
Mistletoe cactus; Spaghetti cactus

Named after its inedible white spring berries, which look like mistletoe, this cactus' other common name describes its green spaghetti-like branched stems. These flowing stems will trail elegantly from a hanging basket and can reach over 1m (3ft) in length, so hang the plant up high enough to allow them space to develop. Creamy-white flowers form at the stem tips and precede the berries.

HEIGHT & SPREAD Up to 1.5 x 0.6m (5 x 2ft).

CARE NOTES See opposite.

RHIPSALIS CEREUSCULA
syn. *Erythrorhipsalis cereuscula;*
Hariota cereuscula
Coral cactus;
Rice cactus

This unusual cactus looks like a mound of green coral, hence its common name. Perfect for a tall pot or hanging basket, the cyclindrical stems are armed with soft, bristly spines, and branch out at the tips. In late winter or spring, tiny creamy-white blooms that look like snowflakes develop at the stem tips.

HEIGHT & SPREAD Up to 60 x 60cm (24 x 24in).

CARE NOTES See opposite.

RHIPSALIS MONACANTHA AGM

syn. *Acanthorhipsalis monacantha;*
Hariota monacantha;
Pfeiffera monacantha
One-spined wickerware cactus

Unlike most *Rhipsalis,* the one-spined wickerware cactus features sharp black spines and white bristles along the edges of its ribbon-like, serrated stems. In late winter or spring, small orange bell-shaped flowers develop next to the black spines, often blooming for a few months. Stems may turn red if the plant becomes stressed due to poor care.

HEIGHT & SPREAD Up to 20 x 45cm (8 x 18in).

CARE NOTES See p234.

WARNING! Wear cactus gloves when handling this plant.

RHIPSALIS MICRANTHA

An elegant *Rhipsalis*, ideal for a large basket, this tropical cactus produces flowing green ribbon-like stems with wavy margins. Grow it where you can appreciate the small white flowers that appear along the stem margins in late winter, and the inedible white berries that follow in spring and summer.

HEIGHT & SPREAD Up to 0.6 x 1m (2 x 3ft).

CARE NOTES See p234.

RHIPSALIS PACHYPTERA
syn. *Hariota pachyptera*

The trailing, flattened stems of this beautiful plant are divided into large leaf-shaped, spineless segments. The segments' lobed edges add a decorative touch to the stems, and they are sometimes also tinged with red. Creamy-yellow or whitish scented flowers form along the edges of the stems, opening from pink buds, which are also attractive. The blooms are followed by inedible round white berries.

HEIGHT & SPREAD Up to 1.5 x 0.6m (5 x 2ft).

CARE NOTES See p234.

RHIPSALIS PILOCARPA
syn. *Erythrorhipsalis pilocarpa*
Hairy-fruited wickerware cactus

With its unusual spaghetti-like stems, which are covered with soft hairs and tipped with fine bristles, this cactus makes for a great talking point. White scented flowers appear in winter or early spring, followed by inedible red berries.

HEIGHT & SPREAD Up to 0.6 x 1m (2 x 3ft).

CARE NOTES See p234.

SCHLUMBERGERA

This small group of tropical cacti comprises about nine species, but only two – *Schlumbergera* x *buckleyi* and *Schlumbergera truncata* – are widely available and both are known commonly as Christmas cacti. These plants are epiphytes, and cling to trees in the rainforests of their native Brazil. They produce fountains of trailing stems, which are divided into leaf-like segments, and are grown primarily for their brightly coloured winter flowers.

TEMPERATURE 12-24°C (55-75°F); reduce the temperature to 12-15°C (55-59°F) after flowering and again in autumn.

LIGHT Position in light shade out of direct sun.

WATERING In summer and late winter, water well when the surface of the compost is just dry. After flowering, keep the compost almost dry, then resume watering more frequently in summer. Reduce watering again just before the flower buds form in autumn, but water more frequently again as soon as you see them developing. Mist stems regularly to raise humidity levels.

FEEDING Apply a balanced liquid fertilizer once a month from spring to early autumn.

COMPOST Plant in orchid compost.

FLOWERING These plants bloom easily but are likely to drop their buds if they are moved at this stage.

PROPAGATION Sow seed or take stem cuttings.

COMMON PROBLEMS Plants are generally problem-free, but check them regularly for mealybugs.

SCHLUMBERGERA TRUNCATA

syn. *Schlumbergera* x *bridgesii*;
Epiphyllum truncatum var. *bridgesii*
Christmas cactus

Prized for its beautiful pink pendent winter flowers, the blooms of the Christmas cactus look like those of a fuchsia and open during the festive season, hence its common name. The flowers appear at the tips of the glossy green stems, which are divided into tooth-edged segments and create a mound of trailing lush green growth throughout the year. You may find hybrids of this species with purple, orange, white, or multicoloured flowers.

HEIGHT & SPREAD Up to 45 x 45cm (18 x 18in).

CARE NOTES See opposite.

STENOCACTUS

These small, globe-shaped, easy-to-grow cacti are perfect for beginners. They flower profusely and make a pretty display on a narrow windowsill when their white blooms appear in early spring. Another attractive feature of some species is their unusual pleated ribs, which makes them look like little round corals. The sparse spines are often long and produced in starry clusters.

TEMPERATURE 5–30°C (41–86°F)

LIGHT Position in full sun for most of the year, but provide some shade in summer.

WATERING During the spring and summer, water when the top 1cm (½in) of compost is dry. In autumn, reduce watering to once a month. Keep plants dry in winter.

FEEDING Apply a half-strength cactus fertilizer once a month from late spring to late summer.

COMPOST Plant in cactus compost, or a 50:50 mix of loam-based (John Innes No. 2 Peat Free) compost and 4mm grit.

FLOWERING Flowers appear freely on mature plants, given sufficient light and a little fertilizer.

PROPAGATION Sow seed or take offsets.

COMMON PROBLEMS These plants will rot in wet compost. Pests to look out for include mealybugs and spider mites.

STENOCACTUS MULTICOSTATUS

syn. *Echinocactus multicostatus; Echinofossulocactus multicostatus*
Wave cactus; Brain cactus

It may be tiny, but the wave cactus has many beautiful features that make up for its diminutive size. Long, curved, cream-coloured spines and short white spines form clusters on spiralling pleated ribs, and in some plants, the flattened globes are also topped by red spines. The flowers appear in spring from the crown of the plant and can be white, pinkish-purple, or violet, with a darker violet to purple stripe.

HEIGHT & SPREAD Each stem grows up to 12 x 15cm (5 x 6in).

CARE NOTES See left.

WARNING! Wear cactus gloves when handling this plant.

STENOCEREUS

Column-shaped or tree-like, these sharp-spined cacti can grow into towering plants, though they will remain slightly smaller when restricted to a pot indoors. Make sure you have a large area to show them off, not least because the sharp spines on the stems need a space where they will not cause injury. The flowers develop near the top of the plant and are mostly nocturnal. *Stenocereus* are easy to grow and also produce edible fruits.

TEMPERATURE 5–30°C (41–86°F); keep cool at 8–12°C (46–54°F) in winter.

LIGHT Position in full sun, but provide some shade in summer.

WATERING During the spring and summer, water when the top 2cm (¾in) of compost is dry. In autumn, reduce watering to once a month. Keep plants dry in winter.

FEEDING Apply a half-strength cactus fertilizer from spring to late summer.

COMPOST Plant in cactus compost, or a 50:50 mix of loam-based (John Innes No. 2 Peat Free) compost and 4mm grit.

FLOWERING Keep plants cool in winter to encourage blooms to form.

PROPAGATION Sow seed or take cuttings.

COMMON PROBLEMS These plants will rot in wet compost. Check plants regularly for mealybugs, scale insects, and spider mites.

STENOCEREUS THURBERI

syn. *Cereus thurberi;*
Pilocereus thurberi
Organ pipe cactus

As the name suggests, the stems of the organ pipe cactus form tall, slim, spiny columns, and mature plants also branch out from the base. The white to pale lilac flowers, which appear in flushes from spring to late summer, open for one night and the following day before withering. The spiny, sweet, edible fruits, known as "pitahaya", are more prized than the blooms in their native Mexico.

HEIGHT & SPREAD Up to 1.5 x 0.15m (5ft x 6in).

CARE NOTES See left.

WARNING! Wear gloves when handling this plant.

SULCOREBUTIA

These small cacti produce globe-shape stems that slowly multiply to form clusters. A few species have dramatic purple or red stems, and while some *Sulcorebutia* are spiny, others have very short, almost imperceptible spines. The spring flowers come in a range of bright colours, including pink and yellow, and develop at the base of the stem.

TEMPERATURE 5-30°C (41-86°F); plants prefer a cool spot at 5-10°C (42-50°F) in winter, and may survive -5°C (23°F) for short spells in dry soil.

LIGHT Position in full sun for most of the year, but provide young plants with light shade. All *Sulcorebutia* need some shade in summer too.

WATERING During the spring and summer, water when the top 1cm (½in) of compost is dry. In autumn, reduce watering to once a month, and keep plants dry in winter.

FEEDING Apply a half-strength cactus fertilizer once a month from late spring to late summer.

COMPOST Plant in cactus compost, or a 50:50 mix of loam based (John Innes No. 2 Peat Free) compost and 4mm grit.

FLOWERING Keep plants cool in winter, and give sufficient light and a little fertilizer to encourage flowering.

PROPAGATION Sow seed or take offsets.

COMMON PROBLEMS These plants will rot in wet compost. Pests to look out for include mealybugs, scale insects, and spider mites.

SULCOREBUTIA LANGERI
syn. *Rebutia cardenasiana*

You may find this little cactus classified as a *Sulcorebutia langeri* or *Rebutia cardenasiana*, so check for both names when searching for it. It is prized for its clusters of tiny dark green globes covered with feathery white spines that create a lacy effect and are soft to the touch. Its sunny yellow daisy-like flowers are often larger than the stems, and appear in spring.

HEIGHT & SPREAD Up to 8 x 15cm (3 x 6in).

CARE NOTES See left.

SULCOREBUTIA RAUSCHII

syn. *Rebutia canigueralii* subsp. *rauschii;*
Rebutia rauschii f. *violacidermis;*
Sulcorebutia rauschii f. *violacidermis*

The beautiful purple and green dimpled stems of this clustering species make it stand out, despite its miniature size. The stems also feature short, black spines that are flattened against the surface in a fishbone pattern. As a bonus, eye-catching magenta-pink flowers appear in late spring, adding to this tiny plant's charms.

HEIGHT & SPREAD Up to 2 x 3cm (¾ x 1in).

CARE NOTES See p241.

THELOCACTUS

Small and spiny, these little globe-shaped cacti often grow to form short cylindrical stems. All species are easy to grow and ideal for beginners, but most are heavily armoured with sharp spines, so display them out of reach of children and pets. Some *Thelocactus* have defined ribs – a few form a spiral pattern – while the stems of others are more unusual, featuring raised areas (known as "tubercles") that divide the surface into hexagonal pillow-like segments. The flowers are funnel-shaped and come in yellow, red, or purple. The blooms develop at the top of the plant and can appear from late winter to late summer.

TEMPERATURE 5–30°C (41–86°F); can tolerate -5°C (23°F) if the soil is dry.

LIGHT Position in full sun, but provide a little shade in midsummer.

WATERING During the spring and summer, water when the top 2cm (¾in) of compost is dry. In autumn, reduce watering to once a month. Keep plants dry in winter. Provide good air circulation to reduce the risk of rot.

FEEDING Apply a half-strength cactus fertilizer once a month from late spring to late summer.

COMPOST Plant in cactus compost, or a 50:50 mix of loam-based (John Innes No. 2 Peat Free) compost and 4mm grit.

FLOWERING Flowers appear on mature plants grown in good light and given a little fertilizer.

PROPAGATION Sow seed.

COMMON PROBLEMS These plants are prone to rotting in wet compost. Check plants regularly for mealybugs, scale insects, and spider mites.

THELOCACTUS BICOLOR AGM

syn. *Echinocactus bicolor;*
Ferocactus bicolor
Glory of Texas

A forest of long, sharp, straw-coloured spines radiates out from the ribs of this popular species, making a striking contrast with the green stems beneath. Plants may be globe-shaped when young but will eventually form short columns. The magenta flowers with red throats open from spring to autumn.

HEIGHT & SPREAD UP Each stems grows up to 20 x 10cm (8 x 4in).

CARE NOTES See left.

WARNING! Wear gloves when handling this plant.

THELOCACTUS MACDOWELLII AGM

syn. *Echinocactus macdowellii;*
Thelocactus conothelos var. *macdowellii*

A prickly coat of long, glassy-white, sharp spines wrap around this small globe-shaped cactus, giving a clear signal that it should be handled with care. The winter flowers are pink with a yellow centre, and emerge from clusters of dark pink buds that push out from between the fierce spines in spring. Some plants may bloom again later in the year.

HEIGHT & SPREAD UP Each stem grows up to 10 x 10cm (4 x 4in).

CARE NOTES See opposite.

WARNING! Wear gloves when handling this plant.

THELOCACTUS HEXAEDROPHORUS AGM

syn. *Echinocactus hexaedrophorus;*
Thelomastus hexaedrophorus

It may be small, but this plant's striking good looks make it very collectable. The olive-green or greyish-green stems feature raised hexagonal segments, which can be tinged with pink or purple when the plant is grown in strong light. Star-shaped clusters of long, curved, reddish-brown spines shoot out from the centre of each segment, while the elegant silvery-white flowers have a pale pink central stripe and appear at the top of the plant.

HEIGHT & SPREAD Each stem grows up to 7 x 15cm (3½ x 6in).

CARE NOTES See opposite.

WARNING! Wear gloves when handling this plant.

SUCCULENTS

As a horticultural term, "succulent" describes a range of different plant types, including some that may surprise first-time collectors, such as *Hoya* (see p283) and *Sansevieria* (see p294). As house plants, succulents are grown primarily for their striking foliage, which comes in a range of shapes and colours. If well cared for, however, many succulents can also be encouraged to flower, providing an added burst of colour. While succulents are generally easy to care for, they can suffer if they do not receive plenty of light, or if they are overwatered.

ADROMISCHUS

With a wide range of unusual leaf shapes to choose from, these succulents make up for their small size with their beautiful colours and varied textures. Some have bright green flattened leaves, others are grey and look more like pebbles or shells, while a few resemble ravioli with crimped edges. Tiny star-shaped flowers are produced on long stems in late spring or summer. However, some people remove the blooms because their nectar can encourage fungal diseases.

TEMPERATURE 5–30°C (41–86°F)

LIGHT Position in bright light out of direct sun.

WATERING From spring to early autumn, water when the top of the compost is dry. Reduce watering in autumn and winter so that the compost is just moist and the leaves do not shrivel.

FEEDING Apply a half-strength cactus fertilizer once a month from spring to late summer.

COMPOST Plant in cactus compost, or a 50:50 mix of loam-based (John Innes No. 2 Peat Free) compost and 4mm grit.

FLOWERING Plants will flower without any special treatment.

PROPAGATION Take leaf or stem cuttings.

COMMON PROBLEMS Plants are prone to rot if grown in wet compost. Check regularly for mealybugs. Remove faded blooms to reduce the risk of them falling onto the compost and rotting, which will encourage fungal diseases.

ADROMISCHUS TRIGYNUS

syn. *Adromischus rupicola*
Calico hearts

Grow this tiny succulent for its elegant flat, paddle-shaped, grey-green leaves with dark purple-brown speckles, which develop around the central stem. It rarely flowers indoors, but since the yellow-green blooms are not considered to be as interesting as the foliage, they are not missed.

HEIGHT AND SPREAD Up to 15 x 15cm (6 x 6in).

CARE NOTES See opposite.

ADROMISCHUS COOPERI AGM

Plover eggs

This succulent takes its name from the dark purple spots that cover its green leaves, rather than the shape of its foliage, which actually resembles a tiny tube of toothpaste. Like most *Adromischus*, this beautiful species is a good choice for those without full sun, as a little shade helps it to maintain its decorative markings. Small pink flowers appear in summer on tall stems that shoot out from the middle of the plant.

HEIGHT AND SPREAD Up to 7 x 15cm (3 x 6in).

CARE NOTES See opposite.

AEONIUM

Admired for their decorative foliage, this group includes tall dramatic plants with woody stems topped with rosettes of fleshy leaves, and smaller, more subtle species, featuring flatter rosettes. All produce small, star-shaped flowers on long stems from late winter to summer. After blooming the flowering rosettes will die, but they usually produce offsets (new shoots) that will grow on to take their place, or you can take cuttings to propagate new plants (see pp334–35). Many *Aeonium* species become semi-dormant during very hot summers but their foliage will not wither if plants are grown outside in light shade.

TEMPERATURE 10–24°C (50–75°F).

LIGHT Position in full sun but provide some shade in summer.

WATERING From autumn to late spring, water when the top 1cm (½in) of compost feels dry; reduce in summer when plants may become semi-dormant. Grow outside in summer after the frosts to increase humidity around plants.

FEEDING Apply a half-strength balanced liquid fertilizer once a month in the growing season from winter to late spring.

COMPOST Plant in cactus compost, or a 50:50 mix of loam-based (John Innes No. 2 Peat Free) compost and 4mm grit.

FLOWERING Plants will flower in spring if fed and watered regularly; young plants may not flower for a few years.

PROPAGATION Sow seed or take cuttings in early spring.

COMMON PROBLEMS Plants are susceptible to root rot if overwatered or left sitting in wet compost. Check plants regularly for mealybugs.

AEONIUM ARBOREUM 'ATROPURPUREUM'

syn. *Aeonium arboreum* var. *atropurpureum*
Dark purple houseleek tree

Mature dark purple houseleek trees form a striking silhouette, their tall branched stems resembling a candelabra holding leafy rosettes. Conical clusters of starry yellow flowers rise up from the rosettes in late spring.

HEIGHT AND SPREAD
Up to 1.5 x 0.9m (5 x 3ft).

CARE NOTES See left.

AEONIUM CANARIENSE var. SUBPLANUM

syn. *Aeonium subplanum*
Canary Island flat giant houseleek

The Canary Island flat giant houseleek is not especially tall for a shrubby aeonium, but its leafy rosettes are exceptionally large, which explains the name. The glossy rounded light green leaves are tinged pinkish-purple in winter when temperatures are low or if the compost is dry, creating an eye-catching two-tone effect. Yellow flower spikes emerge from the centre of the leaf rosettes in spring.

HEIGHT AND SPREAD Up to 50 x 40cm (20 x 16in).

CARE NOTES See opposite.

AEONIUM DECORUM

Green pinwheel

The bright colours of the green pinwheel aeonium will shine out when grouped together with dark-leaved or plain green plants. The sturdy stems hold rosettes of pale green oval leaves with orange–red and red margins, which become brighter when the plant is grown in full sun. Soft pink starry flowers appear in spring. Also look out for *Aeonium decorum* var. *guarimiarense*, which has green leaves with red tips.

HEIGHT AND SPREAD Up to 60 x 50cm (24 x 20in).

CARE NOTES See opposite.

AEONIUM 'BLUSHING BEAUTY' AGM

Blushing Beauty houseleek tree

A sought-after, colourful hybrid, 'Blushing Beauty' is similar in structure to *Aeonium arboreum* (see opposite) but forms a more compact plant. Its green leaf rosettes are tinged with reddish-pink, and large clusters of tiny yellow flowers appear in spring and summer.

HEIGHT AND SPREAD Up to 70 x 60cm (28 x 24in).

CARE NOTES See opposite.

AEONIUM HAWORTHII AGM
Haworth's pinwheel

An elegant and sought-after species, the branched stems of Haworth's pinwheel are topped with rosettes of large, bluish-green leaves, often with red-tinged margins. The flowers, which appear in late spring, are pale creamy yellow, and they too may be tinged pink.

HEIGHT AND SPREAD Up to 60 x 60cm (24 x 24in).

CARE NOTES See p246.

AEONIUM TABULIFORME AGM
syn. *Aeonium berthelotianum; Aeonium macrolepum*
Flat-topped aeonium; Dinner plate aeonium

The flat-topped aeonium looks quite different from its shrubby, branching cousins. The ground-hugging, flat rosettes – made up of tightly packed, overlapping light green leaves – can reach dinner-plate proportions, hence its common name. Small starry yellow flowers appear on tall stems from the centre of the rosettes in spring. Grow it in a shallow pot in a bright room, such as a conservatory, turning it regularly to encourage even growth.

HEIGHT AND SPREAD Up to 10 x 30cm (4 x 12in).

CARE NOTES See p246.

AEONIUM 'ZWARTKOP' AGM

syn. *Aeonium arboreum* 'Zwartkop'
'Zwartkop' houseleek tree;
Black aeonium

Similar to *Aeonium arboreum* 'Atropurpureum' (see p246), the dark burgundy leaf rosettes of this houseleek tree are almost black, with a bright green centre. It is a highly prized cultivar and best grown with more colourful species or a plain green variety that will show up its contrasting hue. In winter, bright yellow flowers create a dazzling combination with the dark foliage.

HEIGHT AND SPREAD Up to 60 x 60cm (24 x 24in).

CARE NOTES See p246.

AEONIUM 'VELOUR'

syn. *Aeonium arboreum* 'Velour'
Velour houseleek tree

A show-stopping *Aeonium* that is guaranteed to turn heads, this plant is coveted for its green-centred, dark purple leafy rosettes, which have a soft, velvety appearance. As the plant matures, more rosettes form on the branched stems, producing a striking effect. Yellow flowers appear in early spring.

HEIGHT AND SPREAD Up to 60 x 50cm (24 x 20in).

CARE NOTES See p246.

AGAVE

Spiky leaves and dramatic silhouettes make the plants in this group deservedly popular in both homes and gardens. They form a rosette of thick, fleshy leaves, which, in many species, are tipped with a sharp spine. *Agave* are grown primarily for their foliage, which can be all shades of green or variegated with yellow or cream stripes. Flowers are rarely produced on house plants, but the nectar of those grown outside is used as an alternative sweetener to sugar. Smaller varieties or young plants are the best choices for a house plant collection, as the mature plants of many species are too big for most homes.

TEMPERATURE -5–30°C (23–86°F); can tolerate freezing conditions if the soil is dry.

LIGHT Position in full sun; place in light shade in summer.

WATERING During the spring and summer, water when the top 2cm (¾in) of compost is dry. In autumn and winter keep the compost almost dry, watering just enough to prevent the leaves shrivelling.

FEEDING Apply a half-strength liquid fertilizer once a month during late spring and summer.

COMPOST Plant in cactus compost, or a 50:50 mix of loam-based (John Innes No. 2 Peat Free) compost and 4mm grit.

FLOWERING Flowers rarely appear on house plants.

PROPAGATION Sow seed or take offsets.

COMMON PROBLEMS These plants will rot in wet compost. Pests to look out for include scale insects and mealybugs.

AGAVE AMERICANA 'MEDIOPICTA ALBA' AGM

syn. *Agave americana* f. *medio-picta alba*
American century plant

The sculptural leaves of the popular American century plant feature creamy white and bluish-grey stripes and make a dramatic statement in a large, bright room. Grown outside, it can reach up to 1m (3ft) in height and width, but remains more compact indoors in a pot. However, it still needs plenty of space if you are to avoid the sharp spines that guard the serrated edges and tips of the leaves. The yellow-green flowers will not appear on indoor-grown plants.

HEIGHT AND SPREAD Up to 1 x 1m (3 x 3ft).

CARE NOTES See left.

WARNING! Wear cactus gloves when handling this plant; the sap can also cause skin irritation.

AGAVE AMERICANA 'VARIEGATA' AGM

Variegated American century plant

This large, handsome century plant puts on a show with its yellow-edged grey-green leaves. Buy young plants to grow indoors and display where you can admire their beautiful foliage without being pricked by the spines. When these *Agave* get too big for their pots, consider planting them outside in a sunny, sheltered spot in free-draining soil, where they will survive several degrees of frost.

HEIGHT AND SPREAD Up to 1.5 x 1.5m (5 x 5ft).

CARE NOTES See left.

WARNING! Wear cactus gloves when handling this plant; the sap can also cause skin irritation.

AGAVE FILIFERA AGM
syn. *Agave filamentosa*
Thread agave

The pointed leaves of the thread agave are covered with white hairs, hence its common name. The foliage of this unusual species is also edged with thin white stripes, adding to the plant's decorative appeal. Greenish-white flowers, which form at the top of towering stems, rarely appear on plants grown indoors.

HEIGHT AND SPREAD Up to 45 x 45cm (18 x 18in).

CARE NOTES See opposite.

WARNING! Wear cactus gloves when handling this plant; the sap can also cause skin irritation.

AGAVE COLORATA
Mescal ceniza

The colourful wavy-edged leaves of the mescal ceniza, together with its relatively small size, account for this plant's popularity. The beautiful frosty grey–blue or light grey leaves are armed with vicious spines, so make sure it has enough space to avoid injury. The flowers are red in bud, and yellow and orange when in bloom.

HEIGHT AND SPREAD Up to 1.2 x 1.2m (4 x 4ft).

CARE NOTES See opposite.

WARNING! Wear cactus gloves when handling this plant; the sap can also cause skin irritation.

AGAVE PARRASANA
AGM

syn. *Agave wislizenii*
Cabbage head agave

One of the smaller species, the cabbage head agave is perfect for a windowsill succulent collection when young. Its short, wide leaves are pale blue-green with thorny, toothed edges and a waxy coating. These plants are spiky, so take care when handling them. Flowers are red in bud, then yellow when open.

HEIGHT AND SPREAD Up to 60 x 60cm (2 x2ft).

CARE NOTES See p250.

WARNING! Wear cactus gloves when handling this plant; the sap can also cause skin irritation.

AGAVE PARRASANA 'FIREBALL'
Variegated cabbage head agave

A rare cultivar of the popular cabbage head agave (see left), 'Fireball' differs from its parent only in the colour of the leaves, which are blue-grey with thin creamy yellow margins. When backlit, these margins make the foliage look as if it is on fire.

HEIGHT AND SPREAD Up to 60 x 60cm (2 x2ft).

CARE NOTES See p250.

WARNING! Wear cactus gloves when handling this plant; the sap can also cause skin irritation.

AGAVE PARRYI subsp. NEOMEXICANA
syn. *Agave neomexicana*
New Mexico agave

The New Mexico agave produces upright rosettes of narrow blue-green to powder blue leaves, armed with dark burgundy spines along the edges. Golden yellow flowers on long stems may appear if the plant is grown outside in summer.

HEIGHT AND SPREAD 45 x 60cm (18 x 24in).

CARE NOTES See p250.

WARNING! Wear cactus gloves when handling this plant; the sap can also cause skin irritation.

AGAVE PARRYI AGM
Parry's agave; Mescal agave

The winning feature of the Parry's agave is its elegant silvery grey-blue foliage, which is tipped and edged with short dark spines. Yellow flowers, tinged red or pink in bud, appear on mature plants grown outside, but are unlikely to develop on house plants.

HEIGHT AND SPREAD Up to 60 x 80cm (24 x 32in).

CARE NOTES See p250.

WARNING! Wear cactus gloves when handling this plant; the sap can also cause skin irritation.

AGAVE VICTORIAE-REGINAE AGM

syn. *Agave ferdinandi-regis;*
Agave scabra x *victoriae-reginae*
Queen Victoria century plant; Royal agave

The compact Queen Victoria century plant forms an eye-catching rounded rosette that looks a little like an artichoke head. The plant features three-sided, mid-green, spine-tipped leaves, with smooth, spineless edges and white or black margins. Creamy-white summer flowers may appear on long stems from the centre of the leaf rosettes of mature plants.

HEIGHT AND SPREAD Up to 30 x 30cm (12 x 12in).

CARE NOTES See p250.

AGAVE STRICTA AGM

syn. *Agave striata* subsp. *stricta*
Hedgehog agave

Unlike its cousins, the unusual hedgehog agave forms a spiky sphere of skewer-like leaves, each armed with a spine at the tip. This relatively compact *Agave* quickly forms offshoots that each produce clusters of leafy rosettes, giving it an even quirkier appearance as each plantlet develops its own ball of foliage. Small red flowers appear in summer on mature plants.

HEIGHT AND SPREAD Up to 40 x 40cm (16 x 16in).

CARE NOTES See p250.

ALBUCA

Not strictly a succulent, although succulent specialist nurseries often sell it, *Albuca* needs slightly different care to most of the other plants in this chapter. The spiralling forms are the most popular, prized for their fascinating leaves, which resemble green corkscrews. *Albuca* plants grow from a bulb, and each one produces a single central flower spike bearing nodding bell-shaped green blooms with pale yellow margins. Plants go dormant after flowering in summer but will start growing again in the autumn.

TEMPERATURE 5–30°C (41–86°F)

LIGHT Position in full sun, but provide some shade in summer.

WATERING From autumn to late spring when plants are in growth, water sparingly, applying it only when the top of the compost feels dry; plants will curl more in drier conditions. When dormant in summer, keep almost dry, then water more frequently when growth appears in the autumn.

FEEDING Apply a general-purpose granular fertilizer in autumn at half the dose recommended on the label.

COMPOST Plant in bulb compost, or a 50:50 mix of loam-based (John Innes No. 2 Peat Free) compost and 4mm grit.

FLOWERING Flowers appear on plants given sufficient water and a little fertilizer.

PROPAGATION Plant bulbs in autumn or divide existing plants.

COMMON PROBLEMS These plants will rot in wet compost. Plants are generally problem free.

ALBUCA SPIRALIS 'FRIZZLE SIZZLE'
Ornithogalum circinatum 'Frizzle Sizzle'
Corkscrew albuca 'Frizzle Sizzle'

An amazing plant not to be missed, the corkscrew albuca 'Frizzle Sizzle' has fast-growing, tightly spiralling dark green leaves. The flower spike, which shoots up through the foliage in late winter or early spring, holds dainty fragrant yellow and green nodding flowers. In summer, when dormant, the foliage will disappear below the surface.

HEIGHT AND SPREAD Up to 20 x 20cm (8 x 8in).

CARE NOTES See left.

ALOE

While most people know of *Aloe vera* (see p259), which among other things is used in sunburn remedies and skin creams, this popular species is just one of many varieties of aloe available to house plant collectors. Most species produce a decorative rosette of large, thick, fleshy leaves, which can be bright green, variegated, or mottled. Plants may be stemless, with the leafy rosette growing at ground level, or taller with branched stems. Clusters of tubular flowers, which are usually yellow, orange, pink, or red, are held on tall stems in spring or summer, although on some species the blooms may not develop when plants are grown indoors.

TEMPERATURE 5–30°C (41–86°F).

LIGHT Position in full sun, but provide some shade in summer.

WATERING From spring to early autumn, water when the surface of compost is dry. Reduce watering in autumn and winter so that the compost is just moist and the leaves do not shrivel.

FEEDING Apply a half-strength cactus fertilizer every month from spring to late summer.

COMPOST Plant in cactus compost, or a 50:50 mix of loam-based (John Innes No .2 Peat Free) compost and 4mm grit.

FLOWERING Plants are more likely to flower when given cool conditions in winter at a temperature of 5–10°C (41–50°F).

PROPAGATION Take offsets or leaf cuttings.

COMMON PROBLEMS Plants are prone to rot if grown in wet compost. Check regularly for mealy bugs and scale insects.

ALOE ARISTATA AGM

syn. *Aloe ellenbergeri;*
Aloe longiaristata
Lace aloe

The lace aloe takes its name from the white spots on its dainty green foliage. These form a horizontal striped pattern that sets the plant apart from it plain-leaved cousins. Its tubular orange-red flowers, which form on long stems in autumn, also appear more reliably than in some other species.

HEIGHT AND SPREAD Up to 20 x 20cm (8 x 8in).

CARE NOTES See left.

ALOE ARISTATA 'GREEN PEARL'

syn. *Aloe* 'Cosmo'
Lace aloe

Sold under the names 'Green Pearl' or 'Cosmo', this pretty lace aloe cultivar has elegant dark green leaves, with dainty white spots dotted along the edges and horizontal bands covering the outer surfaces. Like the species, *Aloe aristata* (see left), it also produces tubular, orange-red flowers in autumn.

HEIGHT AND SPREAD Up to 20 x 20cm (8 x 8in).

CARE NOTES See left.

ALOE ERINACEA
syn. *Aloe melanacantha* var. *erinacea*

Look out for this spiky little plant, which produces ball-shaped rosettes of brownish-green triangular leaves edged with sharp spines. The leaves curve inwards and mature plants may form small clusters of rosettes. Plants grown indoors are reluctant to bloom; those that do will bear bright red summer flowers, which turn yellow after opening.

HEIGHT AND SPREAD Up to 25 x 25cm (10 x 10in).

CARE NOTES See opposite.

WARNING! Wear cactus gloves to handle this plant.

ALOE HUMILIS
syn. *Aloe perfoliata* var. *humilis*
Spider aloe

The spider aloe is a small, compact plant that makes a great companion for other dwarf succulents and cacti. Its pale blue-green leaves grow vertically but curve slightly inwards. They feature grey-green raised bumps and are edged with thin, soft, white spines. In spring, clusters of drooping, tubular, bright orange-red flowers appear on tall stems.

HEIGHT AND SPREAD Up to 20 x 20cm (8 x 8in).

CARE NOTES See opposite.

ALOE PLICATILIS AGM
Fan aloe

This unusual species grows as a shrub or small tree in its native South Africa, and even as a potted house plant can grow to 1.5m (5ft) tall. It produces a woody trunk and spineless, strap-shaped, pale green to blue–grey leaves arranged in a fan shape, hence its common name. Tubular, bright red flowers that fade to yellow–green form on tall stems that rise up from the leafy fans in spring.

HEIGHT AND SPREAD Up to 1.5 x 0.9m (5 x 3ft).

CARE NOTES See p256.

ALOE VARIEGATA AGM
syn. *Aloe variegata* var. *haworthii*
Partridge breast aloe;
Tiger aloe

The striped white and dark green bands on outward-curving leaves give the partridge breast aloe a distinctive look, while its lack of spines or sharp-toothed edges make it a goodcandidate for homes with children or pets. The orange-red flowers appear reliably in spring or summer on tall stems.

HEIGHT AND SPREAD Up to 20 x 20cm (8 x 8in).

CARE NOTES See p256.

ALOE VERA AGM
syn. *Aloe perfoliata* var. *vera*
Barbados aloe

While the rosettes of fleshy dull green leaves with soft spiny margins may not look as exciting as some others in this group, the Barbados aloe is an easy and useful plant to grow at home. The fleshy centres of the leaves can be used to treat mild burns, including sunburn, and any foliage removed for such a purpose will soon be replaced by new growth. The plant's tubular greenish-yellow flowers rarely appear on plants grown indoors.

HEIGHT AND SPREAD Up to 60 x 60cm (24 x 24in).

CARE NOTES See p256.

APTENIA

Native to South Africa, these small shrubby succulents develop trailing or climbing stems covered with tiny heart-shaped leaves. Unlike many succulents, this pretty trailer is grown for its prolific summer flowers as much as for its foliage. The small daisy-like blooms develop at the tips of the leafy stems and come in many colours, including pink, purple, yellow, or white.

TEMPERATURE -7°C–30°C (19-86°F); plants can tolerate a few degrees of frost if the soil is dry.

LIGHT Position in full sun or filtered sun; provide some shade in summer.

WATERING From spring to early autumn, water when the top of compost is dry. Reduce watering in autumn and winter so that the compost is just moist and the leaves do not shrivel.

FEEDING Apply a general-purpose granular fertilizer in spring at half the dose recommended on the label.

COMPOST Plant in cactus compost, or a 50:50 mix of loam-based (John Innes No. 2 Peat Free) compost and 4mm grit.

FLOWERING Flowers appear freely without any special treatment.

PROPAGATION Take stem cuttings.

COMMON PROBLEMS These plants will rot if left in wet compost. Pests to look out for include mealybugs and spider mites.

APTENIA CORDIFOLIA 'VARIEGATA'
syn. *Mesembryanthemum cordifolium* 'Variegata'
Baby sun rose

The beautiful flowing stems of white-edged, heart-shaped leaves and bright pink spring and summer flowers create a year-round feature when this plant it grown in a tall pot or hanging basket. If including this plant in a mixed succulent display, plant it in a separate pot; it is very vigorous and may swamp its neighbours if grouped with other plants in a single container.

HEIGHT AND SPREAD Up to 10 x 90cm (4 x 36in).

CARE NOTES See left.

CEROPEGIA

Most *Ceropegia* are grown for their trailing, wiry stems (a few species are upright) and patterned, heart-shaped, fleshy leaves, which make beautiful hanging basket displays. Very easy to grow, these succulents also produce curious tubular flowers that look like old-fashioned tobacco pipes and develop along the length of the stems in summer.

TEMPERATURE 8–30°C (46–86°F)

LIGHT Position in full sun, but provide some shade in summer.

WATERING During the spring and summer, water when the top 1cm (½in) of compost is dry. In autumn and winter, keep the compost just moist enough to ensure the leaves do not shrivel.

FEEDING Apply a half-strength all-purpose liquid fertilizer once a month from late spring to late summer.

COMPOST Plant in cactus compost, or a 50:50 mix of loam-based (John Innes No. 2 Peat Free) compost and 4mm grit.

FLOWERING Flowers appear freely if plants are watered adequately and given a little fertilizer.

PROPAGATION Sow seed or take stem cuttings.

COMMON PROBLEMS These plants will rot if left in wet compost. Pests to look out for include mealybugs and spider mite.

CEROPEGIA LINEARIS subsp. WOODII AGM

syn. *Ceropegia woodii*
String of hearts

As the name suggests, string of hearts produces long slender stems covered with heart-shaped leaves. These are green and decorated with cream-coloured lacy patterns on the upper surface, and purple underneath, creating a beautiful two-tone effect. The pink and purple tubular flowers appear in summer. Very easy to grow, this plant tolerates neglect and will endure long periods of drought. Place it on a high shelf or in a hanging basket where its long stems can flow freely without becoming too tangled.

HEIGHT AND SPREAD Up to 5cm x 2m (2in x 6ft 6in).

CARE NOTES See left.

COTYLEDON

With their softly textured leaves and colourful flowers, this group of small- to medium-sized African succulents are popular house plants. The foliage of some *Cotyledon* species is covered with a powdery bloom or downy hairs, giving the plants a velvety appearance, while the tubular flowers of these decorative plants are typically orange or pink and usually appear in summer.

TEMPERATURE 5-30°C (41-86°F); will tolerate -2°C (28°F) for short periods if soil is dry.

LIGHT Position in full sun but provide some shade in summer.

WATERING Water from below from late spring to autumn when the top 1cm (½in) of compost feels dry. In winter reduce watering so that the compost is almost dry.

FEEDING Apply a half-strength balanced liquid fertilizer once a month from late spring to late summer.

COMPOST Plant in cactus compost, or a 50:50 mix of loam-based (John Innes No. 2 Peat Free) compost and 4mm grit.

FLOWERING Plants will flower without any special treatment.

PROPAGATION Sow seed or take stem or leaf cuttings.

COMMON PROBLEMS Plants are susceptible to root rot if overwatered or left sitting in wet compost. Check plants regularly for mealybugs.

COTYLEDON ORBICULATA
syn. *Cotyledon ramosa*
Pig's ear; Dog's ear

The pig's ear gets its name from its grey-green oval leaves, which are covered with a white waxy coating and edged with a line of red. A tall, branched shrub, this *Cotyledon* may reach over 1m (3ft) in height, but its size can be restricted by growing it in a pot. Small bell-shaped orange-red flowers, which are also covered with a waxy bloom, appear on long stems in late summer and autumn.

HEIGHT AND SPREAD Up to 1m x 60cm (3 x 2ft).

CARE NOTES See left.

WARNING! This plant is poisonous if consumed.

COTYLEDON UNDULATA
syn. *Cotyledon orbiculata* f. *undulata*
Silver ruffles; Silver crown

Silver ruffles has beautiful fan-shaped grey leaves with crimped edges and a soft silver-white powdery coating, hence its common name. Its orange or yellow flowers appear in summer.

HEIGHT AND SPREAD Up to 50 x 40cm (20 x 16in).

CARE NOTES See left.

WARNING! This plant is poisonous if consumed.

CRASSULA

Many *Crassula* plants are tall branched shrubs with colourful foliage, while others form dense rosettes, and some dwarf varieties take on a geometric shape. The foliage varies depending on the species, and can be round, oval, spear- or heart-shaped. *Crassula* also produces showy clusters of star-like white to pink flowers in spring to summer, although plants grown indoors may be reluctant to bloom. If the brittle stems are broken off, they will make good cuttings and are easy to propagate (see p339).

TEMPERATURE 5–30°C (41–86°F); keep cool but frost-free in winter, although plants will tolerate -2°C (28°F) for short periods if soil is dry.

LIGHT Position in full sun. Provide some shade in summer.

WATERING Water from late spring to autumn only when the top 2cm (¾in) of compost is dry; reduce watering in winter so that the compost is almost dry but the leaves are not shrivelled.

FEEDING Apply a general-purpose granular fertilizer at half the recommended dose in late spring.

COMPOST Plant in cactus compost, or a 50:50 mix of loam-based (John Innes No. 2 Peat Free) compost and 4mm grit.

FLOWERING House plants rarely flower.

PROPAGATION Take stem or leaf cuttings.

COMMON PROBLEMS Plants are prone to rot if overwatered or left sitting in wet compost. Check them regularly for mealybugs.

CRASSULA ARBORESCENS
syn. *Cotyledon arborescens*
Silver jade plant

The silver jade plant is a branched, tree-shaped shrub with thick, round, shimmering silver–grey leaves. The foliage may also be edged with a maroon strip and feature reddish spots on the upper surfaces. Clusters of starry pinkish-white flowers may appear in spring on mature plants grown outside in warm climates. Look out for the popular subspecies, *Crassula arborescens* subsp. *undulatifolia* (pictured below), which has more elliptical-shaped leaves with twisted edges.

HEIGHT AND SPREAD Up to 1 x 0.6m (40 x 24in).

CARE NOTES See left.

CRASSULA OVATA 'HOBBIT'
Jade plant 'Hobbit'

'Hobbit' has the same tree-like habit as its parent, the friendship tree (see left), but it sports curious tube-like leaves. Not quite as large as its parent, it is a better candidate for smaller spaces.

HEIGHT AND SPREAD Up to 90 x 80cm (36 x 32in).

CARE NOTES See opposite.

CRASSULA OVATA AGM
syn. *Cotyledon ovata*
Friendship tree; Jade plant; Money plant

The friendship tree has a quiet charm with its branched stems covered with thick dark green oval leaves, often edged in red. Flat clusters of small, starry white or light pink flowers may develop in late summer on mature plants grown outside.

HEIGHT AND SPREAD Up to 1.5 x 0.9m (5 x 3ft).

CARE NOTES See opposite.

CRASSULA OVATA 'HUMMEL'S SUNSET' AGM
syn. *Crassula ovata* 'Sunset'
Jade plant 'Hummel's Sunset'

A popular cultivar of *Crassula ovata*, 'Hummel's Sunset' has bright yellow-edged green leaves suffused with red that create an eye-catching tricoloured effect. It bears small starry white or pale pink flowers but these are rarely produced on plants grown indoors.

HEIGHT AND SPREAD Up to 90 x 80cm (36 x 32in).

CARE NOTES See p262; leaf colours will fade if kept in poor light.

CRASSULA PELLUCIDA subsp. MARGINALIS f. RUBRA
syn. *Crassula marginalis rubra* 'Variegata'

Look out for this *Crassula* if you need a colourful succulent with long, cascading stems for a hanging basket or tall pot. Tiny red-edged, heart-shaped leaves, which are purplish-pink with a dash of yellow or green, cover the stems to provide year-round interest. White flowers may emerge from the stem tips in summer.

HEIGHT AND SPREAD Up to 15 x 45cm (6 x 18in).

CARE NOTES See p262.

CRASSULA PERFORATA AGM

syn. *Crassula perfossa;*
Crassula nealeana
String of buttons; Necklace plant

Originally from South Africa, the stems of the string of buttons initially grow upright and then sprawl to form a loose fountain shape. Its small oval leaves are grey-green with pink edges, and look a little like buttons threaded on the stem, hence its common name. Tiny star-shaped white flowers appear in spring.

HEIGHT AND SPREAD: Up to 45 x 45cm (18 x 18in).

CARE NOTES See p262.

CRASSULA PERFOLIATA var. FALCATA AGM

syn. *Crassula falcata* 'Rochea';
Crassula perfoliata var. *minor*
Propeller plant; Airplane plant

The unusual arrangement of sickle-shaped, silvery grey-green leaves gives the propeller plant its common name, and its quirky appearance can create quite a talking point. As the plant matures, the foliage grows in more horizontal layers, but still looks amazing. Clusters of small fragrant scarlet flowers may appear in late summer on plants grown outside.

HEIGHT AND SPREAD Up to 90 x 90cm (3 x 3ft).

CARE NOTES See p262.

CRASSULA RUPESTRIS subsp. MARNIERIANA

syn. *Crassula marnieriana*
Jade necklace plant

A good choice for small spaces or a hanging basket, the gently trailing stems of the jade necklace plant are composed of square bead-like green leaves, often suffused with red. Quite the show-stopper despite its diminutive size, it is very easy to care for and a good choice for beginners. Small star-shaped pink flowers may appear in the summer.

HEIGHT AND SPREAD Up to 10 x 20cm (4 x 8in).

CARE NOTES See p262.

CURIO

Trailing or upright, the most commonly grown *Curio* species have intriguing leaves that look either like peas or beads, or fat little fingers. The foliage may be blue-green, grey-green, or bright green, and all species will add texture and colour to a succulent and cacti collection. Plants often become leggy with age, but can be trimmed back annually to keep them bushy.

TEMPERATURE 5–30°C (41–86°F); plants will tolerate -2°C (28°F) for short periods if soil is dry.

LIGHT Position in full sun or light shade; place in light shade in summer.

WATERING During the spring and summer, water when the top 1cm (½in) of compost is dry. In autumn and winter keep the compost almost dry, watering just enough to prevent the leaves shrivelling.

FEEDING Apply a half-strength liquid fertilizer once a year in late spring.

COMPOST Plant in cactus compost, or a 50:50 mix of loam-based (John Innes No. 2 Peat Free) compost and 4mm grit.

FLOWERING Flowers rarely appear on house plants.

PROPAGATION Take offsets or stem cuttings.

COMMON PROBLEMS These plants will rot in wet compost, and the leaves can become swollen if given too much water. Check plants regularly for mealybugs.

CURIO REPENS

syn. *Senecio serpens;*
Senecio talinoides subsp. *mandraliscae*
Blue chalk sticks

Often labelled under their synonym *Senecio serpens*, blue chalk sticks are accurately named, as the white coating on their blue-green cylindrical leaves looks like chalk dust. The leafy stems form large clusters and can quickly fill a wide pot. Small white flowers may appear in summer.

HEIGHT AND SPREAD Up to 20 x 30cm (8 x 12in).

CARE NOTES See left.

WARNING! The leaves are poisonous to humans and pets if consumed.

DUDLEYA

Often mistaken for *Echeveria* (see pp268-72), *Dudleya* thrive on neglect and are extremely easy to care for. They are grown for their colourful leafy rosettes, which are often in tones of green or blue-grey. Some plants are branching, producing groups of rosettes on low-growing stems, while others form solitary rosettes. The spring flowers are usually yellow, enclosed by pinkish-red bracts (petal-like modified leaves), and hold on long colourful stems. *Dudleya* grow on rocky outcrops and cliffs in hot, dry southwestern US states and Mexico, and will become dormant in high summer temperatures.

TEMPERATURE 5-30°C (41-86°F)

LIGHT Position in full sun; place in light shade in summer.

WATERING From spring to autumn, water when the top 1cm (½in) of compost is dry. In winter keep the compost almost dry, watering just enough to prevent the leaves shrivelling.

FEEDING Apply a half-strength liquid fertilizer once a month from late winter to late spring.

COMPOST Plant in cactus compost, or a 50:50 mix of loam-based (John Innes No. 2 Peat Free) compost and 4mm grit.

FLOWERING Flowers will form without any special treatment.

PROPAGATION Sow seed or take offsets.

COMMON PROBLEMS These plants will rot in wet compost. Pests to look out for include mealybugs and aphids.

DUDLEYA BRITTONII AGM
Giant chalk dudleya;
Silver dollar plant

Grow the colourful giant chalk dudleya for its beautiful sea-green leaves, which are covered with a white powdery coating that resembles chalk, hence the name. The coating reflects the sun, helping the plant to withstand heat and drought. Avoid touching the leaves, however, as fingers marks can cause permanent blemishes. In spring, long red spikes of starry yellow or orange flowers, cupped in pink bracts (petal-like modified leaves), rise up from the leafy rosettes. As the plants mature, the old dead leaves hang on to the main stem and can be carefully removed.

HEIGHT AND SPREAD Up to 45 x 45cm (18 x 18in).

CARE NOTES See left.

CURIO ROWLEYANUS
syn. *Senecio rowleyanus*
String of beads; String of pearls

The string of beads is one of a kind. Its eye-catching fountain of green pearl-shaped leaves on wiry, cascading stems will flow gracefully over the sides of a tall container or basket. This easy-care plant is ideal for beginners; the stems are quite brittle but this *Curio* will soldier on regardless if they break off. The only problem is keeping the plant in check – its stems can trail for over 1m (4ft), so hang it up high or place it on a stand.

HEIGHT AND SPREAD Up to 10 x 90cm (4 x 36in).

CARE NOTES See opposite.

WARNING! The leaves are poisonous to humans and pets if consumed.

ECHEVERIA

Loved for their beautiful leaf rosettes, which in some species look like water-lily flowers, *Echeveria* include many easy-care varieties in a spectrum of foliage colours and textures. The rosettes quickly multiply to form small clusters, and the lantern-shaped flowers reliably appear each spring or summer without any special treatment. Ideal for beginners, a range of contrasting *Echeveria* species can be used to create a trouble-free windowsill collection.

TEMPERATURE 5–30°C (41–86°F); some species tolerate short periods below freezing at -3°C (27°F) if the soil is dry.

LIGHT Position in full sun; place in light shade in summer.

WATERING During the spring and summer, water when the top 1cm (½in) of compost is dry. In autumn and winter keep the compost almost dry, watering just enough to prevent the leaves from shrivelling.

FEEDING Apply a half-strength liquid fertilizer once a month from late spring to late summer.

COMPOST Plant in cactus compost, or a 50:50 mix of loam-based (John Innes No. 2 Peat Free) compost and 4mm grit.

FLOWERING Flowers will form without any special treatment.

PROPAGATION Sow seed or take offsets.

COMMON PROBLEMS These plants will rot in wet compost. Check plants regularly for mealybugs.

ECHEVERIA AGAVOIDES AGM
Moulded wax

The curious name of the moulded wax plant refers to the waxy coating that covers its rosettes of thick red-tipped pale green leaves. Also look out for the more colourful cultivar *Echeveria agavoides* 'Red Edge', the leaves of which are outlined in red. Both produce dainty red summer flowers with yellow tips.

HEIGHT AND SPREAD Up to 12 x 30cm (5 x 12in).

CARE NOTES See left.

ECHEVERIA AGAVOIDES 'RED TAURUS'
Moulded wax 'Red Taurus'

'Red Taurus' (sometimes sold as just 'Taurus') has dark red to reddish-green leaves and bears red flowers in summer.

HEIGHT AND SPREAD Up to 12 x 30cm (5 x 12in).

CARE NOTES See opposite.

ECHEVERIA AGAVOIDES 'EBONY'
Moulded wax 'Ebony'

The smouldering good looks of this cultivar are created by an eye-catching colour combination of pale green foliage with dark red tips. The yellow-edged red flowers appear in summer.

HEIGHT AND SPREAD Up to 10 x 15cm (4 x 6in).

CARE NOTES See opposite.

ECHEVERIA AMOENA
syn. *Echeveria purpusii*;
Echeveria pusilla
Hen and chicks

The tiny rosettes of this pretty little *Echeveria* are made up of fat, diamond-shaped blue-green leaves, which may be tinged with pink if the plant is grown in a little shade. In late spring, pale yellow and coral flowers produce a dazzling effect when they appear on the end of bright red stems. The long-lasting blooms are open for about a month.

HEIGHT AND SPREAD Up to 2.5 x 5cm (1 x 2in).

CARE NOTES See opposite.

ECHEVERIA 'BLACK PRINCE'

Hen and chicks
'Black Prince'

A rare but much sought-after *Echeveria*, this little succulent produces rosettes of dark chocolate-brown outer leaves with bright green nearer the centre. The dark red flowers add to the rich colour combination in summer.

HEIGHT AND SPREAD Up to 10 x 20cm (4 x 8in).

CARE NOTES See p268.

ECHEVERIA COLORATA AGM

syn. *Echeveria colorata* f. *colorata*;
Echeveria lindsayana
Hen and chicks

The rosettes of this award-winning echeveria are relatively large, and produce silvery blue-green leaves tipped with pinky red hues. The leaves arch slightly upwards, causing the rosettes to look a little like flower heads. Long-stemmed pink blooms appear in early summer.

HEIGHT AND SPREAD Up to 30 x 40cm (12 x 16in).

CARE NOTES See p268.

ECHEVERIA ELEGANS AGM

Mexican snowball;
Mexican gem

The rosettes of the Mexican snowball are made up of silvery, ice-blue, spoon-shaped leaves that glisten in the sun. Pink flowers, tipped with yellow, appear in early spring on long pink stems, creating a colourful display.

HEIGHT AND SPREAD Up to 10 x 20cm (4 x 8in).

CARE NOTES See p268.

ECHEVERIA LAUI AGM
Hen and chicks

One of the most beautiful species, *Echeveria laui* features chubby, spoon-shaped leaves in a sophisticated shade of pale blue. Although the leaves look soft, try not to touch them, as fingers can leave permanent unsightly marks on the waxy coating. Pink and orange summer flowers make a striking contrast to the pastel foliage colour.

HEIGHT AND SPREAD Up to 10 x 15cm (4 x 6in).

CARE NOTES See p268.

ECHEVERIA LEUCOTRICHA AGM
Chenille plant;
White-plush plant

The soft, downy foliage of the chenille plant gives it a velvety appearance, inviting you to stroke It. The tactile texture is produced by silvery hairs that cover the rosettes, turning brown at the tips of the leaves. These provide a foil for the orange-red flowers when they appear in summer.

HEIGHT AND SPREAD Up to 15 x 30cm (6 x 12in).

CARE NOTES See p268.

ECHEVERIA LILACINA AGM
Ghost echeveria

Prized for its unusual colour, the ghost echeveria stands out from its cousins with its neat rosettes of spoon-shaped leaves in a pearlescent shade of blue, which becomes infused with lilac or purple when the plant is grown in full sun. Showy pinkish-orange spring blooms appear in spring.

HEIGHT AND SPREAD Up to 12 x 20cm (4 x 10in).

CARE NOTES See p268.

ECHEVERIA. SECUNDA var. GLAUCA 'COMPTON CAROUSEL' AGM

Glaucous echeveria
'Compton Carousel'

'Compton Carousel' makes a striking impression with its cream and blue-green patterned rosettes. The margins of older leaves become tinged with pink, adding to the colourful mix. In almost all other respects it is the same as its parent plant (see left), although it is a little smaller in stature.

HEIGHT AND SPREAD Up to 15 x 30cm (6 x 12in).

CARE NOTES See p268.

ECHEVERIA SECUNDA var. GLAUCA

syn. *Echeveria glauca*
Glaucous echeveria

Highly popular and widely available, the glaucous echeveria is aptly named, as it forms clusters of pale blue-grey leaf rosettes. Larger than many members of the *Echeveria* family, it makes an attractive house plant in a wide pot. The red and yellow flowers appear in summer on pinkish-purple stems.

HEIGHT AND SPREAD Up to 30 x 45cm (12 x 18in).

CARE NOTES See p268.

ECHEVERIA SETOSA AGM

Mexican firecracker

The hairy texture of the Mexican firecracker give the tiny leaves a frosted look. This *Echeveria* also produces vibrant red flowers with bright yellow tips in summer, hence its common name.

HEIGHT AND SPREAD Up to 5 x 30cm (2 x 12in).

CARE NOTES See p268.

EUPHORBIA

A huge and varied group of plants, *Euphorbia* range from desert-dwelling cactus look-alikes to leafy hardy perennials and towering tree-like species. The succulents grown as house plants generally fall into the group that resemble cacti, which evolved in African deserts to cope with the same hot, dry conditions as their prickly American relatives. *Euphorbia* are generally grown for their foliage more than their flowers, which are often small and not very showy, although some have colourful bracts (petal-like leaves). All *Euphorbia* have poisonous, milky, latex-like sap, which irritates the eyes and skin on contact and is toxic if consumed.

TEMPERATURE 5–30°C (23–86°F) for tender species; some *Euphorbia* grown as house plants must be kept at 10°C (50°F) or higher.

LIGHT Position in full sun; place in light shade in summer.

WATERING During the spring and summer, water when the top 2cm (¾in) of compost is dry. In autumn and winter keep the compost almost dry.

FEEDING Apply a half-strength cactus fertilizer once a month during late spring and summer.

COMPOST Plant in cactus compost, or a 50:50 mix of loam-based (John Innes No. 2 Peat Free) compost and 4mm grit.

FLOWERING Flowers will appear on house plants without any special treatment.

PROPAGATION Sow seed or take stem cuttings.

COMMON PROBLEMS These plants will rot in wet compost. Pests to look out for include scale insects and mealybugs.

EUPHORBIA BUPLEURIFOLIA
syn. *Euphorbia proteifolia*, *Tithymalus bupleurifolius*
Pine cone plant

The long green leaves of this sculptural plant sprout from what look like pine cones or pineapples, hence the name. The "pine cone" is, in fact, a modified stem (caudex) designed to store water. Attractive yellow–green flowers, held in green bracts on slim stems, appear in spring. This plant is deciduous so don't worry if the leaves fall off in winter, as they will reappear the following spring.

HEIGHT AND SPREAD Up to 30 x 30cm (12 x 12in).

CARE NOTES See left; do not allow temperature to fall below 10°C (50°F) and apply full strength doses of fertilizer rather than half strength.

WARNING! Wear cactus gloves when handling this plant. The milky sap a skin and eye irritant, and toxic if consumed.

EUPHORBIA ENOPLA
Pincushion euphorbia

The sharp bright red spines of this plant are more like swords than pins, and it makes a dramatic statement in a mixed collection. Mature plants develop into large branched shrubs with thick grey-green column-shaped ribbed stems, although they will remain smaller if grown in a pot. Position this euphorbia where it will have space to grow without causing injury.

HEIGHT AND SPREAD Up to 90 x 60cm (3 x 2ft).

CARE NOTES See left; grow in light shade for the brightest spines.

WARNING! Wear cactus gloves when handling this plant. The sap is a skin and eye irritant, and toxic if consumed.

EUPHORBIA HORRIDA AGM
African milk barrel

The blue-green ribbed stems of the aptly named *Euphorbia horrida* are covered with vicious long reddish-brown spines and contain a poisonous milky sap. Its spiny armour, beautiful colouring and small yellow and green summer flowers combine to create an eye-catching focal point.

HEIGHT AND SPREAD Up to 75 x 90cm (30 x 36in).

CARE NOTES See p273.

WARNING! Wear cactus gloves when handling this plant. The milky sap is a skin and eye irritant, and toxic if consumed.

EUPHORBIA OBESA AGM
Basketball; Golf ball

This little beauty produces clusters of ball-shaped blue- or brown-green stems with plaid-like patterning. As the basketball grows, it becomes more cone-shaped, but produces offsets alongside the parent plant, creating fascinating clusters. Tiny flowers appear at the top of the plant, which eventually form fig-shaped seedheads, adding another unusual feature to this unique little plant.

HEIGHT AND SPREAD Up to 20 x 10cm (8 x 4in).

CARE NOTES See p273.

WARNING! Wear cactus gloves when handling this plant. The milky sap is a skin and eye irritant, and toxic if consumed.

EUPHORBIA TRIGONA
syn. *Euphorbia hermentiana*
African milk tree

The tall dark green branched stems of the African milk tree feature three or four prominent ribs, from which sprout sharp spines and small spoon-shaped leaves in spring and summer. This plant is deciduous, which means that the foliage will drop in autumn and reappear the following spring. When grown as a house plant, it will not produce flowers.

HEIGHT AND SPREAD Up to 2 x 1m (6ft 6in x 3ft 4in).

CARE NOTES See p273.

WARNING! Wear cactus gloves when handling this plant. The milky sap is a skin and eye irritant, and toxic if consumed.

EUPHORBIA TIRUCALLI
syn. *Arthrothamnus tirucalli;*
Tirucalia tirucalli
Pencil cactus; Pencil tree

A tree-sized succulent in its native Africa, as a potted house plant the pencil cactus will grow to just 1m (3ft) or so in height. The tangled mass of smooth, pencil-thick, cylindrical stems produce its curious, spindly silhouette. In young plants, the stems are also covered with tiny leaves but these fall off as the plant matures. The yellowish flowers rarely appear on plants grown indoors.

HEIGHT AND SPREAD Up to 90 x 75cm (36 x 30in).

CARE NOTES See p273.

WARNING! Wear cactus gloves when handling this plant. The milky sap is a skin and eye irritant, and toxic if consumed.

FAUCARIA

These unusual succulents produce clumps of rosettes made up of tooth-edged green leaves that are arranged to resemble an open jaw. Its daisy-like flowers, which are usually yellow, bloom for many weeks. *Faucaria* need more water than many succulents during their growth period in spring and summer, but apart from that, they are easy to care for and an ideal choice for beginners.

TEMPERATURE 5–30°C (41–86°F); they can tolerate freezing conditions of -5°C (23°F) if the soil is dry.

LIGHT Position in full sun from autumn to spring; provide light shade in summer.

WATERING During spring and summer, water when the top of the compost feels dry. In autumn and winter keep the compost almost dry, watering just enough to prevent the leaves shrivelling.

FEEDING Apply a half-strength liquid fertilizer once a year in spring.

COMPOST Plant in cactus compost, or a 50:50 mix of loam-based (John Innes No. 2 Peat Free) compost and 4mm grit.

FLOWERING Flowers appear annually if plants are watered and fertilized correctly (see above).

PROPAGATION Sow seed or take offsets.

COMMON PROBLEMS These plants will rot in wet compost. Pests to look out for include mealybugs.

FAUCARIA TIGRINA AGM
syn. *Mesembryanthemum tigrinum*
Tiger's jaws

A great gift for children, the little leaves of the tiger's jaws look like open mouths lined with sharp curved teeth, although these spines are actually soft and harmless. The triangular leaves are light green with white flecks, although they may turn purple if grown in strong sun. In autumn, silky daisy-like yellow flowers bloom over many weeks, opening each day in the afternoon when it is sunny and closing in the evening.

HEIGHT AND SPREAD Up to 15 x 20cm (6 x 8in).

CARE NOTES See above.

FAUCARIA TUBERCULOSA AGM
syn. *Faucaria felina* subsp. *tuberculosa*,
Mesembryanthemum tuberculosum
Warty tiger's jaws

Similar in many respects to *Faucaria tigrina* AGM (see left), the leaves of the warty tiger's jaws are covered with white tubercules (raised bumps), giving this plant the warty appearance for which it is named. It produces yellow flowers that appear in autumn and open only on sunny afternoons.

HEIGHT AND SPREAD Up to 15 x 20cm (6 x 8in).

CARE NOTES See above left.

FENESTRARIA

A native of Namibia, this plant group contains just one species, *Fenestraria rhopalophylla*. It takes its Latin name from the transparent window-like area at the tip of each stemless leaf. In the wild, these leaves are buried beneath the sand to protect them from the heat, while their windows peek out above the surface to photosynthesize and feed the plant. When kept as a house plant, the whole leaf will grow above the soil surface. Golden yellow flowers appear in winter. Often mistaken for *Lithops* (see pp288–89), *Fenestraria* is just as easy to grow.

TEMPERATURE 5–30°C (41–86°F); can tolerate -4°C (25°F) for short periods if the soil is dry.

LIGHT Position in full sun. Provide light shade in summer.

WATERING During the spring and autumn, water when the top 2cm (¾in) of compost is dry. In summer and winter, keep the compost almost dry, watering just enough to prevent the leaves shrivelling. Ensure plants have good air circulation.

FEEDING Apply a half-strength liquid fertilizer once a year in spring.

COMPOST Plant in cactus compost, or a 50:50 mix of loam-based (John Innes No. 2 Peat Free) compost and 4mm grit.

FLOWERING Flowers appear annually without any special treatment.

PROPAGATION Sow seed or take offsets.

COMMON PROBLEMS These plants will rot in wet compost. Watch out for mealybugs.

FENESTRARIA RHOPALOPHYLLA subsp. AURANTIACA AGM
Baby's toes

The stemless pale green leaves of this plant each have the characteristic transparent window at the top. Growing in a pot, these leaves form small colonies that are said to resemble baby's toes, hence the name. The relatively large golden yellow daisy-like flowers appear on short, slim stems from winter to early spring.

HEIGHT AND SPREAD Up to 5 x 15cm (2 x 6in).

CARE NOTES See left.

× GASTERHAWORTHIA

A beautiful hybrid succulent and very easy to grow, × *Gasterhaworthia* is a cross between *Gasteria* (see opposite) and *Haworthia* (see p281). It produces rosettes of fat, triangular leaves, often decorated with spots or subtle patterns. It also produces clusters of tubular flowers on long stems in spring or summer, but these are rarely seen on house plants.

TEMPERATURE 5–27°C (41–80°F); can tolerate freezing conditions of -1°C (30°F) for a short while if the soil is dry.

LIGHT Position in a bright spot, out of direct sunlight.

WATERING During the spring and summer, water when the top 2cm (¾in) of compost is dry. In autumn and winter, keep the compost almost dry, watering just enough to prevent the leaves shrivelling.

FEEDING Apply a half-strength liquid fertilizer once a year in late spring.

COMPOST Plant in cactus compost, or a 50:50 mix of loam-based (John Innes No. 2 Peat Free) compost and 4mm grit.

FLOWERING Flowers rarely appear on house plants.

PROPAGATION Take offsets or leaf cuttings.

COMMON PROBLEMS These plants will rot in wet compost. Look out for mealybugs.

× GASTERHAWORTHIA 'ROYAL HIGHNESS'
syn. × *Gasteraloe* 'Royal Highness'

'Royal Highness' features fat triangular dark green leaves that turn a reddish hue in bright sunlight, but it is the white tubercles (round raised bumps) that have made this cultivar so popular. These spots form a horizontal striped pattern, creating a striking combination of texture and colour.

HEIGHT AND SPREAD
Up to 15 x 15cm (6 x 6in).

CARE NOTES See left.

GASTERIA

Compact and easy to grow, *Gasteria* species have thick strap- or tongue-shaped leaves, arranged in round or linear rosettes, which often feature tubercles (raised bumps) or speckles. Plants produce flowers that are generally pink or red and look like little stomachs with a tube at the end, hence the plant's name (which means "stomach" in Latin). Despite the grisly association, the blooms are quite pretty, and appear in clusters on long stems in spring.

TEMPERATURE 5–27°C (41–80°F); can tolerate freezing conditions of -1°C (30°F) for a short while if the soil is dry.

LIGHT Position in a bright spot out of direct sunlight.

WATERING During the spring and summer, water when the top 2cm (¾in) of compost is dry. In autumn and winter, keep the compost almost dry, watering just enough to prevent the leaves shrivelling. Ensure the plants have good air circulation.

FEEDING Apply a half-strength liquid fertilizer once a year in late spring.

COMPOST Plant in cactus compost, or a 50:50 mix of loam-based (John Innes No. 2 Peat Free) compost and 4mm grit.

FLOWERING Flowers will appear on mature plants, given sufficient water and a small amount of fertilizer.

PROPAGATION Take offsets or leaf cuttings.

COMMON PROBLEMS Look out for mealybugs.

GASTERIA BICOLOR

syn. *Aloe bicolor; Aloe bowieana; Aloe dictyodes; Aloe lingua*

The strappy leaves of this plant are green with white mottled stripes, producing a decorative bicoloured effect. The foliage may turn red if the plant is placed in too much light. Tall stems of reddish-pink and green flowers appear on mature plants in spring.

HEIGHT AND SPREAD Up to 40 x 50cm (16 x 20in).

CARE NOTES See left.

GASTERIA BRACHYPHYLLA

syn. *Aloe brachyphylla*
Ox-tongue

The ox-tongue is a compact species with the blunt strap-shaped leaves arranged in a linear formation that is typical of many *Gasteria*. The smooth, shiny, dark green foliage features pale cream speckles that form a horizontal striped pattern. Pink flowers appear in spring.

HEIGHT AND SPREAD Up to 20 x 20cm (8 x 8in).

CARE NOTES See left.

GASTERIA 'LITTLE WARTY' AGM

syn. *Gasteria batesiana* 'Little Warty'
Ox-tongue 'Little Warty'

'Little Warty' has tongue-shaped leaves with pointed ends. The foliage is dark green with pale olive-green edges and raised white speckles or streaks. The pink and green flowers appear in spring on mature plants.

HEIGHT AND SPREAD Up to 20 x 20cm (8 x 8in).

CARE NOTES See p279.

GRAPTOPETALUM

Elegant and colourful, the leafy rosettes of *Graptopetalum* look a little like water lily flowers, although a few have round, pebble-shaped foliage. Their beautiful colours range from pale lilac-grey and silver to lime and blue-green — some also feature variegated foliage. Unlike most succulents, *Graptopetalum* are best grown out of direct sun all year round to maintain the leaf hues. Plants bear dainty flowers on tall stems in spring or summer and they bloom for several weeks.

TEMPERATURE 5–27°C (41–80°F). Keep cool in winter.

LIGHT Position in full sun.

WATERING During the spring and summer, water when the top 2cm (¾in) of compost is dry. In autumn and winter, keep the compost almost dry, watering just enough to prevent the leaves shrivelling.

FEEDING Apply a half-strength liquid fertilizer once in spring.

COMPOST Plant in cactus compost, or a 50:50 mix of loam-based (John Innes No. 2 Peat Free) compost and 4mm grit.

FLOWERING This plant requires low temperatures of 5–15°C (41–59°F) in winter for flowers to form.

PROPAGATION Sow seed, or take offsets or leaf cuttings.

COMMON PROBLEMS These plants will rot in wet compost. Pests to look out for include mealybugs.

GRAPTOPETALUM BELLUM AGM

syn. *Tacitus bellus*
Chihuahua flower

The small, leafy rosettes of the Chihuahua flower look like grey-green water lily blooms. Its common name is derived from the clusters of pink and red flowers, each bloom of which resembles the pointed face of a chihuahua. The clusters appear on tall stems that grow out of the middle of the rosettes.

HEIGHT AND SPREAD Up to 8 x 10cm (3½ x 4in).

CARE NOTES: See above.

HAWORTHIA

A large and varied group of diminutive succulents, *Haworthia* have small, patterned foliage, which may be decorated with speckles, spots, stripes, or streaks. Some have smooth, chubby leaves; others are spiky with spiny tips. The flowers appear on long stems in summer, but are often green in colour and not very showy. They only appear on a few species grown as house plants.

TEMPERATURE 5–27°C (30–80°F)

LIGHT Position in full sun; place in light shade in summer.

WATERING During the spring and summer, water when the top 2cm (¾in) of compost is dry. In autumn and winter, keep the compost almost dry, watering just enough to prevent the leaves shrivelling.

FEEDING Apply a half-strength liquid fertilizer once in spring.

COMPOST Plant in cactus compost, or a 50:50 mix of loam-based (John Innes No. 2 Peat Free) compost and 4mm grit.

FLOWERING Flowers rarely appear on house plants.

PROPAGATION Take offsets or leaf cuttings.

COMMON PROBLEMS These plants will rot in wet compost. Look out for mealybugs.

HAWORTHIA ATTENUATA
f. CAESPITOSA AGM

syn. *Aloe attenuata*

Zebra plant; Fairy washboard

With its spiky dark green leaf rosettes covered with white tubercles (raised bumps) arranged in distinctive horizontal stripes, the zebra plant lives up to its name. The plant soon forms small clusters of rosettes and it flowers reliably each summer, the tiny green blooms held on long stems forming an elegant display.

HEIGHT AND SPREAD Up to 13 x 25cm (5 x 10in).

CARE NOTES See left.

HAWORTHIA 'BIG BAND'

syn. *Haworthia fasciata* 'Big Band'
Zebra plant 'Big Band'

Very similar to *Haworthia attenuata*
f. *caespitosa* AGM (see p281), 'Big Band'
has more exaggerated raised white stripes,
which make a striking pattern against its
dark green spiky leaves. White bell-shaped
flowers appear on lofty stalks in summer.

HEIGHT AND SPREAD Up to 15 x 25cm
(6 x 10in).

CARE NOTES See p281.

HAWORTHIA CYMBIFORMIS 'GREY GHOST'

syn. *Haworthia fasciata* 'Grey Ghost';
Haworthia retusa 'Grey Ghost'
Window boats 'Grey Ghost'

You may find this elegant *Haworthia*
listed under a range of synonyms, but
the distinctive foliage of window boats
'Grey Ghost' makes it worth the search.
The short thick triangular leaves, which
are pale green with delicate white–grey
markings, looks like they have been
painted with a fine brush. Small white
and green tubular flowers appear on
long stems in summer.

HEIGHT AND SPREAD Up to 15 x 25cm
(6 x 10in).

CARE NOTES See p281.

HOYA

These Asian climbers comprise a large and varied group originating in tropical forests, and include a range of plants that have the distinctive fleshy foliage associated with succulents. Many species are epiphytes, which means that they grow on trees, and the most popular house plant varieties are those with sweetly scented flowers. Most *Hoya* bear unusual heads of waxy star-shaped flowers which, in many species, emit a sweet fragrance. Place perfumed varieties in a large space, such as a hallway, where the heady scent can be enjoyed in passing; they may be a little overpowering in a smaller room.

TEMPERATURE 10–27°C (50–80°F)

LIGHT Position in good light out of direct sunlight, or place in light shade.

WATERING Water regularly from spring to autumn, allowing the surface of the compost to dry out between waterings. From late autumn to late winter reduce watering so that the compost almost dries out. *Hoya* prefer moderate humidity; stand the plant on a tray filled with pebbles and water to increase the moisture in the surrounding atmosphere.

FEEDING Apply a half-strength liquid fertilizer once a month from spring to late summer.

COMPOST Plant in cactus compost with extra horticultural grit.

FLOWERING Flowers should develop when plants are given a little fertilizer. Do not move plants in bud, as the buds may drop off.

PROPAGATION Take leaf or stem cuttings.

COMMON PROBLEMS These plants are prone to rot if grown in wet compost. Look out for mealybugs.

HAWORTHIA TRUNCATA AGM
Truncate haworthia

The truncate haworthia may not be the prettiest plant in this group, but it is certainly one of the most unusual. It forms two rows of fleshy dark green leaves, the tops of which look like they have been cut off to form blunt tips. The small tubular flowers are greenish-white.

HEIGHT AND SPREAD Up to 10 x 20cm (4 x 8in).

CARE NOTES See p281.

HOYA CARNOSA 'TRICOLOR'
Wax plant

The flexible stems of this decorative climber can be trained on to a wire support or trellis for year-round interest. Grown for its colourful variegated leaves, which are green with cream and pink splashes, this hoya also features heads of small star-shaped waxy-looking white flowers with red centres. The blooms emit a rich sweet scent when they appear in summer, and each flower also produces a drop of nectar.

HEIGHT AND SPREAD Up to 1.8 x 0.6m (6 x 2ft).

CARE NOTES See left.

KALANCHOE

Natives of Madagascar and tropical Africa, some *Kalanchoe* species are large shrubs, but those grown as house plants are generally small- to medium-sized evergreen perennials. Popular for their bright, colourful flowers, plants generally bloom in late winter or spring, or at other times when grown indoors. The flowers are set off by the glossy green leaves or soft hairy foliage, depending on the species. You may also find plants with patterned or variegated leaves.

TEMPERATURE 10–27°C (50–80°F).

LIGHT Position in bright light but out of direct sun.

WATERING In spring and autumn, allow the top 2cm (¾in) of compost to dry out between waterings. In summer, allow just the surface of the compost to dry out before watering well. In winter, keep the compost just moist enough to prevent the leaves shrivelling.

FEEDING Feed with a half-strength liquid fertilizer once a month from late spring to early autumn.

COMPOST Plant in cactus compost, or a 50:50 mix of loam-based (John Innes No. 2 Peat Free) compost and 4mm grit.

FLOWERING *Kalanchoe* need a clear dormancy period in order to reflower. Prune back faded stems after they have flowered, reduce watering, and ensure plants spend 14 hours a day in darkness. This may occur naturally in winter, but if the blooms fade at other times, place a box over the plant. After 6 weeks, to stimulate flowering, bring the plant back into good light and resume normal watering.

PROPAGATION Sow stem cuttings.

COMMON PROBLEMS Prone to rot in wet compost. Check regularly for mealybugs and aphids.

KALANCHOE BLOSSFELDIANA AGM

syn. *Kalanchoe globulifera* var. *coccinea*
Flaming Katy

Dark green glossy leaves with scalloped edges provide the perfect foil for flaming Katy's bright starry flowers, which can last for many weeks or even months. They appear in late winter, spring, or summer and come in a range of colours, including red, orange, pink, white, or yellow. The double-flowered forms of this *Kalanchoe* resemble little rosebuds and are particularly attractive.

HEIGHT AND SPREAD Up to 30 x 30cm (12 x 12in).

CARE NOTES See left.

WARNING! All parts are poisonous if eaten.

KALANCHOE HUMILIS

syn. *Kalanchoe prasina*
Spotted kalanchoe; Pen wiper

Grown for its boldly patterned foliage, the spotted *Kalanchoe* produces grey–green wavy-edged oval leaves decorated with maroon spots and stripes. The older leaves on the lower part of the plant soon fall off to reveal the blue-green or purplish stem. Purple to green flowers appear in summer, but they are not very showy. Look out for the cultivar 'Desert Surprise', which has even brighter leaf markings.

HEIGHT AND SPREAD Up to 60 x 60cm (2 x 2ft).

CARE NOTES See left.

WARNING! All parts are poisonous if eaten.

KALANCHOE LACINIATA
Christmas tree plant;
Lace leaf kalanchoe

Tall and elegant, the Christmas tree plant forms a large shrub with slim, divided foliage that looks like the lacy leaves of a conifer. Clusters of bright yellow tubular flowers appear in early spring.

HEIGHT AND SPREAD
90 x 60cm (3 x 2ft).

CARE NOTES See opposite.

WARNING! All parts are poisonous if eaten.

KALANCHOE PUMILA AGM
syn. *Kalanchoe brevicaulis;*
Kalanchoe multiceps
Dwarf kalanchoe;
Flower dust plant

One of the smaller plants in this group, the dwarf kalanchoe produces graceful arching stems of silvery leaves that look like they have been dusted with white powder. In spring, clusters of tiny pink urn-shaped flowers appear on slim stems above the foliage.

HEIGHT AND SPREAD 20 x 20cm (8 x 8in).

CARE NOTES See opposite.

WARNING! All parts are poisonous if eaten.

KALANCHOE THYRSIFLORA

syn. *Kalanchoe tetraphylla*
Paddle kalanchoe; Flapjacks

Unlike its cousins, which produce tall leafy stems, the paddle kalanchoe forms a stemless rosette of paddle-shaped foliage. With its large, rounded leaves in shades of grey–green and dark red, the plant resembles a colourful cabbage when young. Once established, it produces towering stems studded with small scented tubular yellow flowers; these blooms last for many months, but then the plant dies.

HEIGHT AND SPREAD Up to 90 x 60cm (3 x 2ft).

CARE NOTES See p284.

WARNING! All parts are poisonous if eaten.

KALANCHOE SEXANGULARIS

syn. *Kalanchoe rogersii;*
Kawhoe rubinea
Six-angled kalanchoe

Unusual square or ridged stems hold the six-angled kalanchoe's oval, scallop-edged foliage. The pretty green leaves are often tinged red, particularly along the margins of the older foliage, and clusters of bright yellow flowers appear on tall stems in spring.

HEIGHT AND SPREAD Up to 90 x 60cm (3 x 2ft).

CARE NOTES See p284.

WARNING! All parts are poisonous if eaten.

KALANCHOE TOMENTOSA AGM

Panda plant

One of the most popular *Kalanchoe* species, the panda plant is prized for its velvety oval leaves. Grey–green and covered with silvery hair, the foliage also has brown spots on the leaf margins. It is grown more for its foliage than the small tubular yellow–green flowers, which rarely appear on house plants.

HEIGHT AND SPREAD Up to 90 x 60cm (3 x 2ft).

CARE NOTES See p284.

WARNING! All parts are poisonous if eaten.

KLEINIA

Some of these South African natives resemble cacti with spiny stems, while others are more shrub-like with bluish-green fleshy foliage, which may be deciduous or evergreen. A few species are popular for their showy red or white flowers, which usually appear in summer, but not many are grown as house plants. The most widely available is *Kleinia stapeliiformis* (see right), which has intricately patterned stems – you may find it under its old name, *Senecio*, with which it shares many similar characteristics.

TEMPERATURE 10–30°C (50–86°F).

LIGHT Position in full or filtered sun; provide some shade in summer.

WATERING From spring to early autumn, water when the surface of the compost is dry. Reduce watering in autumn and winter, keeping the compost just moist enough to prevent the stems shrivelling.

FEEDING Apply a half-strength cactus fertilizer once a month from spring to late summer.

COMPOST Plant in cactus compost, or a 50:50 mix of loam-based (John Innes No. 2 Peat Free) compost and 4mm grit.

FLOWERING Most plants will flower without any special treatment.

PROPAGATION Sow seed or take offsets.

COMMON PROBLEMS These plants are prone to rot if grown in wet compost. Check regularly for mealybugs.

KLEINIA STAPELIIFORMIS
syn. *Senecio stapeliiformis*
Pickle plant

The spiky ribbed pencil-like stems of the pickle plant, which are bluish-green with purple-green patterning, can be confused with those of a cactus. Slightly cascading when mature, they make a beautiful feature for a hanging basket, especially when the heads of thistle-like bright red to orange flowers heads appear in summer.

HEIGHT AND SPREAD Up to 25 x 20cm (10 x 8in).

CARE NOTES See left.

LITHOPS

Loved by children and very easy to grow, *Lithops* are commonly known as living stones due to their resemblance to little rocks or pebbles. There are many species to choose from, but all produce tiny fat pairs of stemless leaves that are fused down the centre to produce their characteristic stone-like appearance. The foliage is generally in shades of cream, grey, or brown and the different species are distinguished by their patterns or speckles. In winter, new leaves develop and then push out between the existing foliage pairs in spring, at which point the older leaves will wither. Daisy-like flowers, which may be scented, emerge in summer or autumn.

TEMPERATURE 5–30°C (41–86°F); will tolerate -5°C (23°F) for short periods if the soil is dry.

LIGHT Position in full sun; provide light shade in midsummer.

WATERING From spring to early autumn, after the old leaves have withered, water when the surface of the compost is dry. Stop watering after flowering and keep the compost dry from late autumn to late winter.

FEEDING Apply a half-strength cactus fertilizer once in spring.

COMPOST Plant in cactus compost, or a 50:50 mix of loam-based (John Innes No. 2 Peat Free) compost and 4mm grit.

FLOWERING Start watering when the old leaves die off and provide a little fertilizer to encourage flowering.

PROPAGATION Sow seed.

COMMON PROBLEMS These plants will rot if grown in wet compost; overwatering can also cause the leaves to split open. Check regularly for mealybugs and aphids.

LITHOPS KARASMONTANA AGM

Karas Mountains living stone

Originally from Namibia, the Karas Mountains living stone has pale beige or bluish-grey leaves, decorated with brown patterns that look like a cracked glaze. Satiny white flowers appear in late summer or early autumn.

HEIGHT AND SPREAD 4 x 8cm (1½ x 3in).

CARE NOTES See left.

LITHOPS MARMORATA

Living stone

The grey-white or pale grey-green leaves of this living stone, which sometimes have a purplish flush, are mottled with a white marbled effect. In late summer or autumn, yellow-centred white flowers appear, which look like little daisies emerging from between the stone-like leaves.

HEIGHT AND SPREAD 4 x 8cm (1½ x 3in).

CARE NOTES See left.

LITHOPS SALICOLA AGM
Salt-dwelling living stone

The salt-dwelling living stone has olive-green leaves decorated with an olive-brown lacy pattern on the upper surfaces. In some plants, this pattern is outlined in beige, so that the olive area looks like it is glowing. Daisy-like white flowers appear in late summer. Despite this plant's common name, it should be watered with fresh water, as you would do for the other members of the *Lithops* family.

HEIGHT AND SPREAD 4 x 8cm (1½ x 3in).

CARE NOTES See opposite.

LITHOPS PSEUDOTRUNCATELLA AGM
Truncate living stone

The truncate living stone has pale grey or buff-coloured leaves and an intricate spidery olive-brown pattern with matching spots on the upper surface. Sunny yellow blooms appear in summer or autumn.

HEIGHT AND SPREAD 4 x 8cm (1½ x 3in).

CARE NOTES See opposite.

ORBEA

Known for their unusual starfish-shaped flowers, *Orbea* have thick leafless stems that are often edged with spiny teeth or wide thorns. Another feature that will attract attention is the blooms' putrid scent. Designed to attract flies, they smell of dung or rotting flesh, and for this reason many people grow them outside during the flowering period in summer and autumn.

TEMPERATURE 5–30°C (41–86°F).

LIGHT Position in full sun but provide some shade in summer.

WATERING Water regularly from spring to autumn, allowing the surface of the compost to dry out between waterings. From late autumn to late winter, reduce watering so the compost is almost dry but the stems do not wrinkle. Provide good air circulation.

FEEDING Apply a half-strength cactus fertilizer once a month from spring to late summer.

COMPOST Plant in cactus compost, or a 50:50 mix of loam-based (John Innes No. 2 Peat Free) compost and 4mm grit.

FLOWERING Start watering in spring. Apply a little fertilizer to encourage flowering.

PROPAGATION Sow seed or take stem cuttings.

COMMON PROBLEMS These plants are prone to rot if grown in wet compost. Check regularly for mealybugs.

ORBEA VARIEGATA AGM

syn. *Caralluma variegata; Stapelia marmoratum*
Star flower

One of the most popular *Orbea* species, the star flower has long slim block-shaped stems with soft-tipped teeth along each of the edges. Relatively unassuming for most of the year, in summer it puts on a stellar performance when up to five large star-shaped purple-spotted white flowers appear. The blooms look amazing but smell horrible.

HEIGHT AND SPREAD Up to 25 x 25cm (10 x 10in).

CARE NOTES See above.

WARNING! This plant is toxic if eaten. Wear cactus gloves when handling this plant.

PACHYPHYTUM

Chubby-leaved and colourful, *Pachyphytum* are small slow-growing succulents, ideal for a mixed windowsill display. The leaves, which form little rosettes, may be tubular or round like pebbles, and come in a range of colours. Take care not to handle the plants, as the oil or pearlescent coating on the foliage is easily marked by fingerprints. The pretty leaves make up for the small bell-shaped flowers, which are quite plain in some species, and appear in spring and summer.

TEMPERATURE 5–30°C (41–86°F); will tolerate -5°C (23°F) for short periods if soil is dry.

LIGHT Position in full sun but provide some shade in summer.

WATERING Water regularly from spring to autumn, allowing the surface of the compost to dry out between waterings. From late autumn to late winter, keep the compost almost dry, watering just occasionally to prevent the leaves shrivelling.

FEEDING Apply a half-strength cactus fertilizer once a year in spring.

COMPOST Plant in cactus compost, or a 50:50 mix of loam-based (John Innes No. 2 Peat Free) compost and 4mm grit.

FLOWERING Water in the growing season to encourage blooming.

PROPAGATION Sow seed or take offsets.

COMMON PROBLEMS These plants are prone to rot if grown in wet compost. Check regularly for mealybugs.

PACHYPHYTUM COMPACTUM

syn. *Pachyphytum compactum* var. *compactum*
Little jewel

The torpedo-shaped leaves of the little jewel are olive-green with burgundy tips, and decorated with a delicate white marble pattern. Tall stems of pinkish-orange flowers with yellow centres appear in summer.

HEIGHT AND SPREAD Up to 30 x 15cm (12 x 6in).

CARE NOTES See opposite.

PACHYPHYTUM BRACTEOSUM

syn. *Echeveria bracteosa;*
Echeveria pachyphytum
Moonstones

Loose rosettes of silvery, pebble-shaped foliage give rise to this little succulent's common name. The leaves' shimmering colour and powdery texture are produced by a delicate coating that covers the plant and marks easily when touched, so take care when handling it. In spring, elegant bright red flowers open from silver buds coated with the same powdery film as the leaves.

HEIGHT AND SPREAD Up to 12 x 10cm (5 x 4in).

CARE NOTES See opposite.

PACHYPHYTUM HOOKERI

syn. *Echeveria hookeri*
Hooker's fat plant

The olive to blue-green cylindrical leaves of the Hooker's fat plant are like little fingers, while a white powdery coating looks as though the foliage has been dipped into icing sugar. The lower leaves often drop off as they age to reveal the stem beneath, and pinkish-red flowers appear at the top of tall stems in spring or summer.

HEIGHT AND SPREAD Up to 30 x 15cm (12 x 6in).

CARE NOTES See p290.

PACHYPHYTUM OVIFERUM AGM

Moonstones

Among the most popular of the *Pachyphytum* species, these moonstones (a few species have the same common name) have pebble-shaped pale blue-grey leaves. Their chalky coating makes them appear soft to the touch, but resist the temptation if you wish to avoid marking the surface. Reddish-orange flowers develop at the top of tall stems in spring.

HEIGHT AND SPREAD 10 x 30cm (4 x 12in).

CARE NOTES See p290.

PORTULACARIA

In its native South Africa, *Portulacaria* is commonly called an elephant bush because pachyderms consider the plant a delicacy. *Portulacaria* comprises a small group of shrubby plants, but only *Portulacaria afra* is grown as a house plant in cooler climes. The leaves are small and round, and either green or variegated. The plants produce little flowers, usually pink, in summer. They make architectural focal plants when grown indoors and, unlike most succulents, prefer a little shade, allowing you to grow them farther away from the window.

TEMPERATURE 5–30°C (41–86°F).

LIGHT Position out of direct sun in light shade.

WATERING Water regularly from spring to autumn, allowing the surface of the compost to dry out between waterings. From late autumn to late winter, keep the compost almost dry, watering just occasionally to prevent the leaves shrivelling.

FEEDING Apply a half-strength cactus fertilizer once in spring.

COMPOST Plant in cactus compost, or a 50:50 mix of loam-based (John Innes No. 2 Peat Free) compost and 4mm grit.

FLOWERING Flowers appear without any special treatment.

PROPAGATION Take stem cuttings.

COMMON PROBLEMS These plants are prone to rot if grown in wet compost. Check regularly for scale insects and mealybugs.

PORTULACARIA AFRA 'VARIEGATA'

syn. *Portulacaria afra* f. *foliis-variegatis;*
Crassula portulacaria
Elephant bush 'Variegata'

Sometimes confused with *Crassula ovata* (see p263) the elephant bush's round leaves are smaller than those of its close cousin. Plain green species are available but the eye-catching 'Variegata' has additional appeal, sporting pale silvery green foliage with wide cream margins, which contrast beautifully with the dark red spreading stems. In summer, clusters of small pale pink flowers appear at the tips of the stems.

HEIGHT AND SPREAD
Up to 60 x 90cm (2ft x 3ft).

CARE NOTES See opposite.

SANSEVIERIA

A great choice for anyone starting a collection of house plants, few species are easier to grow than *Sansevieria*. Originally from Africa and Southern Asia, they are grown for their spear-shaped or cylindrical green foliage, which in most widely available cultivars features yellow and white stripes and patterns. Many *Sansevieria* are also good for the home environment as they absorb air pollutants. The greenish-white or cream-coloured flowers, which look like spidery lilies, are rarely produced on plants grown indoors.

TEMPERATURE 10–27°C (50–80°F)

LIGHT Position in a bright area out of direct sun, or in light shade.

WATERING Water regularly from spring to autumn, allowing the surface of the compost to dry out between waterings. From late autumn to late winter, keep the compost almost dry, watering just occasionally to prevent the leaves shrivelling.

FEEDING Apply a half-strength cactus fertilizer once a year in spring.

COMPOST Plant in cactus compost, or a 3:1 mix of loam-based (John Innes No. 2 Peat Free) compost and 4mm grit.

FLOWERING Flowers rarely appear on house plants.

PROPAGATION Take offsets.

COMMON PROBLEMS These plants are prone to rot if grown in wet compost. Check regularly for mealybugs.

SANSEVIERIA CYLINDRICA

African spear; Cylindrical snake plant

Less well-known than its cousin (see right), the African spear produces long poker-like tubular leaves, which are dark green with paler green horizontal bands.

HEIGHT AND SPREAD 75 x 30cm (30 x 12in).

CARE NOTES See left.

WARNING! This plant is toxic if eaten.

SANSEVIERIA TRIFASCIATA

Snake plant; Mother-in-law's tongue

The tall sword-shaped leaves of the snake plant are dark green and form a tight rosette. Look out for variegated cultivars such as 'Laurentii', which has yellow-edged dark green leaves and silvery white horizontal bands. Greenish-white flowers may appear in spring or summer.

HEIGHT AND SPREAD 75 x 30cm (30 x 12in).

CARE NOTES See left.

WARNING! This plant is toxic if eaten.

SEDUM

Known collectively as stonecrops, *Sedum* comprise a huge range of species, including many hardy garden plants and some tender African and South American natives that are best grown indoors in cooler climes. All species feature fleshy succulent leaves, which come in a variety of shapes and colours. The house plants include decorative trailing types and small upright species ideal for a windowsill collection. While the leaves are the main attraction, *Sedum* also produce clusters of tiny starry flowers in summer or early autumn.

TEMPERATURE 5–30°C (41–86°F)

LIGHT Position in full sun but provide some shade in summer.

WATERING Water regularly from spring to early autumn, allowing the top 1cm (½in) of the compost to dry out between waterings. From autumn to late winter, keep the compost almost dry, watering just occasionally to prevent the leaves shrivelling.

FEEDING Apply a half-strength cactus fertilizer once every 6 weeks in spring and summer.

COMPOST Plant in cactus compost, or a 50:50 mix of loam-based (John Innes No. 2 Peat Free) compost and 4mm grit.

FLOWERING Plants will flower without any special treatment.

PROPAGATION Take offsets or stem or leaf cuttings.

COMMON PROBLEMS These plants are prone to rot if grown in wet compost. Check regularly for mealybugs.

SEDUM BURRITO
Burro's tail; Donkey's tail

A popular trailing house plant, the burro's tail will add texture and interest to a hanging basket display. Its flexible stems are covered with small spherical grey-green leaves that overlap like the hairs on a donkey's tail. The foliage may turn purplish pink when the plant is grown in strong sun. Little pink flowers appear at the tips of the stems in summer, adding hints of colour to the overall textured effect. Take care when moving this plant, as the leaves are prone to fall off, although this does little harm to the plant, and the foliage can then be used for cuttings.

HEIGHT AND SPREAD 10 x 30cm (4 x 12in).

CARE NOTES See left.

SEDUM MORGANIANUM AGM
Donkey's tail; Burro's tail

Almost indistinguishable from its close cousin, *Sedum burrito*, this species has slightly slimmer teardrop-shaped blue-green leaves. In summer it too produces small pink to red flowers at the tip of the stems.

HEIGHT AND SPREAD 10 x 30cm (4 x 12in).

CARE NOTES See left.

SEDUM PACHYPHYLLUM
Blue jelly bean; Many fingers

The blue jelly bean quickly fills a pot with its sprawling stems of silvery blue–green cylindrical leaves, which resemble chubby little fingers, hence its other common name. The foliage turns pink at the tips in winter and sometimes throughout the year, while large sprays of starry buttercup-yellow flowers appear in summer.

HEIGHT AND SPREAD Up to 30 x 30cm (12 x 12in).

CARE NOTES See p295.

SEDUM x RUBROTINCTUM AGM
Banana cactus; Jelly bean plant

Upright stems of little banana-shaped leaves give rise to this sedum's common name, although they are blue–green with reddish tips, rather than yellow. The stems eventually start to trail slightly as the plant matures. As with other *Sedum* plants, display it where the stems will not be disturbed, as the leaves fall off easily. Small star-shaped flowers appear in summer.

HEIGHT AND SPREAD Up to 10 x 20cm (4 x 8in).

CARE NOTES See p295.

SEMPERVIVUM

The intricate leaf rosettes of these alpine species look like little flower heads or cabbages, and the wide range of colours offers something for everyone. Some species are covered with a fine woolly webbing, others have smooth glossy foliage, while the leaves of a few types are protected by a powdery coating. In summer, a stout stem will push out from the centre of mature leaf rosettes. The starry flowers bloom at the top of this stem, after which that rosette dies, but there are usually a few offshoots growing around it to take its place.

TEMPERATURE -15–30°C (5–86°F).

LIGHT Position in full sun but provide some shade in summer.

WATERING Water regularly from spring to early autumn, allowing the top 1cm (½in) of the compost to dry out between waterings. From autumn to late winter, keep the compost almost dry, watering just occasionally to prevent the leaves shrivelling.

FEEDING Apply a half-strength cactus fertilizer once a month in spring and summer.

COMPOST Plant in cactus compost, or a 50:50 mix of loam-based (John Innes No. 2 Peat Free) compost and 4mm grit.

FLOWERING Plants will flower without any special treatment.

PROPAGATION Take offsets.

COMMON PROBLEMS These plants will rot if grown in wet compost. Check regularly for mealybugs and vine weevils.

SEMPERVIVUM ARACHNOIDEUM AGM
Cobweb houseleek

Highly prized for its woolly coating, the cobweb houseleek is a favourite among collectors, and just as easy to grow as the rest of the *Sempervivum* species. The leaves are green or reddish-green and it produces starry pink flowers.

HEIGHT AND SPREAD Up to 10 x 10cm (4 x 4in).

CARE NOTES See left. Take care when planting not to get compost caught on the webbing. It will be difficult to remove.

SEMPERVIVUM CALCAREUM 'GUILLAUMES' AGM
Houseleek 'Guillaumes'

Originally from the Alps of France and Italy, the leaves of this decorative little succulent are an eye-catching combination of apple green with dark burgundy red tips. The pretty leaf rosettes make up for the pale green flowers, which are not as showy as those produced by some other *Sempervivum* species.

HEIGHT AND SPREAD Up to 10 x 10cm (4 x 4in).

CARE NOTES See left.

SEMPERVIVUM 'OTHELLO' AGM
Houseleek 'Othello'

This sought-after cultivar adds a moody note with its dark red leaf rosettes. In summer, the pink flowers on tall stems provide an exciting colour contrast.

HEIGHT AND SPREAD Up to 10 x 10cm (4 x 4in).

CARE NOTES See p297.

SEMPERVIVUM TECTORUM AGM
syn. *Sempervivum arvernense; Sempervivum densum*
Houseleek; St Patrick's cabbage

This vigorous species will soon form a large clump of blue-green rosettes, suffused with reddish-purple tints around the edges. Starry purple-pink flowers appear on tall stems in summer.

HEIGHT AND SPREAD Up to 10 x 20cm (4 x 8in).

CARE NOTES See p297.

SENECIO

There are a number of tender senecio species in this large group of plants that are ideal for growing indoors in cool countries. They hail from areas of the world with a Mediterranean climate, and many have silvery leaves, while the foliage of some is covered with fine hairs that protect the plants from strong sun and drought. Daisy-like or fluffy looking flowers appear in summer and are usually yellow, or white in some of the trailing tender species. Many *Senecio* have now been reclassified under different species, but they may still appear for sale under their old name.

TEMPERATURE 5–30°C (41–86°F); will tolerate -5°C (23°F) for short periods if soil is dry.

LIGHT Position in full sun but provide some shade in summer.

WATERING Water regularly from spring to early autumn, allowing the top 1cm (½in) of the compost to dry out between waterings. From autumn to late winter, keep the compost almost dry, watering just enough to prevent the leaves shrivelling.

FEEDING Apply a half-strength cactus fertilizer once every 6 weeks in spring and summer.

COMPOST Plant in cactus compost, or a 50:50 mix of loam-based (John Innes No. 2 Peat Free) compost and 4mm grit.

FLOWERING Plants will flower without any special treatment.

PROPAGATION Take stem or leaf cuttings.

COMMON PROBLEMS These plants are prone to rot if grown in wet compost. Check regularly for mealybugs and aphids.

SENECIO HERRIANUS
String of beads

This *Senecio* is confused with its near relation, *Curio rowleyanus* (see p267), which also shares the same common name. You can tell them apart because this string of beads produces wiry trailing stems covered with teardrop-shaped leaves, while the curio has round bead-like foliage. Display it in a hanging basket where you can admire the delicate foliage and its small, white flowers, which look like tiny feather dusters, when they appear in summer.

HEIGHT AND SPREAD 5 x 60cm (2 x 24in).

CARE NOTES See opposite.

WARNING! This plant is toxic if eaten.

SENECIO RADICANS
syn. *Curio radicans*
Creeping berries; String of bananas

Another *Senecio* that may be found under *Curio* when searching, creeping berries produces long, trailing stems covered with banana-shaped foliage, hence its other common name. It grows quickly and will soon form stems up to 60cm (2ft) in length or more, so hang it up high in a basket where the sun will shine through the semi-transparent leaves. White cinnamon-scented flowers appear in summer.

HEIGHT AND SPREAD Up to 10 x 90cm (4 x 36in)

CARE NOTES See opposite.

WARNING! This plant is toxic if eaten.

AIR PLANTS

These tiny treasures can literally be grown in thin air, requiring no soil or compost to put on a performance. Plants come in a wide range of shapes and sizes, some resembling little sea urchins, while others look more like conventional bromeliads (see pp134-37), the family to which air plants belong. When mature, these beauties will burst into bloom, brightening up your home with exotic, colourful flowers. Few plants are easier to care for, so if you are a beginner, they will not disappoint.

TEMPERATURE 15-24°C (60-75°F)
LIGHT Filtered sun
HUMIDITY High
CARE Easy
HEIGHT & SPREAD 10 x 45cm (4 x 18in)

The foliage of these pocket-sized plants ranges from silvery and spiky, to curled and spidery. Most flower annually and the blooms are often surprisingly large and colourful. Plants die after flowering but, like all bromeliads, baby plants form to replace the old ones (see pp342-43).

WATERING Place in a tray of tepid rainwater or distilled water once a week for 30 minutes to an hour, then leave to drain (see p313). Avoid wetting the flowers by propping up the air plants.

FEEDING Mist with a specialist *Tillandsia* fertilizer once a month.

PLANTING AND CARE Display plants in glass jars or shells, or on driftwood, bark, or a decorative tray. Do not use glue. Keep in a humid area out of direct sun and away from radiators and heaters.

Tillandsia aeranthos

This air plant flowers reliably every year, with pink and purple blooms appearing between a spray of stiff green leaves.

AIR PLANTS
Tillandsia species and hybrids

Tillandsia argentea AGM

Tillandsia cyanea

Tillandsia tenuifolia

The thin, spiky foliage of this tiny species radiates out from the centre, resembling a sea urchin. Mature plants also bear a long, slim, red flowerhead, which holds tiny purple blooms that are guaranteed to turn heads.

One of the most popular air plants, the pink quill, as it is commonly known, has dark green strappy leaves and an oval-shaped flowerhead, made up of pink bracts (petal-like modified leaves) and small, violet-blue flowers.

This air plant soon forms a clump of spiky green foliage, and it will also tolerate a little neglect, quickly reviving after watering. The pink flower spikes resemble shooting stars and terminate in a cluster of tubular violet blooms.

Tillandsia bulbosa

Tillandsia juncea

Tillandsia xerographica

Like a spider with curled legs, the long thin foliage of this unusual air plant grows from a bulb-like centre, from which tubular pink and purple flowers emerge in early spring. The foliage also turns red when the buds form.

Small and compact, the silver grassy foliage of this elegant air plant is prone to drying out, so water it regularly every week. The blooms look like rows of tiny violet and pink lipsticks when they emerge from the narrow flower spike.

The silver foliage of this must-have plant sprawls and curls to form a dense clump. As it requires less water than most, mist regularly rather than soaking. The long-lasting spike of violet blooms only appears on mature plants.

CARE AND
CULTIVATION

BUYING A NEW
HOUSE PLANT

It's fun visiting the plant shop or nursery to pick out your favourite plants, but before you start spending, check out these tips to make sure you buy strong, healthy ones that will thrive. While you're there, pick up any tools you might need to care for them too (see right).

Cactus gloves
Covered in spines, cacti and some succulents should always be handled with care. Use special cactus gloves, or wrap bubble wrap or newspaper around stems.

IN THE SHOP

Take a shopping list of the plants you like with you and try to stick to it when you get to the nursery or garden centre. If, when you arrive, you fall in love with a plant that is not on your list, check the plant label carefully or ask the nursery staff first before buying to make sure you can give it the conditions it needs. If you are sure you will be able to look after it well, give your chosen plant a thorough health check (see right), and look under the container to see whether it has drainage holes. If not, repot it when you get home, as a lack of drainage frequently leads to waterlogging and fungal diseases.

GIVE YOUR PLANTS A HEALTH CHECK

Inspect any potential plant purchase carefully using this checklist, and reject any that show signs of distress or damage (see pp352–57).

1 **Check for signs of wilting**, which may be a sign of root problems.

2 **Look out for** dark spots or streaks on the leaves, stems, or flowers that could indicate disease or a virus.

3 **Inspect the undersides** of leaves and stems for signs of invertebrates or damage.

4 **Check the compost** is free from invertebrates.

5 **Tip the plant out** of its pot (if you can) and check that it is not root-bound.

6 **Look out for** any yellowing or shrivelled growth, which could indicate a lack of water or nutrients.

TAKING YOUR PLANT HOME

Depending on where you live, you may need to protect tender plants from the cold in winter by wrapping them in cellophane. Do not expose them to temperatures below freezing point, even for just a short time, as this could prove fatal for tender types. Avoid leaving plants in a baking hot car in summer, too. Pack the plants up securely in a sturdy box to keep them from harm during the journey home. If the odd leaf or flower stem is damaged, cut it off down to healthy growth or the base of the plant to prevent diseases entering through the wounds.

AT HOME

Unwrap the plant, inspect it for any signs of damage, removing any broken foliage or stems as needed. Repot it if necessary (see left), then place it, still in its plastic pot, in a waterproof container, known in the trade as a "sleeve", or on a saucer. Give the plant a good drink if required (see pp312–15) and leave it to drain. Finally, check the plant's other care requirements (see the Plant Profiles chapter, pp132–301) and place it in a suitable spot that provides the optimum light and temperature for it to thrive.

Check for drainage holes
Make sure the plant's pot has adequate drainage to prevent it from rotting. If it does not, repot it when you get home.

HOUSE PLANT TOOL KIT
With the tools and materials below, you will be fully equipped to care for the vast majority of house plants.

Small watering can with rose attachment for watering from above

Decorative waterproof pots and drip trays for drainage

Dibber for making holes in compost for seeds and seedlings

Small trowel for tiny pots

Pebbles

Slim-headed trowel for larger plants

Mister spray

Small sharp knife

Small hand fork

Secateurs for pruning

Soft cloth to wipe leaves

Brush for removing compost from cacti and delicate plants

UNDERSTANDING
GROWTH AND DORMANCY

Many plants have distinct seasons of growth, followed by a period of slower growth or dormancy dictated by the fluctuating light, temperature and rainfall they would receive in their natural habitat. Understanding this is key to caring for your plants through the seasons. When growing indoors, heat levels in particular can remain relatively stable through the year, so it pays to learn your plants specific needs and, if necessary, take steps to provide them with cooler conditions that mimic winter.

KEY

☐ Full sun   ☐ Light shade

☐ Filtered sun   ☐ Full shade

GROWING SEASON

This is the period from spring to early autumn during which many plant varieties experience active growth. The longer days and more intense light levels, together with the additional warmth, provide the ideal conditions for plants to put on new growth and, in some cases, flower.

DAYTIME CONDITIONS

Plants require plenty of sun and warmth during the spring and summer months, so place them relatively near a bright window where their needs will be met. However, they may scorch if displayed too close to a window that receives full, strong sunlight, especially in midsummer, when the light is strongest (see p350). Ensure that plants don't overheat when temperatures exceed 30°C (86°F), as many plants will start to suffer (see p351), and may become dormant.

NIGHT-TIME CONDITIONS

Plants need some fluctuation between daytime and night-time temperatures during their growing season, just as they would experience outdoors. Desert-dwelling cacti, for instance, typically require lower temperatures of between 13–19°C (55–66°F).

SUMMER SUN

Sedum and Echinocereus
These desert-dwelling prefer full sun, so keep them on or near a windowsill, but move them further back if they are at risk of being scorched.

Sansevieria
This leafy succulent can live in filtered sun or light shade, so does not need to be moved between summer and winter (see opposite).

Schlumbergera
As a tropical cactus, this plant needs light shade all year round, so keep it away from the bright summer sun.

OTHER GROWTH AND DORMANCY PATTERNS

While most plants grow and become dormant during the seasons described below, some follow a different pattern. Many epiphytic cacti (those that grow on trees in tropical habitats), such as Epiphyllum (see p208), Rhipsalis (see pp234–37), and Schlumbergera (see p238), are in active growth during autumn and spring, and flower in winter and early spring, when kept at around 10-15°C (50-59°F). They then become dormant during the summer. Always check the Plant Profiles to make sure that you are meeting your plant's light and temperature needs from one season to the next.

One room, two seasons

The illustration below shows the same plant-filled room, with a window letting in natural light, at two times of the year. The left hand side shows summer light levels, with full sun near the window fading to light shade at the opposite side. On the right, during winter, the area of light nearest to the window has weakened to indirect sun, while the area furthest from the window is in full shade.

WINTER SUN

Sedum and Echinocereus
Position these plants as close to the window as possible during winter to ensure they still get plenty of sunlight, making sure that they aren't in cold draughts or near a radiator.

Schlumbergera
Move this plant a little closer to the window during winter, so that it is not left in full shade.

DORMANT SEASON

From the middle of autumn to the end of winter, shorter days and low temperatures prompt most plants to stop growing. This is an important evolutionary adaptation, helping them to survive in their natural habitats and conserve energy, ready for the following year's growing season. Try to emulate these conditions indoors to keep your plants happy.

DAYTIME CONDITIONS

Keep plants cooler during this period, and reduce or stop watering, as recommended for your particular species in Plant Profiles (see pp194-99). Cacti and succulents may still need bright light during this time, so move them closer to the window so that they can make the most of the short days. Make sure they are not in cold draughts or too near a radiator (see p351), both of which could adversely affect plants kept on windowsills.

NIGHT-TIME CONDITIONS

As for the growing season, plants expect a nightly temperature drop during dormancy; many prefer around 10°C (50°F), while some can even cope with light frost if their compost is kept dry. On especially cold nights, do not shut plants on windowsills behind curtains, as the temperature beside the window could drop below freezing.

GET THE
LIGHT RIGHT

Providing your plant with the amount of light it needs is essential for its long-term health. Sun supplies plants with energy – too little may inhibit their ability to flower, while too much can scorch the leaves or lead to wilting, so assess the light levels in your home to find the ideal positions for your plants.

CHOOSING THE PERFECT SPOT

Whether you live in a bright house with windows on all sides, or in a small flat that receives little or no direct sunlight, there is a range of plants to suit your situation. Use this floorplan to help you identify what light levels you have in your living space, so that you can choose the best plants to match those conditions. Remember to take into account neighbouring buildings or tall trees that may cast additional shade throughout the day, and bear in mind that light levels may fluctuate over the course of the year, depending on the season.

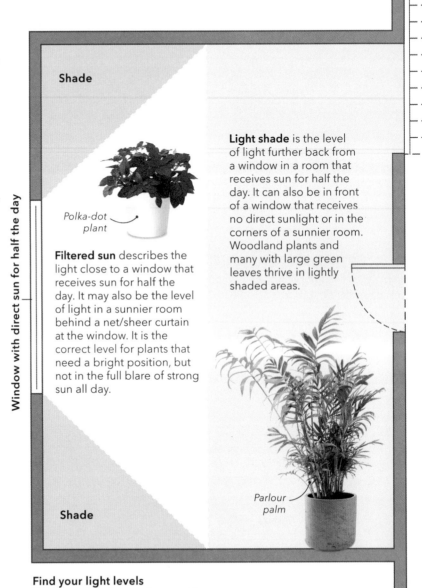

Shade

Window with direct sun for half the day

Polka-dot plant

Filtered sun describes the light close to a window that receives sun for half the day. It may also be the level of light in a sunnier room behind a net/sheer curtain at the window. It is the correct level for plants that need a bright position, but not in the full blare of strong sun all day.

Light shade is the level of light further back from a window in a room that receives sun for half the day. It can also be in front of a window that receives no direct sunlight or in the corners of a sunnier room. Woodland plants and many with large green leaves thrive in lightly shaded areas.

Shade

Parlour palm

Find your light levels
This floorplan shows a home with windows on three sides of the building, each letting in different levels of light, as described in the Plant Profiles chapter (pp132–301). Note that one room may receive up to three different levels of sunlight.

Front door with small window

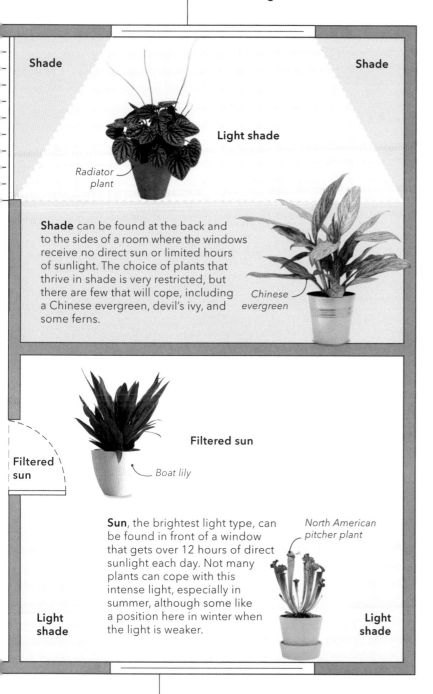

Window with
no direct sunlight

Shade

Shade

Light shade

Radiator
plant

Shade can be found at the back and
to the sides of a room where the windows
receive no direct sun or limited hours
of sunlight. The choice of plants that
thrive in shade is very restricted, but
there are few that will cope, including
a Chinese evergreen, devil's ivy, and
some ferns.

Chinese
evergreen

Filtered sun

Filtered
sun

Boat lily

Sun, the brightest light type, can
be found in front of a window
that gets over 12 hours of direct
sunlight each day. Not many
plants can cope with this
intense light, especially in
summer, although some like
a position here in winter when
the light is weaker.

North American
pitcher plant

Light
shade

Light
shade

Window with direct sunlight
for most of the day

TIPS FOR INCREASING LIGHT LEVELS

1 Clean leaves regularly to increase
the amount of light that reaches
your plant. Use a soft, damp cloth
to remove dust every week, taking
care not to damage the foliage.

2 Turn your plants by 90 degrees
every few days so that each side
receives sufficient sun and grows
evenly, no matter what light levels
your living space receives. This
will prevent the plant becoming
misshapen over time (see p351).

3 Take note of light variations
between seasons. In countries
with marked seasons, sunlight is
stronger in summer and weaker
in winter, when the days are also
shorter. In these areas, plants that
like filtered sun may need to be set
closer to a sunny window in winter.
If this is the case, take care not to
leave them trapped behind curtains
on a cold windowsill at night, as the
extreme drop in temperature could
cause them harm.

4 Boost low light levels in your
living space using artificial lights
(also known as "grow lights"),
which imitate the sun's rays. There
is a range of easy-to-install units
suitable for the home gardener;
but always ask the supplier's advice
before buying, as some may emit
too much or too little light for the
plants you wish to grow.

KEY

Sun

Filtered sun

Light shade

Shade

CHECK THE
TEMPERATURE

While most house plants will grow quite happily in our warm homes, they may suffer in extremely hot or cold spots. Check your plants' preferred temperatures (see pp132–301) and use the advice below to find the perfect spot to display them.

"Keep tropical plants away from heat sources and draughty areas."

PROVIDE OPTIMUM TEMPERATURES

While many house plants will cope with a relatively wide temperature range, always check your plant's specific needs in the Plant Profile chapter (see pp132–301). As many house plants come from tropical areas, few will be able to deal with long periods of very low temperatures. Equally, extended hot spells could cause some plants to dehydrate quickly and wilt. If you have a plant that you cannot identify, the safest range is between 12–24°C (54–75°F), which suits the majority of house plants.

Draughty hallways will suit a few woodland plants, such as the button fern, and tough types like devil's ivy and the umbrella plant. Other plants, including most tropical varieties, should be kept elsewhere, in areas where temperatures are consistently warmer.

Hot, dry areas near radiators, open fires, or heaters, are not suitable for any house plants, so keep them at a safe distance.

Button fern

Away from the window, temperatures will be more even throughout the day, which will suit plants that also prefer lower light conditions.

Bamboo palm

Find the right temperature
Use this illustration to identify different sources of heat and draughts and find the best locations to display your plants.

NORMAL TEMPERATURE VARIATIONS

All plants are adapted to deal with some fluctuations in temperature, but these should not fall below or exceed its minimum or maximum temperature requirements for long periods (see Plant Profiles, pp132–301), as this could harm the plant (see p351).

Day-to-night temperature drops of about 5–10°C (9–18°F) are normal for most plants, as that is what they would experience in nature. However, some plants, such as cymbidium orchids (see right), will only form flowers when there is a drop of more than 10°C (18°F) at night (see p325).

Seasonal temperature variations can be felt by most plants, even inside our heated homes, and in winter, this often leads to a reduction in growth. Some plants have adapted to cold climates by becoming dormant in winter; these will need to be moved to an unheated area at this time of year.

Cymbidium orchid

Heat rises, meaning that rooms will be warmer closer to the ceiling. Water and mist hanging plants more frequently than others in the same room.

Lipstick plant

The ideal spot for most house plants is an area a short distance from sunny windows and away from heaters and radiators.

Angel's wings

Rex begonias

Windowsills can fluctuate a lot in temparature, even those beside double-glazed windows. They can become extremely warm in summer and chilly during the winter. On hot days, open windows or turn on the air conditioning to keep the room cool, and do not trap plants between the window and curtains at night in winter.

HOW TO WATER YOUR HOUSE PLANTS

Watering most house plants can be pretty straightforward provided that you understand their individual needs. By following a few simple rules, you can make sure that they receive just the right amount of moisture to keep them thriving.

HOW TO WATER

To keep your plants in peak condition, check the specific advice for each one in the Plant Profile chapter (see pp132–301) and use the watering method (or methods) appropriate to your plant, as outlined in the six options on the right.

THE GOLDEN RULES OF WATERING

1 Keep plants in pots with drainage holes and tip out excess water from pot sleeves and saucers to prevent waterlogging.

2 Water most plants every 2–4 days (or as required) in spring and summer to keep the compost moist (not waterlogged).

3 Water desert cacti and succulents less frequently (only when the top of the compost feels dry).

4 Reduce frequency of watering in winter when plant growth is slower and temperatures are lower. For desert cacti stop in winter.

5 Check the Plant Profile chapter to see if your plant prefers rainwater or distilled water.

6 Lift the pot just after watering and as it dries out. You will quickly learn to recognise the weight of a wet pot and one in need of watering.

Watering cacti
Desert-dwelling cacti need to be kept almost or totally dry in winter, whereas tropical plants need more water in autumn and winter when they flower. Check your plant's specific needs in the Plant Profiles.

Watering from above
Pour water from above if your plant is happy for its foliage to be doused; most tropical plants and ferns are in this category. Make sure that the compost is also soaked or you risk watering the leaves without any moisture reaching the roots.

Watering from below
Set your plant in a pot with drainage holes in a tray of water about 2cm (¾in) deep. Leave for 20 minutes, then remove and drain. Use this method for plants that do not like wet leaves or stems, such as African violets, or if foliage is covering the compost.

WHEN TO WATER

Most house plants prefer moist compost in spring and summer when they are in growth, but take care not to water too much; soggy, waterlogged compost causes disease and can be fatal, while a little drought is easily remedied. To prevent wet compost, keep your plants in pots with drainage holes at the bottom, so that any excess water can drain out, and tip away any surplus that is sitting in the plant's decorative pot ("sleeve") or saucer about an hour after watering.

STOP THE ROT

Drought-loving cacti and succulents like their leaves and stems to remain dry, so add a layer of grit on top of the compost if repotting. A gravel "mulch" is decorative and helps water to quickly drain away preventing rot. You can use a syringe to water in a tight spot without wetting leaves.

MOISTURE LEVELS EXPLAINED

Almost dry compost should feel dry 2cm (¾in) beneath the surface, but may be slightly damp lower down. Most succulents and cacti require their compost to be this dry between waterings.

A dry top layer of compost should feel dry to the touch on the surface. Many plants should feel dry before water is reapplied; others may only need this level of moisture in winter when growth is slow.

Moist compost should feel damp to touch, but not look wet and glistening. Make sure the plant pot has drainage holes and tip out any excess water about an hour after watering.

Wet compost should be entirely soaked and have a glistening surface. Carnivorous plants are among the few that require this. Plant in a pot with drainage holes and stand in a tray of water.

Misting leaves and aerial roots
Some plants absorb moisture through their leaves and aerial roots. Examples include orchids, Swiss cheese plants and areca palms. Mist the leaves and roots regularly, but also water the compost to keep them healthy.

Watering bromeliads
The leaves and bracts (petal-like modified leaves) of most bromeliads form a cup-like reservoir in the centre of the plant. Fill this up with rainwater or distilled water, replenishing it every few weeks. Also water the compost so that it is moist.

Soaking air plants
Air plants are best soaked in a tray of rainwater or distilled water for an hour once a week. After soaking, leave to drain, and make sure they dry fully within 4 hours to prevent them rotting. Alternatively, mist them 2-3 times a week.

WATERING WHEN YOU GO AWAY

Most plants will survive a long weekend without any water, and many cacti and succulents will be fine for a couple of weeks if you bring them into a cool, bright room and give them a drink immediately on your return. For all other plants, you will need to take action. If you do not have a green-fingered neighbour or friend who can water while you are away, try these simple tricks to keep your plants in good health.

Water bottle method
Cut the bottom off a plastic water bottle, and make a tiny hole in the cap with a tip of hot skewer. Screw the cap onto the bottle and push it into the compost. Fill the bottle with water; this will then drip slowly into the compost. Make sure the plant pot has drainage holes so that the compost does not become too wet.

The wick system
Stand a bowl of water on an upturned pot so that it is higher than the surface of the compost. Weigh down a strip of capillary matting (available from garden centres) in the bowl, then push the other end into the compost. The matting will slowly water the plant. This technique is the best option for watering single plants, or large ones that cannot be moved.

"Use these clever tricks to keep your plants hydrated while you're away from home."

Easy sink method
Fill the kitchen sink with water and place either capillary matting or an old towel on the draining board, with one end in the water. Remove your plants from their sleeves and set them on the wet matting or towel, so that moisture can be drawn up through the drainage holes to the roots.

RAISING HUMIDITY LEVELS

The dry atmosphere in our homes can cause some plants' foliage to dry out and turn brown, inhibiting growth. The many house plants that hail from the tropics are especially vulnerable, as they are adapted to thrive in humid air. Try to replicate this atmosphere in your home using one or two of the methods here.

HUMIDITY LEVELS EXPLAINED

High humidity means that the air is saturated with moisture. Tropical plants thrive in this atmosphere, but they may be difficult to care for in homes with central heating (which can dry out the air). If you want to keep these demanding plants, place them in a humid kitchen or bathroom, or invest in a room humidifier.

Moderate humidity is required by many house plants, including orchids, ferns, some palms, and a large number of foliage plants. Misting them regularly, setting them on a tray of damp pebbles, and grouping a few together will help to raise the humidity to the correct level.

Low humidity is where the atmosphere holds little moisture. Plants from arid regions (such as cacti, succulents, and those from Mediterranean areas) are adapted to these conditions. Most rooms in centrally heated homes have low levels of air moisture, although drought-lovers will not cope well in humid kitchens or bathrooms.

Tray of damp pebbles
An easy way to raise humidity levels is to set your plant on a tray filled with stone or hydroleca ceramic pebbles. Pour in water so that it just covers the pebbles and set your plant pot on top. As the water gradually evaporates, it creates a humid atmosphere around the plant.

Misting plants
Increase the humidity around your plant by misting the leaves and aerial roots every day or two, reducing the frequency to once a week in winter for most plants. Check the advice for your chosen plants in the Plant Profiles chapter (see pp132–301) as some prefer to be misted with rainwater or distilled water.

Grouping plants
All plants release water through a process known as "transpiration", just like we do when we breathe out. You can create a tropical microclimate by grouping a few plants together, where each of them will benefit from the moisture released by their neighbours.

FEEDING
YOUR PLANTS

Put your house plants on a diet of essential nutrients and they will reward you with healthy flowers and foliage. Like us, however, they can suffer if you feed them too much or too little. Knowing what to feed your plants, and how often, will help them stay on track.

"Fertilizer provides the nutrients plants would draw from the soil if planted outdoors."

FOOD ESSENTIALS

While most plants growing in the ground can get all the nutrients they need from the soil, plants in pots rely entirely on you for their food supply. Many composts contain fertilizers, but after your plant has used these up, you will have to step in and start feeding them. The type of fertilizer and dosage depends on the plant, so check its specific needs in the Plant Profile chapter (pp132–301).

Well-nourished plants
A well-fed plant will display vigorous growth and none of the tell-tale signs of over- or under-feeding, such as yellowing or pale leaves.

PLANT NUTRIENTS EXPLAINED

The main plant nutrients are nitrogen (N), phosphorus (P), and potassium (K), also known as potash (see below). Balanced fertilizers contain all three nutrients, together with a range of trace elements that plants needs in smaller quantities. The nutrient content of a fertilizer is often shown on the packaging as a ratio of N:P:K; a balanced fertilizer, for instance, would be 20:20:20. Most plants only need to be fed when they are actively growing, usually between spring and autumn, and they require few or no extra nutrients in winter. Plants also take up fertilizer through their roots in a solution, so dry compost will not only dehydrate them but also limit their ability to absorb fertilizer.

Nitrogen (N) is known as the leaf-maker, because it promotes strong, healthy foliage. This in turn encourages good overall growth, since the foliage feeds the whole plant. It is particularly important for leafy house plants.

Phosphorus (P) is the root-maker, and it is required by all plants to grow and develop. The roots transport food and water to the plant, thus enabling strong and healthy growth.

Potassium (potash) (K) is essential for the development of flowers and fruits. Fertilizers with a high potash content are often given to plants a few months before they are due to bloom to encourage lots of buds to form.

CHOOSING A FERTILIZER

Different plants have different dietary needs, so make sure you are giving the correct fertilizer at the right dosage. Remember that overfeeding plants can be as bad, or worse, than underfeeding them (see p351).

Balanced liquid fertilizer
The majority of house plants need a balanced liquid fertilizer, which you can buy as either a powder or liquid that you then dilute, or as a ready-mixed solution. This type of fertilizer is applied at regular intervals throughout the growing season, usually from spring to autumn.

High-potash fertilizer
This fertilizer is rich in flower-promoting potassium (see opposite). It is usually sold as a liquid that you dilute before use. Tomato fertilizers have a high potash content, and can be used on flowering plants as well as those that produce fruits, such as the Jerusalem cherry.

Slow-release granular fertilizer
Large or woody plants, such as trees, shrubs, and perennial climbers, may benefit from an all-purpose granular fertilizer. Apply undiluted as granules or in tablet form (shown left) to the compost once a year, usually in early spring. Watering breaks down the granules, which then release their nutrients.

This bottle drip-feeds the orchid with a specially formulated fertilizer

Specialist house plant fertilizer
Manufacturers have developed fertilizers that have been carefully formulated for plants with specific needs, such as orchids, cacti, and carnivorous plants. They are usually sold in simple-to-use solutions; some, for instance, come in small bottles that can be inserted into the compost, where they drip-feed nutrients to the plant over time (see above).

CHOOSING COMPOST
FOR YOUR PLANTS

Use this guide to choose the best type of compost for your plant, and any additional materials you may need when potting it up. Always use fresh compost when repotting (see pp320–21); do not reuse old compost from other plants, as this will lack nutrients and could also harbour hidden problems.

WHAT IS COMPOST?

"Compost" (or, more accurately, "growing media") is the term commonly used to describe the soil-like material that potted plants are grown in. There are many different types, made up of a combination of soil (or "loam"), decomposed organic matter (similar to the compost you may make at home in a compost bin), aggregates such as sand and grit, and fertilizers. Specialist composts are made to emulate certain plant types' natural habitats, such as free-draining soil for desert cacti, or moisture retaining for tropical orchids and epiphytic cacti. Look for peat free alternatives, as the extraction of peat threatens the sustainability of natural peat bogs.

Multipurpose compost
Also known as all-purpose compost, avoid brands that contain peat. Made from natural materials, such as coir, bark, and composted wood fibre, most also contain enough fertilizer to feed plants for a few weeks.
BEST FOR Annual flowering house plants

Soil- or loam-based compost
Also known as John Innes compost, this type contains sterilized soil, together with some of the natural materials in multipurpose composts and a range of essential plant nutrients. It is generally used for plants that will live in their pots for more than one year.
BEST FOR Trees, shrubs, and perennial climbers

House plant compost
Formulated to meet the needs of most house plants, this offers a quick and easy solution if you do not know the needs of your plant. Check the labelling to make sure the product is peat-free and contains essential nutrients.
BEST FOR Most house plants, except for those with special needs, such as orchids and cacti (see opposite)

Seed and cutting compost

As the name suggests, this is the best choice for sowing seeds and taking cuttings. It is free-draining to prevent rotting and its fine texture means that even tiny seeds are in contact with the compost, aiding germination.

BEST FOR Sowing seeds; taking cuttings; potting up young seedlings

Specialist composts

Formulated for specific plant groups, such as orchids, cacti, or carnivorous plants, this range of composts takes the guesswork out of making your own mixes for plants that demand very particular conditions.

BEST FOR Orchids, cacti and succulents, carnivorous plants

Ericaceous compost

Similar to multipurpose, this compost is designed for plants that require acidic soil conditions, such as azaleas and blue hydrangeas. After planting, remember to use a fertilizer for acid-loving plants when those in the compost have been used up.

BEST FOR Azaleas, blue hydrangeas, and some ferns

OTHER MATERIALS YOU MAY NEED

The following materials are often mixed with compost to lighten or aerate it, or to help increase drainage. Check the potting advice for your particular plant in the Plant Profiles chapter (pp132–301) to see if it needs them, and the correct quantities to use.

Vermiculite (pictured) and perlite are minerals that have been heated to produce spongy grains. Both increase drainage while retaining and holding water well, then releasing it slowly back into the compost. They are often mixed with compost, or used to cover seeds to keep them moist.

Gravel and grit can both prevent soggy compost. Gravel, if added to the bottom of a pot, creates a reservoir that water can drain into, while smaller grit particles are often mixed with composts to increase drainage, providing ideal conditions for succulents and other drought-lovers.

Horticultural sand is often used in combination with compost to create the free-draining conditions succulents and other drought-loving plants need. Always use washed, sterilized, fine-grade sand; builders' sand contains too much lime for most house plants.

Leafmould is a crumbly dark brown material made from decomposed leaves, and contains a number of essential plant nutrients. It also holds water well, making it a good addition to the potting material of plants that prefer slightly more moisture around their roots.

REPOTTING
YOUR PLANTS

Repotting helps to make sure your plant's roots have the right conditions to grow and thrive, providingng it with adequate drainage, or more space for the roots to expand.

WHEN TO REPOT

Waterlogged compost may indicate that a plant's pot has no drainage, in which case it needs a new one with drainage holes. Plants should also be given a new pot when they outgrow their old one, which is usually every 2–3 years. As the plant grows, its roots fill the container until they become "root-bound", which means they are so compressed that they are no longer able to absorb enough water and nutrients to grow well. If a plant is showing signs of being root-bound (see below), it is ready for repotting.

IS MY PLANT ROOT-BOUND?
The following signs can indicate your plant is ready for repotting:

- Roots are emerging through drainage holes in the bottom of the pot (see below)
- Poor growth or yellowing foliage

- When removed from its pot, the plant's roots are coiled and densely packed
- Very dry compost, as roots take in all available water

HOW TO REPOT

If your houseplant needs repotting, follow these simple steps to transfer it to a larger container. Remember to protect yourself from spiny species using the tools pictured. For larger plants that you want to keep the same size, you can lightly trim their roots, and replace the top layer of compost with fresh compost and fertiliser.

WHAT YOU WILL NEED

PLANT
- Root-bound plant

POTS
- New pot one size larger than the old one, with drainage holes
- Decorative waterproof container and/or saucer (optional)

OTHER MATERIALS
- membrane or gauze, to prevent compost falling through the pot's drainage holes (optional)

- Grit or gravel, for top-dressing
- Compost to suit the plant (see Plant Profiles, pp132–301)

TOOLS
- Spoon or small trowel
- Bubble wrap or cactus gloves (for handling spiny species)
- Sharp scissors
- Soft-bristled brush
- Watering can (fitted with a rose attachment if necessary)

1 Water the plant well about half an hour before repotting, or 2 days before for cacti. Cut a piece of weed-suppressing membrane large enough to cover the new pot's drainage holes and place it in the bottom of the pot. Holding the pot on its side, scoop in a few spoonfuls of compost.

2 Using bubble wrap or cactus gloves if necessary, remove the plant from its old pot and carefully discard any top dressing. Gently tease apart any compressed or coiled roots, then brush away the old compost around the edges of the root ball with your fingers.

3 Check the roots for any signs of rot or invertebrates (see pp350-57). If you notice any dead or damaged roots, remove them with sharp, clean scissors, and remove invertebrates from roots, stems or leaves if you spot them.

4 Holding the part-filled pot on its side, gently place the roots of the plant on the surface of the compost. With a spoon or small trowel, carefully add more compost around the plant's root ball, making sure thecompost is sitting 1cm (½ in) below the rim. Firm the compost gently.

5 Most plants can be watered immediately. Allow cacti and succulents to settle in their pot for a week or two before watering. Add a grit or gravel mulch (see p319) to cacti to help keep their stems dry.

KEEPING YOUR PLANTS
IN SHAPE

If your plant has lost its shape, is threatening to outgrow its space, or has areas of dead or diseased growth, it needs a trim. Regular pruning can also encourage more flowers to form and make plants bushier. Follow these simple pruning techniques to keep your plants neat and in good health.

WHY PRUNE?

1 Reduce the height of the plant to keep its size in check, and to encourage the growth of new shoots further down the stems you have cut.

2 Cut away dead , damaged and diseased stems to reduce the risk of disease setting it.

3 Remove young side shoots that are growing into the centre of the plant where they will not receive adequate space or light to develop well.

4 Trim back leggy, over-long stems to keep the plant compact and encourage bushier growth, and remove any plain coloured leaves on variegated plants.

5 Thin out overcrowded stems to prevent them from rubbing against each other and becoming damaged, which could increase the risk of disease.

6 Encourage more flowers by taking out the old flowering stems, or 'deadheading'. This diverts energy from making seeds into producing more flowers.

BEFORE

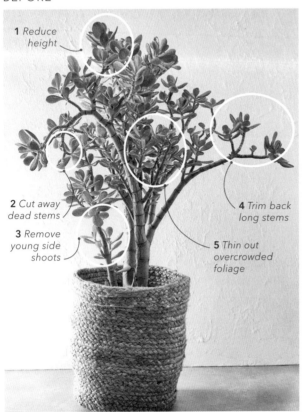

1 *Reduce height*

2 *Cut away dead stems*

3 *Remove young side shoots*

4 *Trim back long stems*

5 *Thin out overcrowded foliage*

AFTER

HOW AND WHEN TO PRUNE

While you can deadhead or remove unhealthy growth at any time, most plants are best pruned during early spring, before they start a period of rapid growth. If you have a large plant, remember that frequent pruning can stimulate growth, so take care if you want to keep it in check.

WHAT YOU WILL NEED

PLANT
- Misshapen or large plant that has outgrown its space

TOOLS
- Cloth, for cleaning tools
- Surgical spirit (rubbing alcohol)
- Secateurs or sharp scissors

1 Use a cloth soaked in surgical spirit to sterilize the blades of your cutting tools before use. This will prevent infections entering the plant when you make your cuts.

2 Inspect the health and shape of your plant to identify the areas you want to prune. Make the first cut, pruning just above a bud (bump on stem) or growth line. Continue making cuts, checking regularly to assess the plant's shape, until you are happy with its appearance.

PLANT MAINTAINANCE

Keeping plants clean and tidy helps them to look their best and stay healthy by improving their ability to absorb sunlight - vital for growth - and catching any problems before they become major plant health issues. Follow the advice below to enjoy your plants for many years to come.

Check plants
Inspect your plants every week or two for signs of poor growth, and other problems (see pp350-57). Don't forget to check the roots as well as the leaves and stems if the plant looks unhealthy.

Clean foliage
Wipe shiny leaves (not those with a delicate coating) with a soft cloth and dust spiny specimens with a small paintbrush once a week to remove dust and dirt. As well as dulling the plant's appearance, dirt can prevent foliage absorbing enough light for the plant to thrive.

Remove dead foliage
Shrivelled, dead, or damaged leaves, flowers, and fruits, not only look unattractive, but can also be a point of entry for rots and other problems if they are not removed. Also dispose of any that fall on to the compost before they rot.

HOW TO MAKE AN
ORCHID REFLOWER

Orchids are usually bought while flowering, and can bloom for many weeks if well cared for. When their flowers do eventually fade and die, encourage them to bloom again after a period of rest by following these simple steps.

BLOOMING HEALTH

The care needed to encourage an orchid to reflower will also keep your plant healthy, as you are offering the optimum conditions for it to thrive. A healthy orchid can live for decades, and bloom every 8 to 12 months.

WHAT YOU WILL NEED

PLANT
- Mature orchid with fading flowers

OTHER MATERIALS
- Pot one size larger than the original with drainage holes in the bottom (optional)
- Compost to suit the plant (see Plant Profiles, pp142–47)

TOOLS
- Secateurs
- Soft cloth
- Watering can
- Mister spray or tray of damp pebbles
- Suitable fertilizer

1 Cut back the flowering stems to just above the second pale horizontal band. This allows the plant to put all its energy into making new leaves, rather than seed, which will supply energy for the next set of flowers.

2 Ensure the plant receives plenty of light, as too little sun will inhibit flower formation. Bring it closer to a window during winter, when the light is weaker, and dust the leaves every week or two to maximize the amount of light they can absorb. Remember to move the plant back out of direct midday sun during summer.

3 Repot the plant if it is tightly root-bound (see pp320–21). Use a pot just one size larger than the original, as most orchids prefer slightly cramped roots.

4 Keep your plant hydrated as necessary, watering less frequently during winter. Mist the leaves and aerial roots every day or two with rainwater or distilled water, or set on a tray of damp pebbles (see p315).

5 Feed the plant using a specialist orchid or balanced liquid fertilizer, applying the correct dosage for your plant (see pp316–17). During winter, either feed the plant less or do not feed it at all, depending on its particular needs.

6 Check your plant's temperature needs, including if it requires a marked drop at night. After 9–12 months (depending on the type of orchid; see pp142–47), move it to a cooler room to encourage buds to form, then bring it back into the warmth to bloom.

KNOW YOUR ORCHID'S NEEDS

Each type of orchid requires slightly different conditions to thrive and reflower, so check yours in the Orchids section of the Plant Profile chapter (see pp142–47) and tailor your care accordingly.

1 Take seasonal variations into consideration. Some orchids from cool, humid forests like lower temperatures, while others, such as moth orchids, flower well in warmer conditions.

2 Look out for orchids that need a marked difference between day and night temperatures to form flowers; *Cattleya, Cymbidium, Dendrobium nobile*, and *Vanda* all fall into this category.

3 Check if your plant needs a high-potash fertilizer instead of a specialist orchid fertilizer to flower.

4 Be patient. While moth orchids could reflower after a dormancy of just 8 months, most orchids will only bloom once a year.

ENCOURAGING
CACTI AND SUCCULENTS TO FLOWER

With the right year-round care, many cacti and succulents can be encouraged to bloom indoors. Although there is no secret solution that guarantees flowering, you can encourage many mature plants to bloom in your home year after year as long as you keep them in good health.

CAN MY PLANT BLOOM?

Before you start thinking about encouraging your cactus or succulent to flower, take a moment to check whether or not it is possible.

NON-FLOWERING PLANTS

Even with the best care, some cactus and succulent species will not bloom when kept as house plants, as their natural conditions cannot be fully replicated indoors. Check the advice in the Plant Profiles (pp194–299) to see if your plant is likely to flower.

IMMATURE PLANTS

Some cacti and succulents will not flower until they reach a certain level of maturity, which can take many years for slow-growing plants. Obvious as it may seem, the easiest way to ensure that a plant is mature enough to bloom is to buy one that is already in flower. Once those flowers fade, continue to care for the plant and it should reward you with more blooms the following year.

Echinocereus rigidissimus subsp. rubispinus

Mammillaria guelzowiana 'Robustior'

Gymnocalycium baldanium

Notocactus ottonis

HOW TO ENCOURAGE BLOOMING

Flowering is a an energy-consuming process that starts long before the first buds begin to form. In order to bloom, you need to ensure that your cacti and succulents have enough energy to start the process.

DORMANCY

Many cacti and succulents need to experience an annual period of dormancy, during which time they conserve their energy for the following growth season, which will include their flowering period. By adjusting your plants' light, temperature, and watering needs as advised in the Plant Profiles, you can give them that all-important rest, before they start into growth again and begin to form flower buds.

NUTRITION

Despite their reputation for thriving on neglect, most cacti and succulents need feeding during their growth period, because nutrients are quickly washed through their free-draining soil when watering. Feeding is only necessary during the plant's growing season (for most, this is from spring to early autumn) when a diluted fertilizer (see right) should be applied once a month, or less frequently for some species. Reduce or refrain from feeding as the plant moves into a period of dormancy.

   Take care not to under- or overfeed plants, or to feed them during their dormant season, as this could lead to health issues, such as poor growth, yellowing leaves and stems, or excessive soft growth that will be prone to rotting (see pp350-51).

GOLDEN RULES FOR HEALTHY CACTI AND SUCCULENTS

1 Check the individual care needs of your plants in the Plant Profiles chapter (see pp194-299).

2 Use containers with drainage holes and allow the top of the compost to dry out before watering. Never leave plants standing in water.

3 Provide plants with the right temperature, depending on whether they are in growth or dormant. Make sure they have good ventilation in summer and keep them away from heaters in winter.

4 Position plants in the right amount of light, providing shading in summer if necessary.

5 Feed plants carefully with a specially formulated fertilizer for cacti and succulents (see right).

6 Keep plants free of dust and remove dead leaves and flowers, which may harbour fungal disease as they decay.

7 Inspect plants weekly for pests and diseases, and deal with them as quickly as possible if found (see pp352-57).

Astrophytum capricorne AGM

Mammilaria magallanii

Echinocereus viereckii subsp. *morricalii*

HOW TO GROW
BULBS INDOORS

Plant bulbs in autumn for beautiful floral house plant displays
in winter and early spring. In cooler countries, tender bulbs,
such as amaryllis, should be grown indoors, while hardy outdoor
types can be "forced" to flower earlier inside by growing them
in a cool spot, then moving them to a warmer room to bloom.

GROWING TENDER BULBS

Amaryllis bulbs (available from late autumn to midwinter) are tender and will die in frosty conditions outside, but they can be planted indoors where, with a little care, they will grow into beautiful house plants.

WHAT YOU WILL NEED

PLANTS
- Amaryllis bulb

OTHER MATERIALS
- Pot with drainage holes, slightly wider and about one and a half times as deep as the bulb
- Peat-free bulb fibre (specially formulated compost for growing bulbs) or multipurpose compost

TOOLS
- Watering can

1 Soak the bulb for a few hours. Set the bulb on a layer of bulb fibre, then fill in around it with more fibre, leaving up to two-thirds of the bulb showing above the surface.

2 Water well and leave to drain. Stand the pot in a bright, warm place. Water sparingly until shoots appear; then keep the compost consistently moist.

3 Turn the pot every day so that stems grow evenly. Move to a cooler room where flower buds will appear 6–8 weeks after planting, and stake the tall stems, if necessary. After blooming, feed the plant weekly with a balanced liquid fertilizer until the leaves die down. Keep in a cool, bright position, and do not feed or water when dormant, from late summer to mid-autumn.

GROWING HARDY BULBS

Outdoor bulbs are often "forced" to bloom earlier indoors than they would normally develop outside in the cold. Suitable bulbs include scented hyacinths (shown here) and grape hyacinths; daffodils and lilies of the valley require slightly different forcing methods (see below). Some bulbs, including hyacinths and paperwhite daffodils, will be labelled "prepared". These have been chilled to imitate a winter season, which they need to go through before flowering, and will bloom in winter, rather than spring. Other bulbs do not require this treatment to flower earlier indoors, but may not bloom until late winter.

1 Place a layer of bulb fibre in a pot. Water the fibre and leave to drain. Wearing gloves (the bulbs can cause skin irritation), space the bulbs evenly on the fibre, making sure the pointed ends face up.

2 Fill in around the bulbs with fibre so the tips are just above the surface. Leave a 1cm (½in) gap between the fibre and top of the pot. Place the pot in a black plastic bag and set in a cool dark place.

WHAT YOU WILL NEED

PLANTS
• Prepared hyacinth bulbs or unprepared grape hyacinth bulbs

OTHER MATERIALS
• Wide pot with drainage holes
• Bulb fibre

TOOLS
• Gloves
• Black plastic bag
• Watering can with a rose attachment

3 Check every week and water lightly if the bulb fibre is dry. When shoots are 5cm (2in) tall (usually 6–10 weeks later), remove the bag and bring the pot indoors into a cool room out of direct sun. Stand in a slightly warmer spot to flower.

FORCING DAFFODILS AND LILIES OF THE VALLEY

To force daffodil bulbs, follow Steps 1 and 2 above, but cover the bulbs with a thin layer of compost. Set in a cool room below 10°C (50°F) for 6–12 weeks in a bright spot out of direct sun, then in a warmer area to flower. The best scented daffodils for forcing are tender paperwhites, which flower within 12 weeks.

Grow lilies of the valley from rhizomes, known as "pips", which are sold in winter with the roots already growing. Soak the pips for 2 hours, then plant in soil-based compost in tall, deep pots with drainage holes, so the top of the pips are just below the surface. Water and leave in a cool room in light shade, out from direct sun. Flowers will appear 3–5 weeks later.

HOW TO
PROPAGATE PLANTS

Filling your home with the plants you love can be expensive, but many are easy to propagate, giving you lots of new plants from your original purchase. Use the guide below to decide which method suits your plants best; many can be propagated from cuttings, while others are better grown from divisions, offsets, or seed. Grafting is a little more technical but can be hugely rewarding.

PROPAGATE FROM SUCCULENT LEAVES

One of the simplest propagation methods, this can produce rooted baby plants in as little as a few weeks. Always select plump, fully grown leaves that show no signs of disease or damage. The best time to take leaf cuttings is in spring when temperatures are on the rise, as cool conditions will slow down the process.

WHAT YOU WILL NEED

PLANT
- Succulent plant with fleshy leaves, such as an *Echeveria* (shown here), *Sedum, Crassula,* or *Kalanchoe*

OTHER MATERIALS
- Small plastic pots with drainage holes in the base

- Cactus compost, or a 50:50 mix of loam-based compost (John Innes No. 2 Peat-Free) and 4mm grit

TOOLS
- Kitchen towel or plate
- Plastic container
- Cocktail sticks (optional)
- Watering can fitted with a rose attachment

1 Choose a plump, mature leaf from near the bottom of the plant's stem. Firmly tug the leaf to one side to detach it, ensuring the whole leaf comes away cleanly from the stem. Repeat until you have as many leaves as you would like to propagate.

2 Place the leaves on a tray or piece of kitchen towel and set them in a warm, dry area out of full sun for a few weeks to allow the base of each leaf to callus over. Do not water or mist them during this time. Roots and shoots may soon start to develop from the base of the leaves.

3 After a few weeks, pot up your leaves, even if they have not yet sprouted. Fill your pots with cactus compost. Carefully push the base of each leaf into the compost, gently burying any roots if they have sprouted. Prop up the leaves with cocktail sticks if necessary to stop them falling over.

4 Water often, keeping the compost moist but not wet. As the new plant develops, the original leaf will start to die off, at which point it can be removed. Once the new plant is established, repot it in a pot one size larger and follow its specific care advice (see Plant Profiles, pp194–299).

PROPAGATE FROM LEAF CUTTINGS

It may seem unlikely that a leaf can produce roots, but many plants will perform this trick. Begonias, like the Rex begonia shown here, are the most frequently used for leaf cuttings, but you can also try Cape primroses, the snake plant, and succulents, such as *Kalanchoe* and *Echeveria*. These other plants require slightly different methods (see opposite).

WHAT YOU WILL NEED

PLANT
- Mature plant with large healthy leaves

OTHER MATERIALS
- Peat-free cuttings compost
- Perlite

TOOLS
- Sharp knife or secateurs
- Cutting board
- 12cm (5in) plastic pots or small seed tray
- Repurposed plastic bags and rubber bands
- Small watering can with a rose attachment
- Small pots
- Spoon
- Peat-free multipurpose compost

1 Select a healthy mature plant with plenty of large leaves. Water it well about 30 minutes before taking your cuttings.

2 Select a large leaf and, using a sharp knife, remove it at the base of the leaf stem. Place on a clean cutting board.

3 Cut out a small circular section around the stem and discard. Divide the leaf into sections about 2cm (¾in) long, each with veins running through them (veins may be more visible on the reverse).

4 Fill a small pot or seed tray with cuttings compost and a handful of perlite. Press down gently to remove any air pockets. Carefully push the leaf segments in, so they are standing up with the veins in contact with the compost.

5 Using a small can fitted with rose attachment, water the cuttings to help to settle the compost around them. Ensure excess water drains away, or the cuttings could rot.

6 Seal the pot with a plastic bag secured with a rubber band and leave in a warm area out of direct sun. Cuttings take about 6–8 weeks to form new leaves and roots. When 2–4 leaves emerge, use a spoon to remove each cutting, keeping the roots intact, and transfer into small pots of multipurpose compost. Water well, and set in a warm, bright spot out of direct sun to grow on.

LEAF CUTTING METHODS FOR OTHER PLANTS

Cape primrose leaves should be cut either side of the midrib vein. Discard the midrib, and insert each side of the leaf into cuttings compost with the cut side down. Then follow steps 4 and 5.

Snake plants can be propagated by cutting a young, healthy leaf horizontally into 5cm (2in) sections. Take each of the sections and plant the edge that was closest to the base of the original leaf into cuttings compost. Then follow steps 4 and 5.

Succulent leaves should be kept whole and set aside for 24–48 hours until the cut ends dry out. Insert these ends into pots filled with a 2:1 mix of cactus compost and sand, then add some grit on top. Do not cover the cuttings. When 2–4 new leaves have emerged, plant them into small pots of cactus compost, water lightly, and place in a bright position to grow on.

PROPAGATE FROM
STEM CUTTINGS

One of the easiest ways to make new plants, this method is suitable for most soft-stemmed house plants. Take your cuttings in spring or early summer, when the plant is growing quickly, and use young, pliable stems, rather than older, woodier growth, which may take longer to root. Many plants, including this silver inch plant, will produce rooted cuttings in 6-8 weeks.

WHAT YOU WILL NEED

PLANT
- Mature plant with healthy young stems

OTHER MATERIALS
- Hormone rooting powder (optional)
- Small plastic pots or seed tray
- Peat-free cuttings compost

TOOLS
- Secateurs or sharp clean knife
- Dibber
- Small watering can fitted with a rose attachment
- Repurposed plastic bag and rubber band or clear seed tray or pot lid

1 In spring or early summer, select a non-flowering stem from a healthy plant. Using sharp secateurs, cut off a 10–15cm (4–6in) section from the tip, just below a leaf joint.

2 Remove the lower 2-3 leaves (or sets of leaves, if they are opposite each other). Take a few cuttings using this method, making sure you leave plenty of stems on the parent plant.

3 Dip the end of each cutting into hormone rooting powder. This is an optional step, as most stems will produce roots without it, but they may take longer.

5 Insert up to 3 cuttings per pot, or plant 6 in a small seed tray. Settle the compost around the stems by watering lightly with a watering can fitted with a rose attachment.

4 Fill a small plastic pot or seed tray with cuttings compost. With a dibber, make a hole in the compost. Place the cutting into the hole and firm around it gently.

PROPAGATE FROM **CACTUS STEMS**

This is a very simple method for propagating cacti, and can also help to save stems that have been damaged or are suffering from disease. The stem is removed and the healthy section repotted, allowing it to survive, while the damaged area is discarded. Of course, you can just take a healthy stem and use this for propagation too. Columnar cacti can be cut at any point along the stem, while segmented cacti stems, such as those of *Schlumbergera* and *Opuntia*, should be cut where two segments meet. Take cuttings in early spring for the best chances of success.

WHAT YOU WILL NEED

PLANT
- Cactus with tall or trailing stems, such as *Cleistocactus* (shown here), *Ferocactus*, *Opuntia*, and *Schlumbergera*

OTHER MATERIALS
- Plastic pots with drainage holes in the base
- Peat-free cactus compost, or a 50:50 mix of loam-based compost (John Innes No. 2 Peat-Free) and 4mm grit

TOOLS
- Bubble wrap or cactus gloves (optional)
- Clean, sharp secateurs
- Dibber
- Wooden sticks
- Watering can with a narrow spout

Damaged stem

1 Using bubble plastic or gloves if necessary, grip the chosen cactus stem and cut it from the plant with secateurs, ensuring the healthy cutting is at least 10cm (4in) long. If the stem is partially damaged or diseased, make the cut at least 4cm (2in) below the affected area.

2 Remove and dispose of the damaged area (if necessary). Place the cutting in a warm, dry, shady spot where the spines will not cause any damage. Leave it for around two weeks, or until until the cut end calluses over.

3 Once the cutting has fully callused over, fill a pot with cactus compost. Use a dibber to make a hole in the compost large enough to fit the base of the cutting.

5 If necessary, push a couple of wooden sticks into the soil to support the cutting and prevent it from toppling over. Water the compost then leave to drain. Place in a warm, dry, lightly shaded area indoors, watering only when the top 1cm (½in) of compost is dry. Once roots form and the cactus begins to grow, follow its specific care instructions (see Plant Profiles, pp194–299).

4 Insert the cutting into the hole in the compost so that 2½–5cm (1–2in) is beneath the surface, depending on the length of the cutting. Use the dibber to gently firm the compost around the cutting until it is secure.

PROPAGATE FROM **SUCCULENT AND CACTUS OFFSETS**

Many mature cactus and succulent species develop offsets: little "babies" produced by a mature "mother" plant. Offsets can be removed and potted up easily to make new plants, offering a great way for beginners to increase a cactus or succulent collection without too much effort. Offsets should be taken in early spring for the best results.

1 Gently remove an offset from the mother plant. Small offsets can be pulled off easily with your hands (wearing gloves if necessary) or a pair of tweezers, while larger offsets may need to be cut away with a sharp knife.

2 Place the offsets in a warm, dry, shady area for about two weeks, or until the ends have callused over. Small roots may begin to appear but are not necessary at this stage for successful propagation.

WHAT YOU WILL NEED

PLANT
- Offset-producing cactus or succulent plant, such as *Mammillaria* (shown here), *Echinocactus*, *Gymnocalycium*, *Matucana*, *Rebutia*, and *Aloe*

OTHER MATERIALS
- Small plastic pots with drainage holes in the base
- Peat-free cactus compost, or a 50:50 mix of loam-based compost (John Innes No. 2 Peat-Free) and 4mm grit

TOOLS
- Cactus gloves (optional)
- Tweezers or a sharp, clean knife (optional)
- Watering can fitted with a rose attachment

3 Fill the pots with cactus compost. Place one offset in each pot, so the base is in contact with the compost. Gently water them from above. Leave the offsets in a lightly shaded area to grow on, watering them only when the top 1cm (½in) of compost is dry. As the offsets mature, move them to a sunnier position and follow the relevant care instructions (see Plant Profiles, pp194–299).

PROPAGATE FROM SUCCULENT STEMS

Succulents with woody stems, such as *Aeonium* and some *Crassula*, are ideal for taking cuttings, while the fleshier stems of *Sedum* and *Kalanchoe* can also be propagated in this way. Stem cuttings are generally quick to root, producing new plants in no time. This propagation technique also helps to prune the "parent" plant, which will benefit from the process (see pp322-23), developing more stems further down the plant. Take cuttings in spring.

1 Remove a leafy side stem at least 7–10cm (3–4in) from the "parent" plant. Strip away any lower leaves so that the bottom 2–3cm (1–1½in) of stem is clear. Repeat with several more cuttings.

2 Set the stems in a warm, dry area out of direct sunlight for a few weeks, until the ends callus over. Fill the pots with compost and gently insert one stem into each, so the leaves are just above the surface.

WHAT YOU WILL NEED

PLANT
- Succulent with stems, such as *Aeonium* (shown here), *Crassula*, *Kalanchoe*, and *Sedum*

OTHER MATERIALS
- Plastic pots with drainage holes in the base
- Cactus compost, or a 50:50 mix of loam-based compost (John Innes No. 2 Peat Free) and 4mm grit

TOOLS
- Sharp, clean secateurs or scissors
- Watering can fitted with a rose attachment

3 Place the cuttings in a plastic tray, water them, and allow to drain. Leave in a warm area out of direct sunlight, watering the cuttings when the top of the compost is just dry.

4 Once the plants take root and new growth develops above the surface, follow the relevant care instructions (see Plant Profiles, pp194–299).

PROPAGATE WITH
WATER

Quick and easy to do, this is a great propagation method for beginners. It is also fun for children, as they can watch the roots developing on the cut stems day by day. A large number of house plants can be increased in this way, especially those with soft, pliable stems, such as the African violet (used here), devil's ivy, and species of *Peperomia* and *Pilea*.

WHAT YOU WILL NEED

PLANT
- Mature healthy plant

OTHER MATERIALS
- Peat-free multipurpose compost

TOOLS
- Scissors, sharp clean knife, or secateurs
- Glass or jar
- Small pots with drainage holes

1 Choose a healthy non-flowering stem and remove it at the base with a knife, scissors or secateurs. Cut the stem below a node (bump on the stem) if there is one.

2 Ensure the leaf has a clear portion of stem at least 5cm (2in) long. If the stem has a number of leaves growing from it, remove the bottom sets to leave the lower stem clear.

3 Place the cutting in a glass of water, ensuring the leaf or leaves are not submerged; rest them on the sides. After a few weeks, roots will grow from the base of the stem.

4 When a good root system has developed in the water, transplant each cutting into a small pot of multipurpose compost. Grow on in a bright area out of direct sunlight.

PROPAGATE BY
DIVIDING PLANTS

Some plant varieties produce a network of fibrous roots that throw up new stems around the sides of the plant. If you see you see new shoots growing around the base of a mature ("parent") plant, use this simple method to divide it up to make two or three new ones. Here, we have divided a snake plant; other suitable plants that are easy to divide include cast iron plants, asparagus ferns, Boston terns, peace lilies, and most *Goeppertia*.

WHAT YOU WILL NEED

PLANT
- Mature healthy plant with shoots growing around the sides

OTHER MATERIALS
- Peat-free multipurpose compost

TOOLS
- Watering can
- Sharp, clean knife
- Plastic pots that match the size of the root balls

1 Water the plant about an hour before removing it from its plastic pot. Using your fingers, remove some of the compost from the root ball, so you can see more clearly where the stems are attached to the roots.

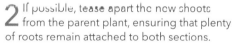

2 If possible, tease apart the new shoots from the parent plant, ensuring that plenty of roots remain attached to both sections.

3 If the root ball is too congested, use a sharp knife to cut it into sections, ensuring that the stems all have some roots (severing a few roots is fine).

4 Fill new pots with multipurpose compost. Plant the divisions in the pots, taking care not to damage the roots. Set them at the same level they were growing at in their original pot; do not bury the stems. Water, and set in a warm, bright spot out of direct sun.

PROPAGATE FROM
OFFSETS

Offsets are young plantlets (known as "pups") that grow from the parent plant. Some plants produce offsets that replace the parent when it dies after flowering; this is the case for all bromeliads (shown here), as well as some cacti and succulents. Mature spider plants, meanwhile, regularly produce offsets from long cascading stems, which can be potted up to create new plants (see opposite).

WHAT YOU WILL NEED

PLANT
- Mature, flowering bromeliad with offsets growing around the base

OTHER MATERIALS
- Hormone rooting powder
- Peat-free cactus compost (or a 2:1 mix of soil-based compost and sand)
- Perlite

TOOLS
- Sharp clean knife
- Soft clean brush
- 10cm (4in) plastic pots
- Short stick for staking
- Small watering can with a rose attachment

1 Check that the offsets around the base of the plant are between one-third and one-half of the size of the parent before removing them. These will root more successfully than younger offsets.

2 Carefully remove the plant from its pot. With a sharp knife, cut off the offset close to the parent. Try not to damage the parent plant; it can be repotted if it has not died back, as it may yet go on to produce more offsets.

3 If there is a papery leaf covering the end of the offset, pull this back to reveal the base and dust with hormone rooting powder. Do not worry if the base does not yet have roots; they are not essential for success at this stage, as the powder will encourage root growth.

4 Fill a 10cm (4in) plastic pot with cactus compost mixed with a handful of perlite. Insert the base of the offset into the compost, taking care not to bury too much of the stem, which may rot. Water lightly to settle the compost around the offset.

5 If the offset is too heavy to stand up on its own, stake it with a short stick. Set the pot in a bright position out of direct sun, and keep the compost moist, but not wet. Roots will develop after a few weeks. Repot when new shoots appear, following the advice for your bromeliad in the Plant Profiles chapter (see pp134-37). Offsets take 2-3 years to mature and flower.

POTTING UP "SPIDER" OFFSETS

Spider plants are easy to propagate from the offsets (known as "spiders", which give the plant its name). These grow at the ends of long stems that cascade down from the parent plant.

1 Wait until your plant has produced a few small leafy offsets at the tips of the cascading stems. Look for those that are healthy and have a few sets of leaves.

2 Select an offset with a tiny root growing from the base. Fill a small plastic pot with cuttings compost, and set the offset into the compost; do not bury it too deeply.

3 Do not cut the offset from its parent yet. Keep the compost moist, and wait for new shoots to appear. This is a sign that the offset has made its own root system, and you can then cut it free from the parent plant.

PROPAGATE FROM
SEED

Many houseplants are surprisingly easy to raise from seed, offering you a great way to increase your plant collection for very little outlay. Annual plants are good choices for beginners, and so are cacti (shown here). Seeds can be sourced online or by visiting specialist nurseries. Buy fresh seeds every year for the best results. Depending on the variety, some seeds will germinate within a few weeks, while others can take up to a year of pampering, so patience may be required. Late winter or early spring is the best time to sow seed, if you have a heated propagator to keep them warm.

1 Fill the small pots, or seed tray, with compost and firm gently. Sprinkle the seeds evenly over the surface; larger seeds may need covering with sieved compost or vermiculite (check seed packs for sowing depths).

WHAT YOU WILL NEED

PLANT
- Packet of seeds

OTHER MATERIALS
- Seed tray with clear plastic lid
- Small plastic pots with drainage holes in the base
- Module seed tray
- Larger pots
- Peat-free seed and cutting compost, or cactus compost
- Peat-free multipurpose compost
- Vermiculite

TOOLS
- Tray, for watering
- Sieve, for compost (optional)
- Plant labels
- Watering can
- Propagator tray or clear plastic bag and rubber band
- Mister
- Spoon or small trowel

2 Place the pots in a large tray and part-fill the tray with water. Leave for 1 hour or until the surface of the compost darkens, showing it is damp, then remove the pots.

3 Label the pots with the name of the plant and the date the seed was sown. Transfer the seed pots to a propagator tray and cover with the clear plastic lid. If you do not have a propagator, cover the pots with a plastic bag secured with a rubber band. Place the pots or propagator in a bright area out of direct sun; the seeds need light to germinate.

4 Leave the seeds to germinate. Remove the propagator lid or plastic bag daily for a brief period, wiping away any excess condensation. Mist the the surface of the compost if it becomes dry. As soon as seedlings appear, remove the lid or bag. Leave the seedlings to grow on, continuing to mist the surface every few days to keep the compost damp but not wet.

5 After a few months, the seedlings should be large enough to handle. Remove them from the pot and gently tease them apart, one seedling at a time, taking care not to tear the stem from the roots.

6 For each seedling, part-fill a clean pot with fresh compost. Holding the pot on its side, lie the seedling down on the compost so that its roots reach into the pot. Carefully backfill with compost until the roots are covered and the seedling is secure but not buried.

7 Repeat steps 4-6 for the remaining seedlings and place them in a warm, bright spot out of direct sun. Turn them every day or two so that the plants grow evenly and do not stretch towards the light. Continue to mist them every few days, allowing cacti compost to dry out between waterings. Keep the compost moist for other plants. Once the seedlings mature, you can transplant them into larger pots. Follow the relevant care advice for your plant (see Plant Profiles, pp194-299).

HOW TO GRAFT CACTI

Not for the faint-hearted, grafting cacti is a little like plant surgery: the base ("rootstock") of one cactus is combined with a cutting ("scion") of another. The result is a unique living creation that, if successfully grafted, could thrive and even flower over many years. Grafting is a great way to accelerate the growth of a cactus that matures slowly by securing it onto one that grows quickly. Flat grafting (shown here) is the easiest method, and can be performed on columnar and round cacti with similar-diameter stems. For slim-stemmed cacti, try side grafting (see opposite). In all cases, for best results, choose two healthy cacti of roughly the same width.

1 Make a horizontal cut through the rootstock at least 2.5cm (1in) below the growing point at the top.

2 Bevel the edges of the cut by slicing off 5mm (¼in) of skin at an angle around the stem's circumference. This prevents the inner flesh shrinking when it dries to a level below the hard skin, which will mean the rootstock will not fit snugly on the scion.

WHAT YOU WILL NEED

PLANTS
- Columnar cactus to be used as rootstock
- Round cactus to be used as scion

TOOLS
- Cactus gloves
- Sharp, clean knife
- Elastic bands
- Watering can with a narrow spout

3 Cut horizontally through the scion at the base. As with the rootstock, bevel off 5mm (¼in) of skin around the edge to help the plants fuse together well.

4 Both the scion and rootstock will have a ring made up of tubes in the centre. These tubes transport water and nutrients, and the rings of both scion and rootstock must line up when they are brought together. If the rings are not aligned, the grafted plant will die.

5 Align the cut surfaces and rotate the scion to disperse air pockets. Secure in place with elastic bands, making sure it is not too tight. Place in a warm, humid area out of full sun – the humidity ensures the flesh does not shrink back. Remove the bands at the first sign of active growth (around 4 weeks).

SIDE GRAFTING

This variation of the basic technique is ideal for grafting slim-stemmed cacti, which often have narrow central rings. Cutting both plants at a shallow angle exposes a larger area of the ring, making it easier to line them up when uniting the rootstock and scion.

1 Using a clean knife cut the rootstock at an oblique angle, about 2.5cm (1in) below the growing point, or until the ring is clearly exposed. Cut away 5mm (¼in) of skin all around the cut to bevel the edge (see Step 2, opposite).

2 Cut through the scion near the base at a corresponding angle and bevel the cut edge.

3 Press the cut surfaces together, aligning both rings and removing air pockets. Secure in place with elastic bands (see below), making sure you do not damage either scion or rootstock in the process.

4 Support the grafted plants with a thin cane and twine if necessary. Remove the bands when the scion has started to show signs of active growth, usually after 4 weeks or so.

WHAT'S WRONG
WITH MY PLANT?

If your plant isn't thriving the way it should, take a look through these pages to identify a cause and find a solution. More often than not, poor plant health is a result of insufficient or incorrect care. This can lead to a range of care-based problems, and can also increase the risk of damage from plant feeding invertebrates.

TROUBLESHOOTING
Once you've identified the most likely cause of your plant's ailment, turn to the following pages to find the solution:

Care-based problems are usually the most likely cause of poor house plant health. **(pp350–51)**

Diseases can also be a potential cause; familiarise yourself with the warning signs and learn how to treat them. **(pp356–57)**

Plant-feeding invertebrates are another possibility, so remove them if you spot any. **(pp352–55)**

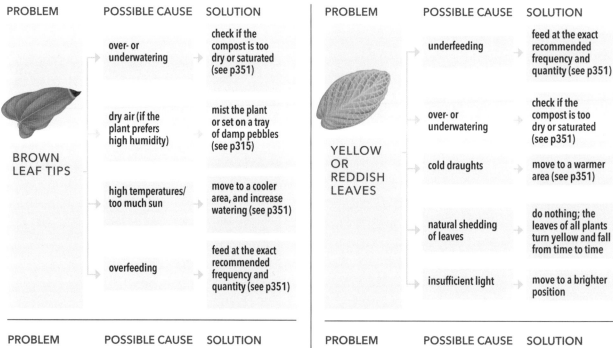

PROBLEM	POSSIBLE CAUSE	SOLUTION
BROWN LEAF TIPS	over- or underwatering	check if the compost is too dry or saturated (see p351)
	dry air (if the plant prefers high humidity)	mist the plant or set on a tray of damp pebbles (see p315)
	high temperatures/ too much sun	move to a cooler area, and increase watering (see p351)
	overfeeding	feed at the exact recommended frequency and quantity (see p351)

PROBLEM	POSSIBLE CAUSE	SOLUTION
YELLOW OR REDDISH LEAVES	underfeeding	feed at the exact recommended frequency and quantity (see p351)
	over- or underwatering	check if the compost is too dry or saturated (see p351)
	cold draughts	move to a warmer area (see p351)
	natural shedding of leaves	do nothing; the leaves of all plants turn yellow and fall from time to time
	insufficient light	move to a brighter position

PROBLEM	POSSIBLE CAUSE	SOLUTION
HOLES IN LEAVES	Invertebrate damage	check leaves and compost (see pp352–55)
	physical damage due to people or pets brushing past	move to a more protected area

PROBLEM	POSSIBLE CAUSE	SOLUTION
CURLED LEAVES	high temperatures	move to a cooler area, and increase watering (see p351)
	invertebrate damage	check leaves and compost (see pp352–55)

PROBLEM	POSSIBLE CAUSE	SOLUTION
SPOTS ON LEAVES	dark brown spots: overwatering	check the compost is not saturated (see p351)
	dry patches: underwatering	water more frequently to keep the compost moist (see p351)
	pale spots: misting with hard water	use rainwater or distilled water to mist the plant
	disease damage	check leaves for signs of infection (see pp352–57)

PROBLEM	POSSIBLE CAUSE	SOLUTION
SUDDEN LEAF FALL	environmental change due to repotting or new position	wait a few days; the plant should soon recover
	invertebrate damage	inspect roots for invertebrates (see pp352–55)

PROBLEM	POSSIBLE CAUSE	SOLUTION
FLOWER BUDS FALL	dry air (if the plant prefers high humidity)	mist the plant or set on a tray of damp pebbles (see p315)
	under- or overwatering	check if the compost is too dry or saturated (see p351)
	wrong temperature	check advice and move if too hot or too cold (see p351)
	invertebrate damage	check buds, stems, leaves and compost for invertebrates (see pp352–55)

PROBLEM	POSSIBLE CAUSE	SOLUTION
WILTED LEAVES AND STEMS AND POOR GROWTH	over- or underwatering	check if the compost is too dry or saturated (see p351)
	root-bound	repot the plant into a container one or two sizes larger so roots can absorb water more easily
	diseased roots	identify the disease (see pp356–57) and treat as suggested
	high temperatures/ too much sun	move to a cooler area, and increase watering (see p351)
	invertebrate damage	check the leaves and roots for invertebrates (see pp352–55)

PROBLEM	POSSIBLE CAUSE	SOLUTION
FURRY GROWTH ON LEAVES AND STEMS	fungal diseases	identify the disease (pp356–57) and treat as suggested

PROBLEM	POSSIBLE CAUSE	SOLUTION
NO FLOWERS	too little light	move into an area with more sun(see p350)
	over- or underfeeding	feed at the exact recommended frequency and quantity (see p351)
	dry air or compost	mist the plant if it likes high humidity and check if the compost is too dry or the temperature is too high
	pot too big	repot to a smaller pot; some plants only flower when roots are restricted
	immature plant	wait for the plant to mature (see pp326–27)

DEALING WITH
CARE-BASED PROBLEMS

The health of houseplants is most likely to suffer as a result of the wrong care or growing conditions. Thankfully, these problems are often easily remedied if identified quickly. Use this guide to diagnose any issues you find and adjust your plant's care conditions accordingly. If there is no improvement after a few days, consult pp352–57 to see if there is another cause, such as disease.

TOO WARM

THE PROBLEM Even in spring and summer, most plants will stop growing at temperatures above 30ºC (86ºF) and all will be vulnerable to scorching (see opposite). High temperatures also cause compost to dry out faster, leading to underwatering (see right) and may also reduce the humidity levels in the air. Symptoms can include brown leaf tips, curled leaves, wilting, falling flower buds, or no flowers.

THE SOLUTION Keep temperatures down by shading windows in summer with a net curtain or moving plants out of bright sun, and opening windows or doors to provide good ventilation. Move plants away from radiators and other direct heat sources. Also water more frequently when temperatures rise to keep the compost moist (but not too wet – see right).

TOO COLD

THE PROBLEM Low indoor temperatures will slow plant growth, but fluctuations in temperature caused by cold draughts and shutting plants behind curtains at night can cause brown marks on the plant's body or foliage, flower buds to drop, or rotting if the compost is wet.

THE SOLUTION Protect plants from cold draughts and move them away from windowsills at night during winter. Check the minimum temperature limits for your plant (see Plant Profiles). Keep watering to a minimum or stop altogether in cool conditions, as recommended for your plant.

Scorched leaves are the result of too much strong sunlight

INSUFFICIENT LIGHT

THE PROBLEM Certain plants flourish in bright sunlight. Given too much shade, they will stretch towards the light and become "etiolated", with elongated, spindly growth that is washed-out or yellow in colour. Where light only comes from one direction, such as on a windowsill, plants can quickly become lopsided.

THE SOLUTION Ensure that your plant is given the correct light levels (see Plant Profiles). Move drawn-out, etiolated specimens to a brighter spot. Turn pots on windowsills every few days to avoid plants reaching towards the sunlight and becoming lopsided.

Plants standing in insufficient light will become misshapen as the stems stretch towards the sun

TOO MUCH LIGHT

THE PROBLEM Although many plants need full sun, even cacti and succulents can get sunburn and plants from shadier habitats will suffer acutely.. Their skin can be damaged, or "scorched", on hot, sunny late spring and summer days, causing affected areas to develop brown corky raised marks or white papery patches that turn pale brown.

THE SOLUTION Hang a net curtain over sunny windows during summer, but also on sunny days in late spring when new growth on plants is soft and prone to burning after their winter rest. Find any shade loving plants a position with more diffuse light. Good air ventilation also helps to prevent scorching.

OVERFEEDING

THE PROBLEM Feed your plants too much and they will grow too fast. Although this doesn't sound like a bad thing, the soft, weak tissue produced by rapid growth is susceptible to rot and fungal diseases and may not flower well. Overfeeding can also cause "reverse osmosis", where nutrients are leached out of the plant into the surrounding compost, which could lead to signs of underfeeding (see below).

THE SOLUTION Feed plants according to their needs (see Plant Profiles). Make sure to use a specialist fertilizer, where and when appropriate.

Underwatered cacti and succulents will eventually shrivel and stop growing

UNDERFEEDING

THE PROBLEM Pale or yellowing plants that put on little growth and don't flower are likely to be deficient in nutrients as a result of underfeeding.

THE SOLUTION Ensure your plants are adequately watered, because roots can't absorb nutrients from dry compost. Feed as recommended (see Plant Profiles), following the instructions carefully to avoid overfeeding (see below).

UNDERWATERING

THE PROBLEM All plants can suffer from a lack of water, even cacti and succulents that are supremely adapted to arid environments. Symptoms include wilting, brown leaf tips, yellow or red leaves, curled leaves, poor or no growth and falling flower buds, or no flowers.

THE SOLUTION Check that your plant isn't root-bound (see p320) and repot if it is. Water plants sparingly from the bottom by setting pots in a shallow dish of water and removing it to drain when the top is glistening with water. This method will gradually remoisten very dry compost without waterlogging. Plants should plump up quickly, but lost buds will not be replaced until the following year.

OVERWATERING

THE PROBLEM The symptoms of underwatering (above) can also be a sign of overwatering, as the roots begin to rot due to the excess moisture, preventing them from taking up water. Overwatering can also cause fungal diseases (see pp356-57) and spots on the foliage, caused by a condition called "oedema" (below), where water-soaked patches on the leaves rupture and turn corky.

THE SOLUTION Pour away excess water in the plant's decorative waterproof pot or saucer, and repot if its root ball is in a container with no drainage holes. Then leave the plant to dry out on a draining board or tray filled with dry gravel.

Yellow stems and leaves can be a sign of underfeeding

Oedema is caused by over-watering and results in corky patches on leaves

DEALING WITH
COMMON PESTS

Small invertebrates will inevitably enter your home through doors and windows, or via newly bought plants. Many of these can be tolerated but others may cause severe, sometimes fatal damage to your house plants. Vigilance is key: familiarize yourself with the signs of invertebrate damage, thoroughly examine the stems, leaves, and roots of new plants before you allow them near the rest of your collection, and check all of your plants weekly so that you can deal with any potentially harmful visitors as soon as possible.

Leafhoppers cause leaves to become lightly mottled

LEAFHOPPER

THE PROBLEM These small, pale green insects are about 3mm (⅛in) long, and can jump from leaf to leaf, flying short distances when disturbed. The creamy white, wingless nymphs (juveniles) and their white cast skins can be easier to spot than the adults. Both cause a pale mottling on leaf surfaces, but the damage does not seriously affect the plant.

THE SOLUTION Tolerate, as leafhoppers rarely cause serious plant health problems.

APHIDS

THE PROBLEM Also known as green- or blackfly some species of these common sap-sucking insects can grow to up to 7mm (¼in) long. They can cause distorted or curled leaves, stunted flower buds, and poor overall growth. Aphids also excrete a sticky honeydew, which can lead to the growth of sooty moulds (see p357).

THE SOLUTION Look for aphids on flower buds, stems (below) and under the leaves. To remove them, wear plastic gloves and gently squeeze them, then wipe them off. Biological controls are available and may work in some cases.

THRIPS

THE PROBLEM Also known as thunder flies, these minute, winged, sap-sucking insects are only 2mm (⅟₁₆in) long and difficult to see unless they are flying around. Their nymphs (juveniles) are wingless. Symptoms are dull green leaves with a silvery discoloration and tiny black dots on the upper surfaces. They can also cause distorted shoots and flower buds, while the flowers may have white markings and lose their colour, or the buds may fail to open.

THE SOLUTION Use sticky traps to help to ensnare these tiny insects. Organic soap-based pesticides are also available.

These tiny flying insects (not shown to scale) cause silvery discoloration on leaves

EARWIGS

THE PROBLEM These nocturnal brown insects are up to 15mm (½in) long, and have distinctive pincers on their rear ends. They eat flowers and leaves, reducing the latter to a skeleton of veins. While they are not a common house plant pest, they may attack some of the flowering types.

THE SOLUTION Inspect your plants at night, and remove any insects you find. Also check inside ornamental containers or pots nearby, where they may be hiding during the day.

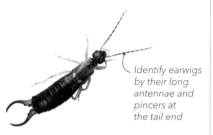

Identify earwigs by their long antennae and pincers at the tail end

FUNGUS GNATS

THE PROBLEM Also known as sciarid flies, these greyish-brown insects grow up to 4mm (¼in). They are sometimes a nuisance, but do not generally eat live plants; they simply fly around them and run over damp compost. Their larvae are white maggots with black heads, slightly larger than the adults, and feed on decaying leaves or roots, and occasionally seedling roots, but rarely mature plants.

THE SOLUTION Check composts are not too wet. Use sticky traps to ensnare the flies, and a drench of the nematode *Steinernema feltiae* to control the larvae.

"Check your plants weekly and, if possible, pick off any insects you find."

MEALYBUGS

THE PROBLEM These sap-sucking pests look like tiny white woodlice, and cause distorted or stunted growth. You will first notice a fluffy white substance in between the leaves and stems or under the foliage – the bugs or their orange-pink eggs are hiding beneath it. They also secrete honeydew, which can lead to sooty mould (see p357), and a few species feed on roots.

THE SOLUTION Often brought in on new plants, check for bugs before buying. A ladybird (*Cryptolaemus montrouzieri*) is available for biological control. Or use pheromone lures to trap the adult males and disrupt breeding. Throw out badly infested plants; pesticides rarely work.

STEM AND BULB NEMATODES

THE PROBLEM These microscopic, worm-like animals are not visible to the naked eye, yet they can cause severe damage, feeding on the plant's fluids and leading to distorted leaves, often with yellow blotches. The stem tips and buds may also turn black and die. Stem and bulb nematodes can infect bulbs, too, leading to similar symptoms in the foliage, as well as yellowish swellings or specks on the undersides of leaves.

THE SOLUTION Remove affected plant parts as soon as you see them, and buy firm, healthy looking bulbs from reputable suppliers. There are no chemical controls.

ROOT MEALYBUGS

THE PROBLEM If your plant stops growing and looks pale and sickly, knock it out of its pot and check carefully around the roots for woolly white clumps of small, woodlouse-like, sap-sucking insects similar to mealybugs.

THE SOLUTION Prevent root mealybugs becoming a problem by inspecting new plants before buying and checking the roots of plants regularly when you get them home. Remove the insects by washing as much soil as possible off the roots. Repot using fresh compost and a clean pot. Heavy populations may be impossible to treat as no effective pesticides are available.

Eelworms cannot be seen by the naked eye; look for distorted yellow leaves instead

A fluffy white substance hides mealybugs and their eggs

ROOT APHIDS

THE PROBLEM These aphids look like greenflies, and feed on plants' roots, sucking the sap from them, just like those that live above the soil. However, because they are hidden, you will often notice the symptoms before the insects. Leaves can become stunted, wilt, and turn yellow as the vigour of the plant is reduced.

THE SOLUTION If watering does not revive a wilting plant, check for root aphids in the soil. Try washing off the compost and aphids outside, then repot in fresh compost, as there is no chemical control.

Root aphids suck the moisture from roots, causing them to wither and die

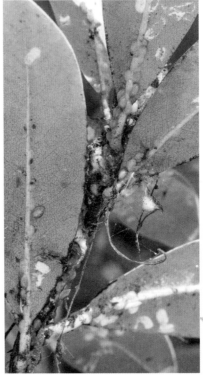

SCALE INSECTS

THE PROBLEM Scales or shell-like bumps up to 1cm (½in) in length appear on stems or beneath the leaves. There are many species of scale insect and some produce waxy, white egg masses. These sap-sucking insects can cause distorted and weak growth, and secrete sugary honeydew, which can lead to the growth of sooty moulds (see p357).

THE SOLUTION Remove affected parts and replace any plants that have becone heavily affected.

GLASSHOUSE RED SPIDER MITE

THE PROBLEM This tiny sap-sucking mite produces a mottled appearance on plant leaves. The foliage also loses its colour and may then fall off; heavy populations can eventually kill the plant. Look out for tell-tale silky webs on plants.

THE SOLUTION Remove and bin affected parts promptly; also replace severely affected plants to prevent the mite spreading. Misting plants regularly can help slow down population build up. Biological controls including predatory mites are available.

While spider mites are too small to see, mottled leaves signal their presence

SLUGS AND SNAILS

THE PROBLEM You will probably be familiar with these slimy molluscs, which eat holes in leaves and munch through stems. While they mostly affect outdoor plants, they can enter your home on new plants or through open windows.

THE SOLUTION You can normally see these pests on house plants, or find them lurking in their ornamental pots. Pick them off and dispose of them.

"Some invertebrates are too small to see easily; check for symptoms of a problem instead."

"Watch out for grubs and nymphs – these can often be just as bad, if not worse, as the adult pest."

CATERPILLARS

THE PROBLEM Not many house plants are affected by these pests; the most common indoors is the Tortrix moth caterpillar, which binds leaves together with fine webbing (below), causing them to dry up and turn brown, then fall off. Other caterpillars eat holes in the leaves, and you will see them usually lurking under the foliage.

THE SOLUTION Pick off caterpillars, or press the affected leaves together to kill the insects and pupae. In most cases there will only be a handful of catepillars so they can be managed by hand.

The root-eating grubs (right) cause more damage than the adult vine weevils

VINE WEEVILS

THE PROBLEM The adult black weevils are about 9mm (½in) long and easy to spot. They nibble leaves, making notches along the margins, but do little serious damage. The white, C-shaped, legless grubs with brown heads (about the same size as the adults) can be more of a problem because they eat the roots, causing plants to collapse and die.

THE SOLUTION Shake plants to dislodge the adults or trap them with sticky barriers around the outer pots. Try to catch the slow-moving weevils before they lay eggs in spring and summer. If you see the grubs, try hosing the roots outside to remove them, then repot in fresh compost, or apply the nematode *Steinernema kraussei* in autumn.

GLASSHOUSE WHITEFLY

THE PROBLEM These white, winged, sap-sucking insects are easy to see, even though they are just under 2mm (¹⁄₁₆in) in length. Clouds of these insects rise up when disturbed, and you may also spot the white, scale-like nymphs on the undersides of leaves. Whitefly causes distorted leaves and buds, and stunted growth. Both adults and nymphs excrete honeydew, which can lead to black sooty mould (see p357).

THE SOLUTION Hang sticky sheets near plants to trap the adults. Parasitoid wasps are available for biological control. Also try standing affected plants outside in summer where beneficial insects will help to control them.

DEALING WITH
DISEASES

When it comes to plant diseases, prevention is far better than cure. Poor care, such as lack of drainage or inadequate ventilation, can provide the ideal conditions for fungal spores to thrive, leading to many common diseases. Healthy plants are better equipped to fight off disease, though no plant can be made fully immune. Good hygeine as part of regular care is always important in preventing disease, especially for grey mould, by removing dead or damaged material from otherwise healthy plants. If a plant does show signs of sickness, move it away from other house plants immediately to prevent any infection spreading, repot it with fresh compost in a disinfected pot, and follow the appropriate advice (see right).

DAMPING OFF

THE PROBLEM Seedlings (see pp344–45) rapidly develop brown rotten areas at their base, collapse and die. A white fungal growth then appears on the compost.

THE SOLUTION Sow seeds thinly, keep compost well-drained, and remove any lid or plastic covering at germination, so that air can circulate. There is no chemical cure.

CORKY SCAB

THE PROBLEM Light brown patches appear on the surface of cacti, which gradually become raised to form scabs. While they will not damage the plant further, they are unsightly. Humidity, poor ventilation, over-watering, and possibly over-fertilizing contribute to the problem.

THE SOLUTION Increase air circulation around affected plants to reduce humidity, reduce watering and feeding, and grow in the recommended amount of light for your plant.

While not fatal, corky scab patches can look unsightly

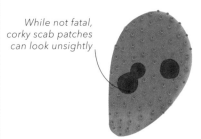

POWDERY MILDEW

THE PROBLEM This disease produces a white, powdery fungus on leaves, stems and flowers, and is often caused by lack of water and poor ventilation.

THE SOLUTION Check that your plant is not stressed due to underwatering or irregular/inconsistent watering, which increases the risk of infection. Remove affected parts as soon as you see them, and make sure the air is well ventilated.

DOWNY MILDEW

THE PROBLEM This fungal disease causes green, yellow, purple or brown blotches on the leaves, and a mould-like growth under the foliage. The leaves can also turn yellow and fall.

THE SOLUTION Remove affected parts, and bag and bin severely infected plants. Avoid wetting the leaves which can increase the likelihood of mildew developing. There is no chemical cure.

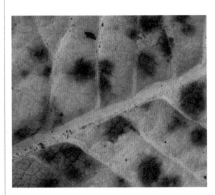

FUNGAL LEAF SPOT

THE PROBLEM Dark brown or black spots appear on the leaves, and the foliage may then fall off, leaving scars.

THE SOLUTION Remove affected leaves as soon as you see them, along with any foliage that has fallen onto the compost. Provide more ventilation around the plant and water from below to avoid splashing the plant. Badly marked plants are best thrown away.

GREY MOULD

THE PROBLEM The first sign of this fungal disease is a fuzzy grey mould on the plant's stems and leaves, which soon leads to their decay.

THE SOLUTION Remove affected parts, provide more ventilation around the plant and water plants from below to avoid spreading fungal spores. Badly affected plants should be thrown away. No chemical controls are available.

SOOTY MOULD

THE PROBLEM A black or dark brown fungal growth appears mainly on the leaves. It is caused by fungus growing on the sugar-rich honeydew produced by sap-sucking organisms, such as aphids.

THE SOLUTION Remove the pests (see pp216-219) if possible, and wipe off the fungus with warm water. There is no chemical cure.

STEM AND CROWN ROT

THE PROBLEM Brown patches with a wet appearance and sometimes a bad smell develop at the base of the plant. The plant will begin to show signs of wilting and then start to decay.

THE SOLUTION Due to the location of these rots at the base of the plant they are usually fatal, because the infected area can't be removed without destroying the plant. There are no chemical controls. Throw away infected plants and keep new plants in drier conditions.

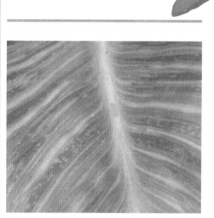

ROOT ROT

THE PROBLEM Often unnoticed until the plant wilts and will not recover after watering, this fungus is caused by poor drainage or overwatering. The roots look dark brown or black, then rot.

THE SOLUTION If caught early, remove the dark, rotten roots and repot the plant with fresh compost and good drainage. If all roots are affected, throw the plant away.

RUST

THE PROBLEM The rust-coloured pustules caused by this fungal disease appear mainly on the undersides of leaves, which then turn yellow and die. Rust mostly affects garden plants, but can infect pelargoniums grown indoors.

THE SOLUTION Avoid over-feeding, which increases the risk of infection. Remove affected leaves as soon as you see them. There is no chemical cure.

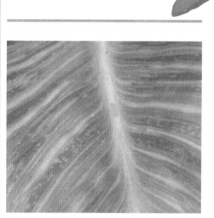

VIRUS

THE PROBLEM Pale green or yellow spots, streaks, mosaic patterns, or rings appear on the leaves, and overall growth may be stunted or distorted. The flowers may also have white or pale streaks.

THE SOLUTION Bag up and bin infected plants promptly to prevent spread. Do not use a plant with a suspected virus for propagatation. There is no chemical cure.

INDEX

ACKNOWLEDGMENTS

RHS Practical House Plant Book

AUTHOR ACKNOWLEDGMENTS
Fran Bailey would like to give a big thank you to Amy Slack and Philippa Nash at DK for their encouragement and support; to Nigel Wright and Rob Streeter whose vision and expertise really brought the projects to life; and to Katie Mitchell (@bymekatie) for her macramé expertise.

Zia Allaway would like to thank the whole team at DK for their dedication to the detail in producing this book, with particular thanks to editor Amy Slack for her support with the words and her infinite patience, and to Christine Keilty, Mandy Earey, and Philippa Nash for their beautiful designs. Thanks also to photographer Rob Streeter and stylists Nigel Wright and Janice Browne of XAB Design for the stunning images, and to Managing Editor, Stephanie Farrow for commissioning her and scrutinizing each page to ensure the quality was never compromised. And thanks to Christopher Young of the Royal Horticultural Society for his editorial input and fact checks. Last but not least, a huge thank you to her husband Brian North and son Callum Allaway North for their patience and support while she was writing this book.

PUBLISHER ACKNOWLEDGMENTS
DK would like to thank Julie Aylett, Kathy Sanger, Sue Unwin, and Irene Morris at Aylett Nurseries for their advice and assistance in sourcing plants; Jamie Song, John Bassam, and Jo for the hire of their homes; Jan Browne at XAB Design for behind-the-scenes help with co-ordinating photoshoots; Rosamund Cox and Emma Pinckard for editorial assistance; and Vanessa Bird for indexing.

For their work in creating *RHS Practical House Plant Book*, DK would also like to thank Philippa Nash, Mandy Earey, Lee-may Lim, Sunil Sharma Robert Dunn, Rajdeep Singh, Stephanie Farrow, Christine Keilty, Maxine Pedliham, and Mary-Clare Jerram.

RHS Practical Cactus and Succulent Book

AUTHOR ACKNOWLEDGMENTS
Fran Bailey would like to thank all at DK, in particular Stephanie Farrow for giving her the opportunity to contribute to this book and Amy Slack for her unflagging support and word wizardry. Thank you also to Rob Streeter, Ruth Jenkinson, and Nigel Wright for their skill and expertise in bringing the book to life. Finally, thank you to the team at Forest and Fresh Flower for keeping the ship afloat in her absence.

Zia Allaway would like to thank the whole team at DK for their help in producing this stunning book, with particular thanks to editor Amy Slack for running the project so smoothly and checking the words, and to Christine Keilty and Sara Robin for their beautiful designs. Thanks also to photographer Rob Streeter and stylists Nigel Wright and Janice Browne of XAB Design for the beautiful images, and to Managing Editor Stephanie Farrow for commissioning her. Thanks to Daniel Jackson of Ottershaw Cacti for his help and advice, and for allowing the team to photograph his amazing plants, and to Christopher Young of the Royal Horticultural Society for his editorial help and for checking the facts. Zia would also like to thank her husband Brian North for his patience and support while she was writing this book.

PUBLISHER ACKNOWLEDGMENTS
DK would like to thank all the marvellous people who have helped make this book possible: Daniel Jackson of Ottershaw Cacti for welcoming us into his nursery and answering our many questions; Jan Browne of XAB design for her marvellous behind-the-scenes help with co-ordinating photoshoots and sourcing plants from across the country; the DK Delhi team for their tireless retouching work; Philippa Nash for her illustrations; Anne Fisher, Mandy Earey, and Jade Wheaton for design assistance; Naorem Anuja, Poppy Blakiston Houston, and Oreolu Grillo for editorial assistance; and Vanessa Bird for indexing.

For their work in creating *RHS Practical Cactus & Succulent Book*, DK would also like to thank Sara Robin, Glenda Fisher, Harriet Yeomans, Satish Chandra Gaur, Anurag Trivedi, Rajdeep Singh, Sunil Sharma, David Almond, Stephanie McConnell, Stephanie Farrow, Christine Keilty, Maxine Pedliham, and Mary-Clare Jerram.

ABOUT THE AUTHORS

Fran Bailey grew up on a cut flower nursery near York, where her Dutch father Jacob Verhoef encouraged her love of all things horticultural. After studying at the Welsh College Of Horticulture, she moved to London to work as a freelance florist. In 2006 she opened her first flower shop, The Fresh Flower Company, in South London. In 2013 she expanded into house plants with the opening of her shop Forest, which she runs with her daughters, and which is packed to the rafters with lush greenery.

Zia Allaway is an author, journalist, and qualified horticulturist who has written and edited a range of gardening books for the RHS and DK, including the *RHS Encyclopedia of Plants and Flowers*, *RHS How to Grow Plants in Pots*, and *Indoor Edible Garden*. Zia also writes a monthly column on garden design for *Homes and Gardens* magazine and is a contributor to the *Garden Design Journal*. She runs a consultancy service from her home in Hertfordshire and offers practical workshops for beginners.

ABOUT THE BOOK

This book is adapted from **RHS Practical House Plant Book** and **RHS Cactus and Succulent Book**, both written by Fran Bailey and Zia Allaway and published by DK.

The Royal Horticultural Society is the UK's leading gardening charity dedicated to advancing horticulture and promoting good gardening. Its charitable work includes providing expert advice and information in print, online and at its five major gardens and annual shows, training gardeners of every age, creating hands-on opportunities for children to grow plants and sharing research into plants, wildlife, wellbeing and environmental issues affecting gardeners.

For more information visit www.rhs.org.uk or call 020 3176 5800.

PICTURE CREDITS

The publisher would like to thank the following for their kind permission to reproduce their photographs:

(Key: a-above; b-below/bottom; c-centre; f-far; l-left; r-right; t-top)

13 GAP Photos: Friedrich Strauss (tr, bl). 15 Fran Bailey: (tr, cr). 17 GAP Photos: Friedrich Strauss (ftl, tl). 21 Fran Bailey: (cl, tl). GAP Photos: (tc); Juliette Wade (tr); Friedrich Strauss (bl). 22 GAP Photos: Howard Rice (br). 23 GAP Photos: Friedrich Strauss (bl). 27 Fran Bailey: (tr). 31 Fran Bailey: (crb, bc). GAP Photos: Dianna Jazwinski (br). 355 Dreamstime.com: Sarah2 (ca)

All other images © Dorling Kindersley

Use sustainably sourced moss wherever possible. That may involve sourcing from a reputable retailer or gathering moss from your own, or a friend's lawn, with their permission. Be wary of sphagnum moss as it may not be harvested from sustainable sources. Sustainably farmed moss (paludiculture) is more and more available, as is moss gathered rotationally from UK forests.

Authors Fran Bailey, Zia Allaway

DK UK
Project editor Amy Slack
Editor Ankita Gupta
Managing editor Chitra Subramanyam
Senior art editor Nidhi Mehra
Managing art editor Neha Ahuja Chowdhry
DTP Coordinator Pushpak Tyagi
DTP Designer Manish Upreti
Pre-production Manager Balwant Singh
Creative head Malavika Talukder
Production editor David Almond
Production controller Rebecca Parton
Jacket co-ordinators Jasmin Lennie, Abi Gain
Editorial manager Ruth O'Rourke
Art director Maxine Pedliham
Publisher Katie Cowan

Editorial Alice McKeever
Photography Rob Streeter, Ruth Jenkinson
Photographic art direction Nigel Wright
Consultant gardening publisher Chris Young

ROYAL HORTICULTURAL SOCIETY
Consultants Christopher Young, Simon Maughan
Publishers Rae Spencer-Jones, Helen Griffin

First published in Great Britain in 2023 by
DK, One Embassy Gardens, 8 Viaduct Gardens,
London, SW11 7BW

Based on content first published in RHS Practical House
Plant Book (copyright DK 2018) and RHS Practical Cactus
and Succulent Book (copyright DK 2019)

The authorised representative in the EEA is
Dorling Kindersley Verlag GmbH. Arnulfstr. 124,
80636 Munich, Germany

MIX
Paper | Supporting
responsible forestry
FSC™ C018179

This book was made with Forest
Stewardship Council ™ certified
paper - one small step in DK's
commitment to a sustainable future.
For more information go to
www.dk.com/our-green-pledge